Wisdom in Love

RICK ANTHONY FURTAK

Wisdom in *Love*

Kierkegaard
and the Ancient Quest
for Emotional Integrity

UNIVERSITY OF NOTRE DAME PRESS

NOTRE DAME, INDIANA

Manufactured in the United States of America

Library of Congress Cataloging-in-Publication Data
Furtak, Rick Anthony.
Wisdom in love : Kierkegaard and the ancient quest for
emotional integrity / Rick Anthony Furtak.
p.   cm.
Includes bibliographical references (p.   ) and index.
ISBN 0-268-02873-7 (cloth : alk. paper) --
ISBN 0-268-02874-5 (pbk. : alk. paper)
 1. Emotions (Philosophy)   2. Conduct of life.
 3. Kierkegaard, Søren, 1813–1855.   4. Stoics.   I. Title.
B105.E46F87   2004
128'.37—dc22
                                        2004026367

∞ *This book is printed on acid-free paper.*

in memory of

Jabe MacMillan Darby

1974 – 1997

artist, skeptic, friend

CONTENTS

Acknowledgments   ix
Preface   xi

PART I   STOICISM AND ITS DISCONTENTS

            1   Making Sense of Emotion   3
            2   The Structural Critique (Stoic Virtue)   17
            3   The Fundamental Thesis (Stoic Values)   24
            4   Integrity without Apathy?   34

PART II   STRUCTURAL CORRECTIONS

            5   Interlude: The Relevance
                of Kierkegaard's Writings   41
            6   Aesthetics and Sentimentality   52
            7   Virtues of Ethical Resolution   65
            8   The Romantic Imagination   78

PART III   FUNDAMENTAL QUESTIONS

            9   Love as Necessary Premise   91
            10 Suffering as Logical Consequence   108
            11 Value on the Other Side of Nihilism   119
            12 Conclusion: The Tragicomedy
                of Passionate Existence   137

            Notes   143
            Bibliography   205
            Index   225

ACKNOWLEDGMENTS

I owe thanks to many people. To my parents, for home and support. To Martha Nussbaum, for inspiration and guidance, and to everyone else who took the time to read and comment on this work while it was still "in progress": Niels Jørgen Cappelørn, Arnold Davidson, Jonathan Ellsworth, Alastair Hannay, Charles Larmore, Jonathan Lear, Edward Mooney, James Reid, Jennifer Schuberth, and one anonymous reader for the University of Notre Dame Press. To others who, in various ways, have helped me to develop my thoughts on this topic: Noel Adams, Ewa Atanassow, Jeremy Bendik-Keymer, Ted Cohen, Joseph Donohue, Chad Flanders, Jeff Gainey, Matthew Geiger, Jürgen Habermas, Geoffrey Hill, Victor Kestenbaum, Ulrich Knappe, Sheela Kumar, David Michael Levin, Alyssa Luboff, Gordon Marino, Jean-Luc Marion, David Miller, Marjan Moshayedi, Paul Muench, Thomas Nørgaard, Sarah Pessin, Christopher Ricks, John Riker, Ettore Rocca, J. P. Rosensweig, Anthony Rudd, Matt Schwartz, Roger Scruton, Brian Söderquist, and Pia Søltoft. To the Hong Kierkegaard Library at Saint Olaf College in Minnesota for funding a research visit during the summer of 2001. To the American-Scandinavian Foundation and the Lois Roth Endowment for providing me with generous fellowship aid which enabled me to spend August through December of 2002 in Copenhagen, and to everyone at the Kierkegaard Research Center for their hospitality during my stay. To the students who took part in my Kierkegaard seminar at Colorado College in the spring of 2003, for many stimulating discussions. To every other person, named or unnamed, who has been a part of the emotional background to what is written here; philosophical writing is always to some extent a personal confession, but especially when it comes to a topic like this one. To the bodies of water that gave me sustenance outside my apartment windows while I was working on this project, Lake Michigan and Gentofte Sø. To R., for making me wonder. And, most of all, to S., for wanting to stay.

Emotions color human experience in various ways: they seem to be connected with whatever matters most to us, and yet they are often so unpleasant or disconcerting that we find ourselves wishing we could be rid of them altogether. According to Stoic moral psychology, emotions (or passions) are cognitive responses to perceived value in the world, and therefore we can eradicate them by changing our beliefs about what really matters in life. Stoicism is the ancient source for a perennial bias against the emotions, and it has so thoroughly left its mark on conventional wisdom that it is acceptable in contemporary English to use the word "philosophical" to describe a person with a stoical or calm disposition. And the stoical approach to life is always being reinvented in bestseller nonfiction, which tells us not to sweat the small stuff and then adds that everything ought to count as small stuff—in other words, as no big deal.

For the person who believes this, life becomes much easier, but only at the cost of becoming meaningless. Stoicism offers us a bleak view of things according to which emotional problems can be resolved only through the complete avoidance of emotion. Now, we may agree that some types of emotion are worth trying to overcome. When we experience intense anger at being stopped in traffic, we may rightly feel that we are not at our best either morally or rationally. But the anger of the liberating officer who has just walked into a concentration camp is not so easily dismissed as an emotion that it would be better to avoid. Being rational cannot be equated with remaining dispassionate, if there are cases in which human life is touched by phenomena that are worthy of emotional response.

My aim in this work is, through a critical engagement with certain figures in the history of ideas, to develop a conceptual account of what emotions are, in what sense they could be false or unreliable, and whether they could ever be acceptable. In other words, do our emotions provide us with a reliable source of guidance in life? After beginning with a consideration of normative

Stoicism, I draw upon the writings of Søren Kierkegaard to develop an alternative philosophy according to which the emotions can be understood as embodying a kind of authentic insight—and even, perhaps, enabling us to attain a uniquely truthful way of seeing the world. The outcome of this guide for the emotionally perplexed is a conception of what it would mean to trust oneself to be rational in being passionate.

When we draw a categorical distinction between reason and passion, we forget that it makes sense to talk about whether our emotions are internally coherent and whether they correspond to external states of affairs. When we classify every mental state as a belief or a desire, we disregard the fact that beliefs can be evaluative, and that our cares are not always desirous. When we measure emotions in hedonistic terms, we neglect to consider that what is painful may nonetheless be true. One uncomfortable truth which emerges from this inquiry is that we cannot sustain the emotions that hold us together without accepting the risk of suffering emotions that tear us apart. In order to get to this conclusion and appreciate what it means, it is necessary to move through a progress of thought in which certain presumptions are reconsidered and certain words are redefined. "Integrity," for instance, signifies for the Stoics a soundness of character that resembles an invulnerable citadel fortified against emotion. In Kierkegaard's writings, however, to have integrity or moral soundness means to be edified by love in a way that is less rigidly secure but also more real: it is more open to significant experience, and more in accordance with the ground of our being.

In what follows, I open in Part I with a discussion of Stoicism and its failings. Then, in Part II, I endorse a virtue ethics based upon cultivating an awareness of emotional responses over time. Finally, in Part III, I argue for a religious acceptance of love as the basis of moral agency and, in a deeper sense, of all value in life as we know it. This conception of the self as radically passionate, I believe, does justice to what is best in us as the fragile, unique, and situated creatures we are. Love and wisdom need not be at odds with one another: even if we could, we would not want to live without emotion. Ultimately, my goal is to find out how it might be possible to make the best of our condition as emotional beings, rather than attempting to deny or rise above it.

PART I

STOICISM AND ITS DISCONTENTS

What is all this for? What does it signify? What is the *meaning* of life? It's usually an easy enough question to evade. . . . But last week, a student who had studied metaphysics and epistemology and Søren Kierkegaard, the student who read Immanuel Kant and brought fresh fruit to class, killed herself with a single gunshot to the head, sitting at home, at the kitchen table. She left no note, no explanation, and no one can make any sense of it. Her professors lean heavily against the classroom walls and cannot speak.

—Kathleen Dean Moore, "The Testimony of the Marsh"

After dinner in the evening, at which he ate little, he said he would go for a walk. So he went out and spent the next three hours—as we learnt from him later—tramping round and round Port Meadow (which is an enormous, rather damp field beside the river Thames on the outskirts of Oxford). Since we were by this time rather worried about what could be on his mind, when he came back at about eleven o'clock we sat him down in an armchair and asked him what the trouble was. It appeared that he had been reading Camus's novel, and had become convinced that *nothing matters*.

—Richard Mervyn Hare, "Nothing Matters"

CHAPTER I

Making Sense of Emotion

It has been said that philosophical argument is empty unless it pertains to human suffering.[1] When it does, it ought to begin with a concrete illustration of whatever kind of common experience it purports to address. For this reason, it is fitting that this study should begin with a portrayal of two students of philosophy: one who has apparently suffered too much, and another who has lost the ability to suffer. In the epigraphs to this chapter, we hear two narratives related by concerned teachers, showing two possible extremes of emotional suffering. From the Oregon forest comes a story of overwhelming passion; from the marshes of Oxford, a tale of unbearable apathy. Hearing such tragedies described, and reflecting upon our own experience, we may wonder: what is the meaning of all this? Is it rational to be vulnerable to emotion, or not to be emotional at all? If philosophy is the love of wisdom, then what would it mean to attain wisdom in this area of human existence? Such questions are relevant to every one of us, yet we find no coherent answer to them in our pre-philosophical thinking, riddled as it is with clichés that range from *follow your heart* to *don't get hysterical*. If our understanding is to surpass these superficial and conflicting slogans, then we must look more critically at what emotion is, and consider how to live with (or without) it.

It would be rash and unreasonable to establish an attitude toward emotion (or, in other words, "passion"[2]) without attempting to understand what it *is*. If emotions were merely sensations rather than perceptions, we might safely regard them as meaningless fluctuations. But unlike a sore leg or an itchy scalp, an emotion is a way of seeing the world: when we get angry or when we grieve, we feel anger *at* someone or grief *about* something.[3] If I am annoyed, then something must be annoying me; and I could not sincerely claim to be afraid of you unless I believe that you are frightening. My subjective experience of emotion cannot be fully described without reference to objects external to myself: it may be that I am annoyed by a conversation at the next table, or worried about the direction in which you are pointing your gun. If someone says that he is afraid that he might win the lottery, we ought to ask him why he views this as an undesirable prospect. Unless he believes that money corrupts a person, or something of the sort, then it is unclear why he should describe his emotion as fear rather than as hope.[4] In short, emotions involve evaluations or appraisals which may in some cases be mistaken. Anger, for instance, is inappropriate if it is based upon a false belief, and it would be irrational for me to be angry at someone for a crime that I know he did not commit.[5] There is a whole vocabulary of adjectives which we apply to emotions, yet which could not be assigned to mere sensations: emotions can be described as sensible or foolish, warranted or unwarranted, right or wrong. As Robert Solomon points out, it would not make sense to use such terms in reference to cramps and itches.[6]

In recognizing what might be called the intelligence of emotions, Solomon and other contemporary philosophers are reviving an ancient way of thinking.[7] Aristotle defines emotions as mental states with a pleasant or distressing quality, in which certain objects appear to loom large with importance.[8] Chrysippus, the early Stoic philosopher, contends that an emotion is nothing other than a judgment of value (that is, a *fresh* judgment of *apparent* value) concerning something outside of a person's own control, experienced as an agitation of the mind.[9] Although it is not new, the idea that passions are in some sense cognitive phenomena is rather unfashionable; without explanation, it is likely to be misunderstood. It does not require a denial of the obvious fact that, for instance, when I am disappointed I may experience something like a hollow ache. Nor does it imply that I could undergo this emotion without an amygdala or a hippocampus, not to mention a beating heart. It only adds to these observations the further insight that I cannot be disappointed in you unless I believe that you have let me down. Admittedly, in feeling this way

I could be mistaken in a number of ways: my expectations of you might have been unreasonable, my beliefs about your actions may be based on false information, and I might be wrong in identifying you as the person who has let me down. Perhaps the emotion I am experiencing would be more accurately described as a general dissatisfaction with my life or a discouragement about my chance of improving it. Maybe it is more of a future-oriented despondency than a disappointment about something in the past. The point is that when we call an emotion "irrational," what we are pointing out is not a necessary property of every emotion, but a contingent fault in this particular one. Emotions are always "rational" in the sense that they incorporate beliefs, and they are sometimes "rational" in the sense that these beliefs are true.

Aristotle generally recognizes that emotions involve rational appraisal, but no one before the Stoics is consistent in arguing that the only necessary condition of having an emotion is assenting to a particular kind of mental impression. Chrysippus sees emotions as part of rational activity itself, and puts forward a monistic view of the human mind according to which emotions are not the product of some other faculty that either adds raw potency to our thinking or else confounds it.[10] According to his theory, I could not be disappointed without the belief that someone has let me down. Of course, I could not be disappointed by someone unless I saw her actions or attitudes as important in some way. In every instance of passion, a similar formal structure must exist: (X) a dispositional attitude about the significance of what is beyond one's own control and (Y) an episodic response to some contingent event involving a significant object.[11] So, for example, I may be (x) afraid of bears because I believe that they are dangerous and then (y) frightened by the appearance of an actual bear in my backyard. There is a difference between a *primary* disposition of fear and a *secondary* episode of fright. Believing in the value of contingent "externals" (which need not be outside a person's body, just outside of his or her control) disposes a person toward a range of emotional responses. "Given a deep attachment to something outside one's own control," Nussbaum writes, "the very accidents of life, combined with that attachment to an object, will bring the person who is so attached now into intense joy, when the beloved object is at hand, now into fear, when it is threatened, now into grief, when catastrophe befalls it," and so on.[12] Once a person has developed a primary affective disposition, he or she is thereby susceptible to all the varieties of passionate experience.

Emotions, therefore, rely upon some kind of *axiological* belief about what is of value, as well as a *volitional* boundary between what is under one's own control and what is not. According to Chrysippus, passions arise from "beliefs about what is good and what is bad," while for a later Stoic such as Epictetus the "most important" moral distinction is that between what is up to us and what isn't.[13] The historical Stoics' descriptive account of the cognitive elements of emotion is their main contribution to moral psychology, and in this chapter I will be drawing upon it in order to develop a conceptual account of emotions as what I will term "perceptions of significance." I will first focus, on the concept of significance; then, I will try to clarify what kind of perception it is that registers this significance. We will see, as the discussion proceeds, why I have chosen this phrase: but a few remarks should be made right away.

It is essential to retain from the Greek *pathos,* which is the source of our word "passion," the sense that *passivity* is a distinguishing feature of emotion:[14] although we are responsible for shaping our dispositions, in the moment of emotion we are acted upon by some feature of the world that we do not control. The word "perception" nicely suggests both a subject who is perceiving *and* an object which is there to be perceived. Likewise, the reason for my preference of "significance" over such related terms as "value" and "meaning" is that it more obviously implicates both self and world: a significant circumstance is one in which there is value (or meaning) for *me,* in *this.* Moreover, when we speak of significance it is clear that we do not mean to denote something substantial, like peanut butter or carbon dioxide. Rather, we call attention to the dynamic process in which an object comes to be significant for a subject.[15] Significance is a property of any relation in which whatever is perceived matters to the perceiver. Moreover, it includes both value and disvalue: an earthquake that kills a thousand people is a significant disaster, if not a positively "valuable" one. These reasons for favoring certain terms do not mandate a technical exclusion of the others; however, it is worth keeping in mind that there are some connotations which I would prefer to avoid.

What exactly *is* significance? To care (or, to be concerned) about something, to view it as important, or to take it seriously, is to find significance in it. It is not necessary for the significant object to be a person, although it often is: it might be a project, an idea, a loved item, or a state of affairs. In any case, what matters about the object is not merely that it exists but that it is significant. Human life is a complex of meaningful relations, and it is only in the context of these relations that meaning, or significance, can be found. We tend to describe our own concern as a non-arbitrary fact, and the importance of whatever it is that we care about may even be portrayed as an objective quality: this *is* significant, we say, meaning that it ought to be taken seriously and that we are only responding appropriately to this objective warrant. Even so, it is also possible to look at ourselves as if from a distant vantage point and, in a mood of incredulity, see how insignificant our lives "really" are. But naïve realism and blasé relativism go equally wrong with regard to significance by assuming that it must reside solely in either the object or the subject. In seeing things in light of our cares, we do not forcibly project value onto the world; nonetheless, outward conditions do allow us room for some variability in interpretation.

Undeniably, it is a remarkable fact about us that "we are creatures to whom things matter," as Frankfurt points out.[16] Yet it is also a remarkable fact about the world that it matters to human beings. Many of us are familiar with the experience of vanity famously lamented in the book of Ecclesiastes, in which one feels estranged from a world that seems empty because nothing is significant.[17] If we are fortunate, then what we find egregious about this condition is the absence of something that is normally present. We remember what it was like to be meaningfully involved in a world that did not seem to be devoid of value, and it is in contrast with this memory that the experience of vanity stands out sharply. Something has gone wrong in the relation between self and world: significance has vanished. At some times we think that the world is to blame for this, and at other times we blame ourselves. But significance, insofar as it does seem to exist, is more likely to require both a perceiving subject and an external world to be perceived: it is neither a property of "objective reality" as viewed from nowhere nor a weirdly self-projected light that radiates out from us onto a featureless environment.

So when a person perceives significance for himself in some component of the outside world, he is both active and acted upon. The way the self reaches out beyond itself to form attachments of care is plainly a dynamic capacity: yet this process is typically not initiated by an act of will. In becoming concerned, we are extended beyond ourselves by an influence that is not positively within our control. We find ourselves drawn outward into relations of concern; and, inwardly regarded, it is not wholly within our power to care or not to care. Often, it is only in a moment of upheaval that we first discover that something or someone has become significant for us: until I heard about the accident, I didn't realize how much she meant to me. In ordinary experience such concerns have an inveterate tendency to form—almost on their own, as it were—as long as we accept them and do not resist. When

Heidegger speaks of "taking care" as a way of "letting things be relevant," he captures both aspects of the idea that significant engagement in life arises from the active cultivation of a passive mode of receptivity.[18]

The question of what we find significant is a crucial one in human existence: it defines the way in which our happiness is at stake. By virtue of our cares, we find ourselves in the midst of a network of concern, which extends out into the world and defines our moral identity. In other words, as love bonds us to objects, it sets up the conditions of our vulnerability to all other emotions. This constructive process is depicted in a stoical image by a philosophical anthropologist:

> You get a good feeling for what the self "looks like" in its extensions if you imagine the person to be a cylinder with a hollow inside, in which is lodged his self. Out of this cylinder the self overflows and extends into the surroundings, as a kind of huge amoeba, pushing its pseudopods to a wife, a car, a flag, a crushed flower in a secret book. The picture you get is of a huge invisible amoeba spread out over the landscape, with boundaries very far from its own center or home base. Tear and burn the flag, find and destroy the flower in the book, and the amoeba screams with soul-searing pain.[19]

The risk in all of this, as the screaming amoeba indicates, is that once we have become attached to significant objects, our well-being is bound up with those objects in a very intimate way. The wife, the car, and the flag are so many hostages to fortune: by virtue of our underlying love for them, we are liable to be affected correspondingly by whatever may affect them for good or evil. In other words, care is a condition of vulnerability; our happiness is at stake wherever we perceive significance. This is the sense in which emotions have their source in the outside environment: anger, for instance, "does not come from nowhere, nor does it come only from the overheating of the organism itself."[20] If we do not personally care about something, or if we take it for granted, then we do not feel a passionate sense of its value as a contingent external good.

Because what moves us to care is also what disposes us to be at the mercy of what is outside of ourselves, it is an urgent task for us to establish an appropriate attitude toward this susceptibility. Is the burgeoning of concern a development we ought to cultivate, or does it need to be weeded out by some other mental faculty? While we must acknowledge the "propensity of human beings to make strong affectional bonds to particular others,"[21] this psycho-logical description does not amount to a normative justification. Episodes of gratitude or sadness or any other passion might be subject to some criteria of accuracy and appropriateness, but the original formation of care cannot be subject to the same kind of criteria. What makes an emotion more or less appropriate, in a simple case such as worry about missing the bus, is whether or not one is indeed running late. But in what sense are we right or wrong to perceive things as significant—to find value in the world—in the first place? The Stoics force us to ask this kind of question, claiming that nothing is worse than giving our assent to false impressions about moral reality.[22]

The difference between particular mistakes and comprehensive mis-takenness brings into contrast the two aspects of the dynamic of passion: the *primary* bond of love, or care, that proceeds out from the self to establish emotional relations with the world, and the *secondary* episodes of passion that ensue from these relations—recall (X) and (Y) from the discussion above. As Nussbaum puts it, "once one has formed attachments to unstable things not fully under one's control," one has "background" emotions that set the stage for "episodic or situational" emotions.[23] Augustine covers both of these as-pects with a statement that can be interpreted in two ways. It comes after he has defined love as the ground of all other emotions: for instance, fear is a re-action to a threat to one's love, and elation is the sense of having one's love fulfilled. Generally speaking, the value of a particular emotion is determined by the rectitude or wrongness of the fundamental love upon which it is predi-cated: as Augustine puts it, *mala sunt ista si malus amor est, bona si bonus.*[24] In other words, depending on whether the reader introduces a definite article, these particular emotions are either:

(1) bad if [the] love is bad, and good if it is good, *or*
(2) bad if love [itself] is bad, and good if it is good.

The first version states that various loves may be better or worse, without disputing the primary validity of loving; the second says more radically that particular emotions must be either potentially good or categorically bad, de-pending upon whether or not our basic human capacity to love is a good thing.[25]

Embarrassment, for example, is a passion in which I respond to a con-crete situation in light of certain morally relevant facts, such as that I care about my reputation in the eyes of those who are present. Whether or not I have correctly perceived the situation as embarrassing, and responded in the appropriate degree, is a legitimate question only after it is granted that I am already concerned about this. But what about the initial process of my becoming concerned: is it fortunate or deplorable that this has taken place? This question proposes a profound distrust with regard to the earliest emergence of significance, and we cannot easily answer it, since we do not begin to care through a process in which skepticism arises and is then refuted. We do not begin to care by finding reasons for caring. These observations might lead an irrationalist to proclaim that life "is contra-rational and opposed to clear thinking," because the emotions through which we participate in life are "anti-rational."[26] But such an argument is predicated upon a false opposition. Even though perceptions of significance do not compel agreement from anyone and everyone, as do the truths of geometry, the fact that they are not impersonally transitive doesn't mean that they are untrue—unless we confuse being truthful with having an objective consensus. Once we abandon that bias, we see that emotion manifests a logic of its own: it may be true that I love someone, without it being a mental omission on anyone else's part not to love that same person.[27] Axiological perception rests upon a kind of axiomatic grounding: that is, in a human being's primary care for the external world.

There is a sense in which caring needs to be recognized as a basic mental process: in *becoming concerned* about particular objects, a person is not responding to those objects *in terms of* a previously established relation of care. Coming to love someone, for instance, is not a secondary process derived from other considerations. But when I become afraid for someone's safety, I must already care about the person in question.[28] This fundamental cognitive process is what Scheler calls the movement of the heart, which is set in motion by objects and which grounds our "many sided interest in the things of this world."[29] We might describe it, from the subjective point of view, as a dynamic force which motivates our engagement with the world outside of the self.[30] It may manifest itself in romantic passion as well as in "love for parents and children, friendship and love for humanity in general, and also devotion to concrete objects and to abstract ideas." These words are Freud's,[31] and it seems fitting to agree with him that we can do no better than use the word "love" to designate the emotion which is prior to all other emotions. If love did not lead us to care for the people, places, and things of this world, we would not be disposed to respond to one set of circumstances with jealousy, to another with joy, and so on. It is our standing attitudes of love and concern that establish in us a readiness for being affected.[32]

Again, all other emotions (the secondary emotions that follow from love, which is their primary condition) are consequences of the way that we encounter the world in light of our cares. If I have no particular interest in someone, then I cannot see a situation as saliently good or bad with reference to her; I will not have emotions associated with her at all. This initial taking-an-interest is a manifestation of love: that is what we either accept or reject, depending upon how we comport ourselves toward the origin of significance. The Stoics speak of "pre-emotions" [*propatheiai*], immediate value-impressions that have not been accepted as true or rejected as false, and locate our liberty at the moment in which we either endorse or oppose them.[33] This freedom of assent places primary cares somewhat within the control of the moral agent whose emotional liabilities are decided by whether or not he or she assents to the tacit propositions ("this child is precious") embodied in these impressions. But this freedom may be limited: part of the mental agitation of an emotion is its intrinsic claim to its own truth, and (as Epictetus admits) we are not always free to oppose this claim, to say: "no, I do not love, do not care for this child."[34] Yet if our background evaluations are mistaken—if the good we think we perceive is illusory—then our situational passions will be chronically false.

By analyzing the dynamics of significance, we have come to see that passion works both ways: it involves the love that moves us to care about anything in the first place *and* the reactions that follow from events beyond our control touching upon what we already care about. In the one case, we awaken to the primary awareness that something is meaningful; in the other, we recognize that something already seen as meaningful is now at stake in an important way. This distinction between the fundamental and the derivative is central to the dual-aspect theory of emotion which is being developed here. To the psychoanalytic observation that "love strives after objects," we can add the complementary point that the objects among which we find ourselves also make a claim upon us, finding their way into our hearts without any decision on our part.[35] This process may be called arbitrary in the hypothetical sense that, had we found ourselves in different surroundings, we would have formed different attachments. But since our identity depends largely upon the cares that we *have* developed, we cannot coherently hold ourselves apart from our love and complain that its genesis was proto-rational: for who are *we* to do this? It only makes sense that significance ought to be bound up with contingencies of time and place, as a narrative passage by Willa Cather suggests (tenderly, if somewhat fatalistically):

This was the road over which Ántonia and I came on that night when we got off the train at Black Hawk and were bedded down in the straw, wondering children, being taken we knew not whither. I had only to close my eyes to hear the rumbling of the wagons in the dark, and to be again overcome by that obliterating strangeness. The feelings of that night were so near that I could reach out and touch them with my hand. I had the sense of coming home to myself, and of having found out what a little circle man's experience is. For Ántonia and for me, this had been the road of Destiny; had taken us to those early accidents of fortune which predetermined for us all that we can ever be. Now I understood that the same road was to bring us together again. Whatever we had missed, we possessed together the precious, the incommunicable past.[36]

However contingent these accidents of fortune might be, it would be ungrateful not to appreciate the definitive impact of whatever has become significant in our lives. Like the emotional associations that color the atmosphere around Cather's narrator, significance is a quality that permeates the human world.

To describe emotions as "perceptions of significance" is not to suggest a reduction, but to demand a more expansive view of cognition which does not prohibit us from appreciating the meaning of our passions.[37] Strictly attending to either physiological minutiae or phenomenal qualia is insufficient for identifying a particular emotion as, say, anger. Granted, my anger is (in one sense) a chemical episode, and there is something it is like for me to be angry, but neither of these details considered by itself is enough to justify the conclusion that what I am undergoing is anger. The physical aspect and the raw feel of an emotion may be variable and hard to decipher: rather, what will be common to all cases of anger is a certain kind of intentional attitude.[38] This not only licenses the use of mental language in discussions of emotion, but it also reminds us that whatever organic configuration we need in order to be identified as human beings is prerequisite to even our non-emotional thoughts. And if some of what we tend to describe as "emotion" or "passion" lacks this intentional structure, then it must be sensational, not perceptive, and (therefore) outside the domain of the present discussion.

Why, then, should emotions often involve "a more conspicuous participation of the body than do other mental states"?[39] To risk a bit of speculative biology, it may be that emotions involve the body more noticeably because of their connection with matters of urgent concern in one's existence—even if they do not always mean that one's bodily survival is literally at stake. What is more difficult to account for from a mental perspective is the way that emotions also seem to be influenced by the weather, by diet and exercise, and so on. One of the most difficult, and crucial, distinctions to make in this area is that between meaningless sensations and meaningful perceptions. There is a categorical difference between being euphoric for no reason and being elated *by* something. In either case, however, the mood may paint our experience so completely that we cannot discern whether what we see as rosy is being tinted by a discoloration in the lenses of our eyes. We also should not mistake effects for causes and examine the physiology of sadness as a basic problem without any reference to the object of that emotion: this would leave us no way of distinguishing between a sadness that is reasonable and a depression that is best understood in medical terms.[40] Robust, meaningful emotions can be ascribed to persons, not to brains or any other subpersonal systems. If a strictly physical stimulus causes a person to experience a simulacrum of emotion, then what is going on is a sensation, without any object.[41] Yet such arousal may bear a felt resemblance to actual passion, even though it is not *about* anything. Therefore, in describing an ideal of clarity in emotional perception, we must recognize the value of being able to tell what is merely noise and what deserves to be heard: even long-standing moods are often fraught with significance,[42] and what seem to be objectless emotions may in fact be about something which remains to be identified.

Apart from this caution toward the possibility of mistaking cognitively irrelevant feeling for actual passion, specifically physiological issues will be bracketed from consideration in what follows.[43] Measuring the amount of manganese in our tears will not tell us why we are crying, and this is the kind of question we are concerned about. All that we need to know in order to proceed is that a certain kind of rational attitude is necessary for the existence of emotion, properly speaking, so that the eradication of all such attitudes will eliminate the risk of emotion altogether. And if we have defined cognition in a broad sense that respects the embodied and contextual character of thought, then we can legitimately speak of "perceptions of significance" as a category of rational experience. Emotions may be associated with specific bodily feelings, but the somatic excitement of the child who hopes to get a bicycle as a birthday present may subside at times during the weeks preceding, without it ever being true during that time that the child has ceased to care or to hope. Likewise, personal love involves such concepts as attention, loyalty, and trust: to talk about it only in terms of bodily phenomena would be to tell a small part of the story, if not to miss the point entirely by way of a category mistake.

In order to accommodate emotion into our philosophy of mind, we also need to reject the presumption that nothing less refined than the ability to formulate propositions and use language should qualify as thinking.[44] We need to focus, instead, on a capacity for seeing-as which is not limited to adult human beings. It may be the case that many human emotions would be unavailable to a being incapable of perceiving things in a linguistically sophisticated way, but this does not mean that a person's evaluative outlook does not exist until it has become articulate, or that the emotions of adulthood are never influenced by unformulated ideas. We have loves and cares before we learn to formulate anything in language: and if the impression that *this person is important* or *that object is dangerous* qualifies as an intelligent perception, then prelinguistic infancy has no shortage of such perceptions. Articulation can be transformative, but finding words to express an emotion, while it may clarify the emotion, does not bring something into existence out of nothing. Instead, we say: *this* is what I've been feeling, including before I was able to express it in language, even if *it* has been changed along the way.[45] It may be that I just couldn't find the right words until now.[46] Also, the difficulty of altering long-standing beliefs of any kind should lead us to expect that the disposition to such unwanted passions as (for instance) racially motivated fear will, once ingrained, be hard to remove. Paying lip service to more enlightened beliefs does not free a person from attitudes that run contrary to those beliefs: the former racist who still experiences hatred toward non-whites ought to view his response as evidence of a residual belief, rather than to dismiss it as something other than rationality.[47]

In order to make sense of emotion, in other words, we need to think of conceptual understanding as a taking to heart of what something means. To accept the truth of a proposition, then, is to register its full significance, to feel its truth at a visceral level. Nussbaum gives a description of a woman faced with the fact that someone she loves has just died, who claims that she is not upset:

> Chrysippus will say, This person is in a state of denial. She is not really assenting to that proposition. She may be saying the words, but there is something in her that is resisting it. Or if she is assenting to something, it

is not to that same proposition. She may be assenting to the proposition that a mortal human being has died: even (just possibly) to the proposition that X (the man she loves) has died; what she has not assented to is the proposition, that the person whom she loves and values above all others, has died. For to recognize this is to be violently disturbed.[48]

Given a certain care, the acknowledgment of a certain fact cannot be made with equanimity. Yet it is possible for the care to exist without being articulate, and for the fact to be stated without being deeply acknowledged. These observations can be coherently reconciled only within a broad account of cognition that makes room for gut feelings, dim suspicions, unacknowledged thoughts, and other ways of seeing that do not involve sophisticated linguistic assertion. Only such an expansive account of rationality can do justice to the full spectrum of human emotions.

We can now see more precisely why perceptions of significance ought to combine activity with passivity. Some theories emphasize the idea that emotions proceed from active decisions on our part. The common mistake of such theories is their tendency to speak as if passions could be mustered up one way or another at any moment. Yet the cares that define our distinct emotional dispositions do not come into being all at once, but develop over time. We enter every situation with a particular character and a readiness to be affected in specific ways. Is grief at a person's death an emotion that it is easily within our power to have or not to have? Or is it not the case that, by the time we hear the news of such a death, our response has already been decided? We are, of course, responsible for the development of our concerns over time, but the dispositions we embody in a given instant are not so plastic that we can spontaneously judge an event to be cheerful or disturbing or whatever we will. Unless our consciousness is only an assortment of value-neutral facts, we cannot be assured of having total command over our thoughts and responses.[49] The Stoics, as we have seen, locate our greatest control at the moment of "assent" to an impression. Perceiving something as significant includes an initial action. Although objects actively impress themselves upon us, they do not force us to give assent to them in one way or another.[50] But once we do, it is as if we have set a cylinder rolling: our mental states take on a momentum of their own.[51] If we have assented falsely, then our minds will be corrupted as a result of this mistake.

We are passive, then, with respect to situations: our care extends further than our control, and in that sense our emotions reveal the ways in which the world acts upon us. It is not the passions themselves, but the objects of concern beyond ourselves, to which we are passive.[52] And, since we have some power of assent regarding what we care about and how we see things, we are not entirely helpless with respect to our own emotional liabilities. We can, to some degree, assess and alter the conditions of our passivity by reconsidering the way in which we perceive the world, liberating ourselves from such prejudices as, for example, that envy and pride are "manly" passions.[53] If we continue to find ourselves taken by storm with emotions, these can only be an indication that something is of vital concern to us: and why shouldn't this kind of perception pull our attention away from everything else?[54] Self-disruptive upheaval, far from being an irrelevant distraction, might signal an opening of awareness toward new rational understanding: it is abstract ratiocinations lacking passionate force which are most likely to be irrelevant. If emotions are our way of perceiving significance in our lives, then it is dispassionate cognition which ought to be regarded with distrust in the realm of human values.[55]

The Structural Critique (Stoic Virtue)

The Stoic view of emotion includes a normative principle which is typically formulated as an epistemological claim. Passions, the Stoics argue, are false, and it is within our power to eradicate them in the name of preserving our cognitive integrity.[1] As we have seen, both early and late Stoic thinkers agree that nothing matters except what is within our control.[2] We tend to care for many things, thereby rendering ourselves liable to being affected; instead, say the Stoics, we ought to "make the best of what is up to us" while accepting everything else the way it is.[3] If we educate ourselves about what is truly of value—that is, our own moral volition—then we will not be susceptible to passions.[4] The objects of our care would not cause us to become upset if it were not for our own attitude toward them. As Marcus Aurelius says: "If you are disturbed by something outside yourself, it is not the thing which troubles you but your own conception of it, and it is within your power to obliterate this immediately."[5] This statement may exaggerate the ease of undoing a perception of significance, but it suggests that we *can* transform the judgments that render us liable to be affected—and, to the extent that we are able to do so, that we may eliminate the conditions of emotion. This strategy ought to appeal to anyone who is suffering too much, such as the young woman whose tragic story was related in the first epigraph to Part I. At certain times, even a poet can feel its charm:

17

It's when I'm weary of considerations,
And life is too much like a pathless wood
Where your face burns and tickles with the cobwebs
Broken across it, and one eye is weeping
From a twig's having lashed across it open.
I'd like to get away from earth awhile
And then come back to it and begin over.[6]

It is hard for even a non-Stoic to accept that the considerations which provide our lives with meaning also cause us so much pain. Stoic morality offers us a way of dissolving this paradox: if it is wrong to care about anything beyond one's own control, then we should not be torn between beauty, insight, and instability on the one hand and drab insensibility on the other. Instead, as Seneca says, we should recognize that the emotional life is wavering and unstable, beauty is not to be found among externals, and the untroubled state of mind that results from driving out the passions is stern, but happy.[7] The proto-Stoic teachings of Diogenes the Cynic portray this state as one of peaceful simplicity which is ruined when we believe that we must have luxuries in order to be happy; for Zeno, the founder of Stoicism, the goal of uprooting such beliefs is to get rid of the stupidity from which so many emotions arise.[8] To avoid this kind of stupidity is a virtue, or an admirable state of character.

What enables the Stoics to frame their normative thesis in epistemological language is a method of arguing that sees wisdom as a kind of mental health and foolishness as something akin to insanity. On this view, moral and intellectual virtues cannot be neatly distinguished; as a number of contemporary philosophers have also recognized, epistemological terms are inescapably evaluative.[9] From the assessment that a given proposition is *false,* it is a small step to conclude that anyone who believes the proposition to be true is *wrong.* The falsity is a characteristic of the proposition, the wrongness a fact about the person. Now, in order to find significance in anything one must assent (explicitly or implicitly) to a value-ascribing proposition. If I am angry at you for slashing my tires, then I must believe a number of things, including (1) that I have tires, (2) that they have been slashed, (3) that you are the one who did it, and (4) that this should matter to me. The Stoics aim their critique at this last belief, a version of which can be found in every instance of passion: namely, the idea that something outside of one's own control is significant. Since they argue that this cannot be true, they conclude that the passions—which, by definition, involve this kind of belief—must always be false. It is for the sake of our mental integrity, then, that we should attempt to get rid of the passions entirely. The state of *apatheia* which would result from this expulsion is one in which not only our passions but also our susceptibility to passion have been taken out by the roots. This is the condition in which an exceptionally virtuous person will sustain himself or herself: anyone who wrongly finds significance in contingencies is viewed by the Stoics as irrational, or even insane.[10]

Instances of false or mistaken passion illustrate the ways in which we can be wrong in being passionate—that is, the ways in which our emotions can be erroneous. Our emotional lives become contemptibly and oppressively stupid, first of all, when we allow ourselves to care about what Seneca refers to as petty incidents. It is madness, he says, to become incensed by such trivialities as a disarranged couch cushion or a table imperfectly set.[11] His examples occasionally sound dated, but the tendency he describes is perennial: in a similar spirit, the philosophical anthropologist quoted earlier follows his portrayal of the self as an amoeba with this admonition:

> Usually we extend these pseudopods not only to things we hold dear, but also to silly things; our selves are cluttered up with things we don't need, artificial things, debilitating ones. For example, if you extend a pseudopod to your house, as most people do, you might also extend it to the inventory of an interior decorating program. And so you get vitally upset by a piece of wallpaper that bulges, a shelf that does not join, a light fixture that "isn't right."[12]

The triviality of emotion is linked with the weakness that it exposes in us, when we allow ridiculous things to become significant to us. We often resemble the person who, when advised not to complain that life is sometimes unpleasant, whines to Epictetus: "Oh, but my nose is running!"[13] When we are too soft to tolerate even a mild annoyance, we compromise our dignity and render ourselves pathetic. If we guarded against these petty concerns, rather than taking them to heart, we would free ourselves from the passions that handicap us with their banality. Only then could we turn our attention toward what is truly significant.

Sometimes the Stoics go no further than to censure emotional responses that are disproportionate because we are excessively concerned about paltry objects. This argument might be called a *structural* critique, since it depends upon the ability to discern the comparative significance of particular externals (as opposed to the *fundamental* thesis which dismisses all externals as categorically unimportant). And it is a valuable one, since even a non-Stoic moral philosophy should not regard emotions as invulnerable to rational criticism: they are certainly fallible, and they may be especially prone to distortion, bias, and excess.[14] At one point, Chrysippus defines the passions as diseases not just because they see certain things as good, but because they do so to an unnatural extent.[15] Someone who builds his or her entire life around the pursuit of fashionable outfits could, on this account, be accused of going too far, even if being dressed is worth a bit of attention. And we often go much too far with regard to petty things—caring too much about what other people think of us, for instance, or about how much money we have in the bank.[16] Normally, though, the Stoics will not grant that a person who has lost a daughter should be more upset than one who has lost a kitchen utensil: for anything but a dispassionate response will be seen as excessive. "The man who would fear losing any of these things cannot be happy," Cicero reminds us. "We want the happy man to be safe, impregnable, fenced and fortified, so that he is not just largely unafraid, but completely."[17] And we are liable to suffer as long as we believe that aspects of the world outside of our control are significant *at all*. By telling ourselves that these things do not "really" matter, we can annihilate this liability.

The thoroughgoing Stoic does not, therefore, force a staid demeanor from the top down. She does not have emotions that she holds in check. Her tranquillity arises without conflict out of a deep freedom from any cares that would dispose her toward being moved. Stoics, in other words, do not triumph over passions as they occur, but shun whatever may lead to emotion. And the method is effective: if we monitor ourselves in this way, we can evade much suffering that we would otherwise experience. Sincere care for anything subject to chance entails the possibility of suffering; by loving we become susceptible to all kinds of emotional torment. To return to Augustine's terminology for a moment, if the passions are bad (as the Stoics believe), then the love that underlies them must be a dubious influence which ought to be resisted.[18] Even if love does not always lead to the kind of violence portrayed in tragic drama,[19] it can nonetheless bring fierce emotions into every mundane situation. We sometimes find ourselves striking out at inanimate objects, as when we kick a stone in anger after absentmindedly walking into it.[20] Believing that even apparently major events should not arouse a passionate response, the Stoics accordingly find the most grotesque excess in vehement passions that are instigated by paltry concerns.

The allegations against emotion—that it renders us trivial and weak, that it usually becomes disproportionate and always puts us in a precarious relation to what is out of our power—justify the Stoic attempt to mitigate our cares (and perhaps to get rid of them entirely). But there is yet another type of charge directed by stoical authors at the category of passion: that, compared with other forms of cognition, it is notoriously prone to confusion.[21] Emotions do not only focus the mind; they can also cloud it in such a way that "it does not see things in their whole context."[22] Seneca's caricature of what anger does to a person extends a theme introduced by Chrysippus, who insists that a false belief can grow into a disorder that "penetrates the veins and attaches itself to the viscera," becoming ineradicable once embedded.[23] Our belief-forming procedures are often flawed, as the Skeptics recognized: how often might we be perceiving confusedly in the moment of emotion? Our passionate reactions could be influenced by biases which were established in our minds through some unreliable process yet which persistently affect our thinking. Considering the risk of such error in our emotional responses, we might be tempted to forgo all but apathetic modes of cognition.

There is also the risk of what could be called emotion by association: I return to the town where I was once in love with a certain person, in order to visit her again under quite different conditions. But the associations of the place remind me of what it was like, and soon I am confused into almost believing myself still in love. The intentionality of the former passion is not reestablished, but in remembering I live it again confusedly. "If the mind has once been affected by two emotions at the same time," Spinoza cautions, "when it is later affected by the one it will also be affected by the other."[24] This can precipitate a whole cluster of confused, or self-deceived, emotions. When many significant concerns are touched upon at once, ambiguity is likely to ensue; likewise, whenever unclear thoughts are brought to bear upon a situation, we will perceive it in a vague way. Again, the Stoics offer a solution to this predicament: if we stop caring about what is beyond the scope of our own volition, then all of these difficulties will disappear. "What is external to my mind is of no concern," Marcus Aurelius says; and Epictetus adds that "whatever happens, if it is outside the realm of choice, then it is nothing to me."[25] Caring about inconstant objects is "a certain recipe for disappointment, anxiety, and unhappiness": if we never question appearances of value, if we do not avoid concern about external things, then we are bound to suffer as a result.[26] The Stoic avoids this suffering by withdrawing his care from the realm of chance events and cultivating an impersonal point of view. This method makes it easier to deal with "the ups and downs of life":[27] it can help us moderate or even avoid selfish jealousies, misplaced blame, road rage, frustration at work, or turmoil over sudden changes of fortune.

Another reason for eradicating our particular attachments is that intense passions for certain objects can limit the scope of our moral awareness. Selfish cares can be overcome if we develop an impartial regard for humanity instead.[28] It is only in this way, the Stoics argue, that each of us can live in harmony with the rational order of the universe. Rather than celebrating the accidents of time and place that lead us to form specific affinities, Seneca encourages us to consider ourselves part of a greater community, "where we look not to this or that corner, but measure the boundaries of our state by the sun."[29] If our moral purpose is uniquely worthy of respect, then our highly personal concerns are not an expression of what is best in us. The Stoics tell us that we can read in the nature of the cosmos a moral imperative which bids us to care equally for all rational beings.[30] And no less compassionate a person than Gandhi has agreed with the Stoics that our individual passions may blind us to the plight of those who are not within our circle of concern.[31] In other words, the passions that Stoic teachings urge us to overcome may be distinctly at odds with humanitarian charity.

Diogenes the Cynic is reported to have compared himself to a chorus leader who pitches a note too high so that the others may stretch their voices toward it.[32] Similarly, the aphorisms of the Stoics are strong and uncompromising in order that they may have a transformative effect. Taken at face value, however, these prescriptions would enable a person to be in control of his or her world. When we open ourselves to emotion, we lose that assurance. In the words of Pierre Hadot, the elimination of the passions through stoical exercise "raises the individual from an inauthentic condition of life, darkened by unconsciousness and harassed by worry, to an authentic state of life, in which he attains self-consciousness, an exact vision of the world, inner peace, and freedom."[33] By withdrawing the bonds of care that attach us to objects beyond ourselves, we anticipate the risk of being injured when these appendages are torn away:

> There is no more certain proof of greatness than to be in a state where nothing can possibly happen to disturb you. The higher and more well-ordered part of the universe, nearest to the stars, is not condensed into a cloud or lashed into a tempest or churned into a whirlwind; it is free of all

tumult. It is only in the lower regions that lightning strikes. In the same way the lofty mind always remains calm, at rest in a tranquil haven.[34]

This calm anchorage is the state of *apatheia,* or the absence of *pathos,* that should result from obedience to the precepts of normative Stoicism. Since passions are perceptions of significance, a person for whom nothing in the world is significant will (as a logical consequence) rest in a condition of apathy. As Epictetus points out, it is only by altering our beliefs that we can rid our lives of sorrow and disappointment, and of such cries as "Woe is me!"[35]

Complete freedom from emotion is taken by the Stoics to be necessary for emotional integrity. They trace all false evaluations to mistaken ways of thinking about the nature of reality, seeing in the logic of the cosmos a model of rational order that should be mirrored in the human soul.[36] Apart from the perfection of the soul, they recognize no other good as truly worth pursuing. This enables Marcus Aurelius to say that what is truly valuable in us cannot be damaged under any circumstances, "even if wild animals tear to pieces the limbs of this claylike matter which has grown around you."[37] As the Stoics consistently encourage us to believe, our true self is not touched by such incidents. Seeing that our emotions are in need of clarification, they urge us toward a goal which is attainable by any of us, regardless of our situation.[38] In return we are promised not only freedom and peace, but also consistency over the course of life and sincerity of character.[39] As a later advocate of self-reliance would agree, we achieve peace of mind only when we rise above contingency and cease to look outside of ourselves. "A political victory, a rise of rents, the recovery of your sick or the return of your absent friend, or some other favorable event raises your spirits, and you think good days are preparing for you. Do not believe it. Nothing can bring you peace but yourself."[40]

CHAPTER 3

The Fundamental Thesis
(Stoic Values)

Unquestionably, the Stoic program for the eradication of passion is a sound practical method with a number of advantageous results. But there may be another, less attractive side of the story as well. It is a virtue of Stoicism to subject the passions to a qualified structural critique, not to get rid of them altogether. Yet this is the fundamental thesis of Stoic ethics: since nothing outside of oneself is truly of value, emotions are false perceptions of significance that does not exist. Faced with the question "whether it is better to have moderate passions or none," Seneca responds unequivocally that the Stoics "expel the passions entirely."[1] I will argue in this chapter that consistent adherence to the principle of total extirpation would prohibit a person from perceiving meaning in the world, leading necessarily to a condition of absurdity.[2] In other words, the achieved calm of the sage who can drift through any situation without the risk of being moved is attained at a price: to be free from the burden of perceiving significance in life is to be closed off to the experience of value. Complete independence from contingent events can be preserved only by a person who remains in a state of dangerous estrangement. But it is as *participants,* not as bystanders, that we are able to find meaning in the world. Stoic morality is consistent with, and may even entail, an existential despair like that of the young man whose wanderings around Oxford were related in the second epigraph to Part I.

It is fair enough to point out cases in which our emotions are in need of moderation. The argument that nothing in our lives deserves to be taken too seriously,[3] however, betrays a chilling disdain for human existence. Such is the tone of Schopenhauer, when he draws the grim conclusion that "the world and life can afford us no true satisfaction, and are therefore not worth our attachment to them."[4] In the midst of brutal emotional suffering we may indeed wish that we might never again experience the fiery surge of jealousy or the incapacitating blankness of sorrow: but must we scorn the world quite so coldly? Seneca is being humane when he says that wisdom does not require us to be infuriated at everything that could plausibly be seen as infuriating—if it did, then a perceptive person would be constantly upset.[5] But he sounds quite antihumanistic when he says in praise of laughter that it "involves slight emotional commitment and indicates that nothing in the appurtenances of life is important or serious or even pitiful."[6] Stoicism is not a soothing tonic for moments of distress: it is a comprehensive philosophy which offers us the somber consolation that we should not be emotional because our lives are utterly insignificant.[7]

As we have seen, when the Stoics want to show that emotions are prone to triviality, they select examples of objects that are unworthy of our care or that are cared about excessively. This rhetorical strategy relies upon a contrast with other objects which are not so trivial: the contents of my mind, for example, as opposed to the contents of my laundry basket. But if nothing outside of my own volition is significant, then these apparently worthier objects must be just as unworthy of care. Stoicism requires us, not merely to renounce trivial objects of concern, but to let this renunciation become the first step on a progress toward accepting that everything under the sun is unimportant. Epictetus prescribes a meditation intended to help us learn that the art of losing isn't hard to master:

> This is what you ought to practice from morning until night. Begin with the most trivial and fragile things, such as a pot or a cup; then move on to a cloak, a puppy, a mere horse, a piece of land; then on to yourself, your body and its members, as well as your children, wife, and brothers. Look around in every direction and hurl these things away from yourself. Purify your judgments, lest something that is not your own may be attached to you, or joined together with you, which may hurt when it is torn away.[8]

By limiting the boundaries of our care, we gain a kind of self-contained security: yet we may wonder if something worth holding onto has not been lost along the way. While it may be wrong to care more about a pot than a pet, more about a possession than a person, it is not obviously wrong to care *at all* about *either*. In order to be comprehensively apathetic, though, we must reduce all values to zero—if everything outside of one's control is equally insignificant, then even our children must be no more precious than our dishes. As Seneca admits, in order to recognize that some things affect us more than they ought to, it is necessary to depart from the Stoic position that nothing should affect us at all.[9] The attack on triviality makes sense only if not everything is trivial.

When Epictetus poses the rhetorical question, what difference does it make what object a person has a weakness for and depends upon,[10] we might reply: it makes *all* the difference. In a certain sense, what we love defines who we are; when we refrain from caring we do not attain personal integrity but condemn ourselves to personal disintegration. From this perspective, the process of detachment from one's world of concern is not a triumph but a tragedy: "As I chop away at the chains that bind me to loved others, asserting my freedom, I move into a wilderness of strangers and loneliness, leaving behind all who cared for me and even, perhaps, my own self."[11] In a striking parallel to Epictetus, an anti-stoical thinker offers this alternative view:

> Yes, he knew that he was now withdrawing from everything: not merely from human beings. A moment more and everything will have lost its meaning, and the table and the cup, and the chair to which he clings, all the near and the commonplace, will have become unintelligible.[12]

Rilke's narrator is horrified to witness the dying man become so estranged that he can no longer perceive his world as significant. Even if some things are not worth caring about, it may be that others are. This is a modest observation, but it requires us to make a whole range of evaluative distinctions. Emotions reveal the connections that determine the meaning of our life as moral agents,[13] and it would be a good idea for us to pay attention to what they show us. To a great degree, our identity is defined by relations of concern extending into the world:[14] disowning every attachment would leave us in a state of hollow isolation.

The morally vacuous narrator of Camus's *The Fall* argues that "to be happy it is essential not to be too concerned with others."[15] Granted, the Stoics do not make their point about the happy life in quite these terms, but could they consistently disagree with this statement? They agree that unconcern is the proper attitude toward externals, and that dispassionate self-sufficiency is commendable. When the antihero of *The Stranger* begins his narrative by flatly announcing that his mother has died,[16] shouldn't the reader recognize this as the voice of someone who accepts the idea that life and death are equally indifferent? Meursault's lack of grief would presumably be applauded by Epictetus, who specifically tells us that we should think of even our closest family members in such a way that we will not be disturbed when they die.[17] The Stoic may in fact be the more terrifying character, since he can give reasons for believing that *nothing matters*.[18] Although we may admire the historical Stoics for cases in which they demonstrated a bit of warm human affection, as when Marcus Aurelius "is thinking nostalgically of those whom he has loved, and whose departure has left him profoundly alone,"[19] we ought to admit that in such cases they departed from their own arguments. Chrysippus says that the way to console a person who is mourning is to convince him that his grief depends upon a false judgment.[20] To care about the presence or absence of another person is not compatible with Stoic doctrine.

When we consider its intersubjective implications, Stoicism begins to appear more like an abomination than a tenable moral philosophy. A person who doesn't care one way or another for any contingent matter is not a "citizen of the universe" but an intruder to the human community—as Meursault calls himself, after showing that he is just as indifferent to the sufferings of others as he is to the outcome of a soccer game.[21] Here we see the darker consequences of adopting the motto sung by a character of Byron's:

> To feel for none is the true social art
> Of the world's Stoics—men without a heart.[22]

The speaker tells Juan that he has not found himself troubled by friends since his conversion, and this is no surprise. Seneca claims that the wise Stoic with his skill in the art of making friends can fill the place of someone he has lost, just as a sculptor can immediately carve another statue if he loses one.[23] Whatever solace this image may offer for someone who has lost a friend, it is unfortunately based upon a denial of the distinctive singularity of another human being. To encounter others merely as dispensable objects, and not as irreplaceable individuals, one must resist their claim to be recognized as loving and suffering beings, not merely as potential threats to one's own equanimity.

Furthermore, the failure to respond to another person can sometimes betray a deficient perception of what is going on: having noticed that the person in front of me appears to be in pain, I can be dispassionate toward him only if I do not care about his suffering.[24] Moral perception which does not engage the emotions is at risk of missing significant features of the situation. For instance, if two companions of Socrates observe that he is pale, one may be ignorant that this pallor is the symptom of a fatal disease, while the other is a doctor who cannot help but take note of this additional fact. Once he has noticed it, his only way of remaining dispassionate in his observation is through indifference to his companion's potential sickness and death. If this doctor is a Stoic, he will view health, and life itself, as "indifferent" in any case, not subscribing to "the frivolous and arbitrary belief" that these are good things which ought to be valued.[25] He may "prefer" health over sickness, life over death, but not so much as to be even minimally disappointed when his patient grows ill and dies.[26] Of course, if he has actually experienced severe physical pain, like the unorthodox Stoic known as Dionysius the Renegade, he may find it impossible to go on believing that pain is something indifferent.[27] Again, this is a departure from the party line: the consistent Stoic must remain in control of his or her world, and cannot acknowledge the reality of human suffering.

It is true that universal regard for humanity requires us to go beyond our private cares, but this does not require apathy at the level of individual psychology. The lesson we learn from exceptionally compassionate human beings is not how to be unconcerned but how to extend our concern beyond the most private of attachments. The image proposed by Hierocles—of drawing our circles of concern ever closer so that we care about foreigners as much as we do our fellow citizens, about those in our family as much as we do ourselves—is admirable, but ought to be recognized as heterodox.[28] For he tells us to strive fervently to increase our affection for the members of each group, and to reduce the distance of all relationships in a way that can only increase our emotional liabilities.[29] More consistent with the goal of apathy is Seneca's suggestion that we step back and laugh at the human condition,[30] since from a distant vantage point everything that generally affects us appears small and insignificant. But can genuine concern for others be reconciled with such a dismissive and condescending attitude?[31] With enough deadening of sympathetic affection, one might even be able to regard a human torso as uninhabited matter:

> To observe the contortions of the human body in the air, upon the blowing up of an enemy's ship, may raise laughter in those who do not reflect on the agony and distress of the sufferers; but the reflecting on this distress could never move laughter of itself.[32]

The example is harsh, but is there not a similarity between the laughter of the aloof Stoic and that of the person who cannot see his blown-away enemy as a suffering human being? Sympathetic emotion is avoided in both cases by assuming a point of view from which the movements of other people's bodies are no concern of my own. In order for the Stoic to secure tranquillity, he must adopt a perspective from which the sufferings of others are invisible.

For the non-Stoic, there is no dispassionate way of acknowledging the pain of another person: only through ignorance or indifference can we remain unemotional in the face of the other.[33] Or is it possible to care for someone without being moved when he or she is unhappy?[34] With regard to sympathetic affection, Epictetus is the spokesman for orthodox Stoicism:

> "But I have just parted from someone, and he is terribly wounded." Yes, but why did he regard what was not his own as his own? Why, when he was fortunate enough to see you, did he not consider that you are mortal and likely to go away? And therefore he is paying the penalty for his own foolishness.[35]

The hard-core Stoic cannot even have pity for those who are unenlightened. Here, the interlocutor is instructed to think only of his own imperturbable mind and to dismiss any thought of how his friend might feel about the separation. If he cannot replace you as easily as he would replace a broken cup, Epictetus says, that's his problem.

But if the true Stoic cannot acknowledge the legitimacy of another person's emotion, there will be consequences beyond the realm of intimate relations. Such a person will not be able to see the evil of human cruelty, since this involves an injury that he is committed to viewing as insignificant. If it is insane to get upset about anything, then we must never feel sorrow on behalf of another person, nor afraid for someone who is in danger. Of course, not all fears are appropriate—but, as Aristotle says, there are nonetheless some things that a person ought to fear.[36] Even the emotion of anger, so prone to excess and so badly chastised by Seneca, might have its place in certain situations. Negative emotions often call our attention to a disparity between what is and what ought to be—how "sane" would it be to close ourselves off from that form of moral perception?[37] Stoicism bears a resemblance to other philosophies of absurdity because it asks us to view the world beyond ourselves as devoid of value: the Stoic's motto ("it is nothing to me") is practically equivalent to "nothing matters,"[38] and it may lead directly to the same axiological vacuum that the existentialist is lamenting.

Camus writes that the absurd "depends as much on man as on the world,"[39] but it seems that by merely following his own precepts the Stoic is capable of singlehandedly reducing himself to a condition of absurdity. Any person for whom all emotions are false is either in a meaningless world or is incapable of recognizing significance outside of himself. When we do not care about anything, we cannot perceive the world except as insignificant: the absence of love is all that is needed for vanity to consume everything. While it is not within our power to make ourselves love just any object, it may be possible to blind ourselves to the significance of things. If the Stoic goes into situations with her mind already made up about how (not) to feel, then she is closing herself off to the experience of value. The prejudice that nothing is worth caring about can easily become a self-fulfilling prophecy, leading to a condition of nihilistic indifference.[40] What can we say about those who have contrived to escape suffering? "Yes, it is true that they have escaped. They have also escaped having any insight into life and have escaped into meaninglessness."[41]

By attempting to remain in control of our moral world, we not only cling to an unachievable ideal of omnipotence but also lose touch with something that is worthy of being included as part of our lives.[42] Seneca says that love is incompatible with wisdom, since we ought to avoid a condition of powerless dependence.[43] But the ability to love could be seen as a positive virtue, compared with which stoical composure looks like an impoverished goal—a cynical defensiveness in which one guards oneself from genuine investments of concern. If we do not intervene with any emotion-opposing tactics, then our lives as situated agents tend to involve passion. Tranquillity can be assured only through nonparticipation: unless we are detached from the world, we must be susceptible to emotional upheaval. Although Epictetus says that tragedy arises "when accidents happen to fools," we might interpret this as another way of saying that participation in life is a necessary condition of tragedy.[44] Our choice is between the risk of tragedy and the guarantee of absurdity—given that the absurd is "essentially a divorce" between self and world,[45] and that disengagement is precisely what is required in order for us to preclude any tragic experience.

The Stoic may claim that God wants us to be spectators and interpreters,[46] but this questionable appeal to authority could be countered with the argument that we are and ought to be participants as well. At one point in his narrative, the sometimes stoical Thoreau worries that it might not be good to occupy a perspective withdrawn from moral engagement:

> However intense my experience, I am conscious of the presence and criticism of a part of me, which, as it were, is not a part of me, but spectator, sharing no experience, but taking note of it; and that is no more I than it is you. When the play, it may be the tragedy, of life is over, the spectator goes his way. It was a kind of fiction, a work of the imagination only, so far as he was concerned. *This doubleness may easily make us poor neighbors and friends sometimes.*[47]

The "fool" takes part in life and thereby opens himself to passionate experience; the Stoic withdraws in order to avoid being hurt. On these terms, there is something to be said for the fool: the spectator disowns his mundane particularity in order to become a nonspecific, godlike subject. By refusing to identify himself with anything beyond the vanishing point of his moral purpose, the Stoic sneaks out of the world in order to preserve his integrity as a pure rational agent. But alienating oneself from significant features of the world is a high price to pay for the elimination of unhappy passions. The Stoics argue that the cosmos is fiery and alive, and that our end is to live in accordance with nature, since human nature is part of the nature of the universe.[48] That this example should convince us to pursue indifference is an odd interpretation, to say the least. By identifying only with our volition, we cut ourselves off from the movement of the universe, and from any other transcendent power.

The Stoics make just a few remarks about how it is possible to take part in ordinary life in spite of believing that all external goods are insignificant. Although moral agency tends to involve emotion, the exemplar of stoical wisdom can act *as if* practical goals were worth caring about.[49] How it is "psychologically possible" to make "seemingly evaluative distinctions" within the class of "indifferents" is another question.[50] When the Stoics speak of preferring health to sickness without *really* caring one way or the other,[51] it must be the case that either they are indifferent or else they are endorsing a mild value judgment and thereby opening themselves to the risk of moderate emotion. But the Stoics disassociate themselves from those philosophers who "make a point of claiming that the wise man will be . . . measured or moderate in his emotional response, rather than free from any affect altogether."[52] As for the "good passions," a category which provides a loophole to the Stoic pursuit of apathy, it is unclear whether these are really emotions, or whether this term simply refers to the reasonable disposition of a tranquil Stoic.[53] Epictetus and Marcus Aurelius have little interest in this qualification, which can be found in early Stoicism: in any case, it is difficult to imagine what unfamiliar "emotions" could exist for the Stoic sage who could remain unperturbed while being tortured on the rack.[54] But for the rest of us, even infinitesimal passions arising from barely discernible preferences are obstacles to the goal of apathy.[55] Again and again, the Stoics insist that we must be vigilant in rejecting any appearance of value.[56] The follower of their teachings may find himself agreeing with Aristo of Chios that preference and indifference are not compatible— that is, unless he nominally affirms that external goods are not truly valuable while shuddering at the prospect of their loss, as Augustine accused some of the Stoics of doing.[57] Either way, one must look elsewhere in order to find a defense of acceptable passions which are recognizable as such.

Just as there is an insincerity in words that are spoken but not meant, there can be an insincerity in empty gestures which suggest affection.[58] Someone whose heart is hardened against passion, but who goes through the motions of a passionate life nonetheless, is showing this kind of insincerity. Consider, then, what Epictetus is advocating when he says that a person can pass through life "free from pain, fear, and perturbation, at the same time maintaining with his companions the natural and the acquired relationships, of son, father, brother, citizen, husband, wife, and neighbor."[59] When Kant praises the "sublime way of thinking" that is expressed in the Stoic form of friendship, he recognizes that such a relationship is not based upon sympathy.[60] Of course, someone who closes himself off from emotional connectedness can only be so much of a friend: how much can you possibly care about a person whose death you could endure without becoming upset? Like the sentimentalist, who "desires to have the luxury of an emotion without paying for it,"[61] the person who desires affectionate friendship without the risk of grief is wishing for an impossibility.

Stoicism presents us with a vivid picture of human suffering and then suggests that a remedy can be found in passionless detachment. If we look back at the two students whose sufferings were described in the epigraphs to

Part I, it seems that the Stoics are responding to the predicament of Moore's emotionally tortured student in a way that leads directly to the apathetic estrangement of Hare's. Their remedy, in other words, is just as bad as the initial affliction: it introduces new problems of its own, not least of which is its patronizing denial of any legitimacy to the passions that we sometimes experience in the thicket of value-rich existence. Instead, they send us into a different landscape altogether: one reminiscent of a poem by Robert Frost in which the speaker looks out over a wintry field with a sense of desolation and impending doom. As he watches the darkness "falling fast," he fears that his feeling of loneliness

> Will be more lonely ere it will be less—
> A blanker whiteness of benighted snow
> With no expression, nothing to express.[62]

If we value our capacity to care, then we must admit the risk of experiencing passions: there is no reason to believe that the pursuit of emotional integrity must necessarily lead us into an emotionless wasteland. The incapacity to care for what is external to oneself is a vice; to seek to eradicate one's capacity for caring is to cultivate a vice; and to do this in the interest of achieving peace of mind is to have a selfish motive for deliberately cultivating a vice.

Epictetus at one point concedes that, once a child is born, "it is no longer in our power not to love it or to care for it."[63] His mistake in this case is to fail to see that most of our moral life falls into this pattern in a way that renders anticipatory maintenance not only undesirable but impossible. If there are attachments that we cannot help but form, losses that we cannot ignore, then a moral philosophy which tells us to be dispassionate may only encourage us to rationalize a kind of dishonesty about how we feel. Emotional perception is itself a valuable part of moral life, not merely an avoidable distraction. We do ourselves an unfortunate sort of damage when we refuse to care about other human beings any more than we care about silverware. It may be the case that passions are sometimes unreliable, but it does not follow that they are always false. However much we may admire the Stoics for placing emotion at the heart of philosophy, it is difficult to maintain that admiration after seeing the way in which their normative program reduces to absurdity. Just as coldheartedness is not an indication of moral integrity, calmness is no guarantee of wisdom.

CHAPTER 4

Integrity without Apathy?

Stoicism offers a vision of moral integrity uncorrupted by false emotion—but only by classifying all emotions as false. The premise which establishes that classification is not obviously true: it may be that not all beliefs that Z is significant, where Z is something outside my control, are therefore erroneous. But if it is not the case that every emotion must (by definition) be mistaken, then it is essential to assess all of the other ways in which our emotions could be amiss. How could we root out those passions that (in Nietzsche's words) drag us down with their stupidity—without doing away with passion altogether?[1] The critique of apathy as a moral ideal does not amount to a defense of the opposite strategy. Indiscriminate emotionalism is no more defensible than indiscriminate passionlessness: the urgent task, both conceptually and existentially, is to distinguish within the category of emotion between those that are acceptable and those that ought to be rejected. How is it possible to live passionately without being a fool? When are we prone to have emotions that are confused, obtuse, disproportionate, inappropriate, self-deceived, sentimental, or otherwise unsound? To point out the need for these evaluative terms is to turn from the descriptive theory of what an emotion is to the practical issue of how to be passionate without being irrational. "Reasonable" emotion, of course, would not mean emotion which has been sanctioned by some other intellectual faculty, but that which is trustworthy in itself. The desired end of avoiding flawed emotion might be reached via the negative way of identifying the flaws that our emotions are likely to contain.

This, however, will require a critical investigation of our entire moral life. Because our temporal existence is implicated in our emotional dispositions, there is little to say about the moment of emotion without a thorough analysis of the way in which emotions arise in the midst of our being in time. What would it take to pursue the ideal of emotional integrity, yet to acknowledge that not every emotion is false? In grappling with this question we handle what has been called "the prickliest fruit on the giant cactus of emotion theory,"[2] for although the Stoics' fundamental thesis has been found wanting, their qualified critique of emotion remains cogent. So we are left with two major questions. How could our emotional dispositions and responses avoid the kinds of inaccuracy to which they are liable? And, more fundamentally, how can we be sure that it is not wrong to find significance in the external world? Stoic philosophy, as Long points out, holds that "from propositions asserting how things are we can derive propositions concerning what is good," and this is because its concept of nature "is first and foremost a normative, evaluative, or, if you will, a moral principle."[3] This means that a different view of the world might lead us to adopt a different moral psychology than the one which is endorsed by the Stoics. Perhaps it is possible to develop an alternative philosophy that preserves the virtues of Stoicism while denying the idea that rational understanding must be dispassionate.

Any constructive defense of emotion must not only give an account of how to judge that something is objectively disappointing; it must also focus on the subjective expectations that determine what will count as grounds for disappointment. What is it all right for us to care about? How much unpredictable risk can we accept, how many concerns can we sustain, without being torn apart? Even if we have refused to adopt the view that nothing is worth caring about, it is possible and may be morally essential "to distinguish between things that are worth caring about to one degree or another and things that are not."[4] As we have noted, our caring is not entirely pliable: nevertheless, our emotional dispositions can become more or less articulate, and to the extent that we are aware of them we have some ability to criticize and to reconsider, to cultivate some while attempting to eradicate others.

The portrait of a soul that cannot be touched, however, is not going to be resuscitated in this inquiry. Our litany of the inadequacies of normative Stoicism has left no uncertainty as to why one contemporary author should associate Epictetus with images of deterioration while characterizing *detachment* and *serenity* as "vague, almost empty words, except in those moments when we would have answered by a smile if we had been told we had only a few minutes to live."[5] On the other hand, the Stoic ideal should not give way to a less exacting one: it rather needs to be replaced by a conception of a self that is able to maintain its integrity even though it is open to emotion.[6] The cardinal virtue of our renovated ethics would be nothing less than the readiness to be always affected in the right ways, based upon a care for the right things.[7] To possess the reflective foresight to have developed a clear sense of the nature and extent of one's cares, along with the concrete insight needed to comprehend an immediate situation in all of its complexity, would be to embody an extraordinary sort of wisdom. It would be to have earned the right to trust oneself in becoming passionate. The epistemological picture of a subject as "rational" to the extent that he has separated himself from his environment would then need to be thrown away as a misguided paradigm which builds a bias against valued engagement into the definition of what it is to be rational; If rationality means, not being calm, but reasoning accurately, then emotions could become a form of reliable cognition.

Attaining this ideal would require a commitment to intense self-scrutiny, and the eradication of all varieties of false belief. To affirm a life in which one seeks fulfillment through emotional relationships[8] is to see the world as, more than anything else, a fabric of attachments: such that, within the human mind, nothing is more real than the emotional force that establishes those attachments. Allowing our convictions to be formed by love does not amount to abdicating moral responsibility: it only means that we cannot aim at the psychological impossibility of being the all-powerful creators of ourselves. When the Stoic tells us that we ought to revere whatever is best in us, as an expression of what is best in the universe at large,[9] we may agree entirely with the appropriateness of that reverence while disputing his identification of abstract practical reason as what is worthy of such an attitude. Epictetus may be wrong to say that we cannot attend both to externals and to our own governing principle at the same time.[10] It could, in fact, be specifically in giving attention to what is not within our control that we are acting in accordance with our highest capacity.

The Stoics offer a tenable conception of human dignity, and their program for the eradication of passion is based upon a view of the universe which some have found satisfactory. For such a person, my description of what Stoicism prohibits might be taken as evidence in favor of being a Stoic. But I think that its deficiencies are sufficiently troubling to justify an inquiry into the possibility of an alternative—and that the nonapathetic exemplar of emotional integrity (insofar as we can conceive of such a person) represents a compelling ideal. Accepting the validity of passionate experience, affirming the truth of love in spite of every argument for resisting it, may enable a person to attain a state just as truthful, yet more admirable and courageous, than the apathy of the Stoic sage. To suggest what this state of being might be like, I quote from a biographical portrait of a great musical composer:

> He did not turn away from life toward some mystical nirvana. He forgot none of the joy, the effort, or the pain. He abandoned nothing. What he achieved is something much more wonderful than an old man's serenity. . . . There were no feigned or borrowed emotions, and nerve-storms never took the place of feelings. He had no need to complicate his joy with bitterness or to distort his rapture with cynicism. These are the devices of a man who wishes to come to terms with his suffering without facing it in all its starkness. But Beethoven had the innocence of his courage.[11]

It is fair to say that in Stoicism and its imagined alternative we are presented with different visions of wisdom—and different ideals of human existence. The stance we end up taking with regard to our own emotional nature will be determined by, or will itself determine, how we conceive of self and world. Our attitude toward emotion reveals quite a bit about our overall way of thinking: if we believe that nothing in this vain sublunary realm can affect us, then we will regard emotions as basically mistaken. If, on the other hand, we believe that a responsive engagement with the world is more truthful, then we cannot dismiss our proclivity to care as misleading. While we might not always use religious language in talking about the ultimate categories in which we understand ourselves, our attitude toward passion is nevertheless connected to our most general beliefs about the nature of reality. And if we do not agree with the Stoics, if we think that our capacity to love what is beyond our control should not be eradicated, then the reverence that Marcus Aurelius asks us to direct toward what is best in us will need to be reoriented.

In his spiritual exercises, Ignatius of Loyola lists rules "to aid us toward perceiving and then understanding, at least to some extent, the various motions that are caused in the soul: the good motions, that they may be received, and the bad that they may be rejected."[12] He submits a list of criteria for evaluating a given experience: for example, in a person who is making spiritual progress, a bad movement of soul will be sharp, noisy, and disturbing. It may or may not be possible to develop this kind of phenomenological method for assessing a moment of emotion: but even the Ignatian rule draws upon the idea of moral improvement in making its distinctions. The formation of the self over time must be taken into account if we are to set terms of evaluation within experience. Because of the intentionality of emotion, the reliability of our affective dispositions is dependent upon the coherence of our world of cares and commitments. In our situated existence, we embody an ongoing history of love and suffering, bearing witness to what has moved us.[13] What future movements should we admit, and which should we (as far as we can) strive to resist? In order to decide what passions we ought make space for, we must determine what in the world is worthy of love. Outward extends the simple fact of attachment; from that, a diverse array of passions is liable to ensue. And caring for the right things is not enough: we must also be aware of our limitations, not least of which is the limit to how much we can honestly afford to care about. As our cares increase, they are more and more likely to conflict with one another—and, even in the absence of any such conflict, we can bear only so much reality. If we accept the risk of emotion, we should remember the Stoic images of dismemberment: our integrity *is* very much at stake wherever there is an attachment of love.

If we are going to care, then, we had better be careful.[14] A solid proof that, all in all, the emotional life is worth living, is not forthcoming. But this does not mean that there is nothing to be said about various alternatives. What *can* be demonstrated, in the logical sense of showing what follows from what, are the consequences of living—whether tacitly or explicitly—in accordance with certain principles. I have already done this with certain tenets of normative Stoicism; in what follows, we will consider some other ways of thinking about emotion. From a non-Stoic point of view, it ought to be possible to develop some process of legitimation in which some emotions would drop away, but others would be amplified. In other words, it could be that *something* will remain after all false emotion has been rooted out.[15] The careful education of our emotional dispositions would perhaps leave us with something in ourselves that could be trusted. Our passions would be clarified and refined: we would understand what our sufferings were all about, and would know that they were legitimate.[16] This is a lofty goal, but if attained it would enable us to live with a kind of emotional wisdom that the Stoic will never know.

PART II

STRUCTURAL CORRECTIONS

How, then, should I become affectionate?

—Epictetus

Quiet friend of many distances,
feel how your breath is increasing space.
Among the rafters of dark belfries let
yourself ring out. Whatever eats you up

will grow strong upon this offering.
Be acquainted with transfiguration.
What is your most suffering experience?
If your drinking is bitter, turn to wine.

Be, in this immeasurable night,
magic at the junction of your senses,
be the meaning of their odd encounter.

And if the world has forgotten you,
say to the quiescent earth: I flow.
To the running water speak: I am.

—Rainer Maria Rilke

CHAPTER 5

Interlude
The Relevance of
Kierkegaard's Writings

How can we overcome the defects of normative Stoicism without succumbing to its powerful critique of emotion? The only way to resolve this problem is to find a way of distinguishing what is acceptable from what needs to be jettisoned within our passionate experience. In what follows, I will attempt to develop a moral philosophy of emotion that could stand as a positive alternative to Stoicism. The thinker who provides the organizing principles and the particular insights that will together become skeleton and flesh of my argument is one who has seldom been brought into dialogue with Hellenistic philosophy: namely, Søren Kierkegaard. But a passionate alternative to Stoicism can indeed be found in Kierkegaard's writings: his creative engagement with ancient philosophy influences his own radically original conception of emotion and its place in human life. Underlying the diverse terrain of his many works, both those he attributed to pseudonymous "authors" and those to which he signed his real name, is a shared knowledge of ancient philosophy. As a later Danish scholar has noted, "Kierkegaard's pseudonyms are just as well acquainted with Greek thought as is Kierkegaard himself."[1] Long after finishing his dissertation on Socrates and irony to the satisfaction of his principal reader, the classicist and philosopher F. C. Sibbern,[2] Kierkegaard continued to possess great respect for the Greek mentality, which he saw not merely as a historical mode of thought, but as a disposition that could be adopted in any era by a person with the right attitudes and beliefs.

What does Kierkegaard have in mind when he expresses admiration for the spirit of classical philosophy? In the modern age, he claims, people ought to become "a little more Greek in the good sense of the term, that is, more human, and not fantastically inordinate with systematic babble, which no *human being* cares about."[3] The implied contrast is with what had become the dominant style of philosophy in the Germanic intellectual climate which surrounded Kierkegaard in Copenhagen, and which he openly loathed.[4] Hegel, for instance, states that philosophical truth does not lie in edifying insights, but in a system of conceptual knowledge.[5] In opposing himself to this "systematic babble," which he saw as irrelevant to the urgent concerns of existing human beings, Kierkegaard sought to revive a conception of philosophy based upon the care of the self and the cultivation of wisdom: "In the old days people loved wisdom," he laments, "now they love the name of philosopher."[6] According to "Vigilius Haufniensis," pseudonymous author of *The Concept of Anxiety,* the Greek motto *know thyself* has become debased in modern philosophy, as if it referred to something other than the self-awareness of a particular individual.[7] In other words, thought has become detached from life in a way that it was not among the Greeks, for whom a thinker was always "an ardent existing person impassioned by his thinking."[8] But even if this notion of philosophy has become unfashionable, it is precisely what is needed in the present age.

This conviction lies behind the repeated allusions to Greek philosophy throughout Kierkegaard's writings. In the midst of their own predominant topics, his works continually incorporate references to ancient thinkers: not only Socrates, Plato, and Aristotle, but also Chrysippus, Plotinus, Diogenes the Cynic and Zeno the Stoic, Sextus Empiricus, Diogenes Laertius, Aristophanes, and Xenophon, among others.[9] Although he successfully petitioned to write his dissertation in Danish instead of scholarly Latin, Kierkegaard also read a number of Latin authors—especially those who stayed close in spirit to Greek thought, such as Cicero and Seneca.[10] He often invites comparison with ancient philosophy in less direct ways, as when he opens the first set of papers by "A" in *Either/Or* with an epigraph that echoes the *Meditations* of Marcus Aurelius, or when he avows in *Purity of Heart Is to Will One Thing* that every one of us must face the ascetic task of paying attention to himself.[11] To those who try to explain all the categories of human life without understanding themselves, he says "go hang," repeating what Epictetus is reported to have said to a person who wanted to learn philosophy only in order to solve a logical paradox.[12]

Such a puzzler would be laughed to scorn in Greece, Kierkegaard suggests, because he lacks subjective concern. A moralist through and through, Kierkegaard does not accept the idea that science is higher than existence.[13] Yet he fears that modern philosophy has become frivolous in its castle-building, and unable to give sustenance to the person in search of wisdom who is not waving but drowning.[14] Our passionate, concerned rationality is not engaged by logical chess games or by systematic abstraction—what human beings need is practical wisdom, "cognition that displays how the world is *seen,* known by *this* self, and moved by *these* emotions."[15] Socrates is therefore praised above Plato for pursuing his unscientific inquiry in the mundane world of human concern and attachment, as Epictetus would later do.[16] Much like Seneca, who upbraids philosophers who spend their time fooling around with questions of no importance, Kierkegaard argues that an earnest person will refrain from wasting time on irrelevant riddles.[17] In true Hellenistic style, his pseudonym "Anti-Climacus" uses the medical imagery of sickness and physician in his description of spiritual illness and of the person who may be able to diagnose it.[18]

Because they are animated with such a sense of pertinence and urgency, Kierkegaard's writings make the reader feel that he or she is being addressed as an individual and challenged on the spot. Kierkegaard would agree with the Stoics that those who give nominal assent to moral beliefs but "are not at all changed in their hearts"[19] are in a condition of untruth, no matter what position they may nominally endorse:

> Don't ever believe it, my friend; they have not understood it, for if they had in truth understood it, their lives would have expressed it also, then they would have done what they had understood.[20]

To know the truth means to acknowledge it deeply and completely, to allow it to permeate one's being.[21] For an existing individual, this is the fullest sense in which the truth can be said to exist; therefore, truthfulness should be attributed to persons and not to propositions.[22] By contrast, it is ridiculous to construct an abstract castle of "understanding" that one does not inhabit:

> A thinker erects a huge building, a system, a system embracing the whole of existence, world history, etc., and if his personal life is considered, to our amazement the appalling and ludicrous discovery is made that he himself does not personally live in this huge, domed palace but in a shed alongside it, or in a doghouse, or at best in the janitor's quarters.[23]

In matters of the spirit, we are told, this is always a decisive objection: if our thoughts are not the building in which we live, then something is wrong.[24] Here we might hear echoes of Epictetus telling us never to look for our work in one place and our moral progress in another, as if it would help to memorize a philosophical treatise without being affected by what it says.[25] In short, Kierkegaard's attention to the entire person in his or her concrete situation, his impatience with rumination that has nothing to do with significant issues, and his belief that we can attain the truth only as particular embodied beings, all bring him close to ancient philosophy—especially to Socrates and to Hellenistic schools such as Stoicism.

Kierkegaard also resembles the Stoics in laying heavy emphasis on the category of passion: but, unlike them, he aligns himself with the speech of Socrates in the *Phaedrus* which praises the value of sacred madness.[26] The unsettling question, then, is: when is a person fit to receive the influence of "madness" or passion without perverting it from a blessing into a curse? If a spiritual census of all humanity is ever taken, Kierkegaard claims, "there will be a far greater number under the rubric of the flabby than under the rubrics of thieves, robbers, and murderers reckoned together."[27] The flabby of spirit cannot justifiably trust their emotions, for (as the Stoics would agree) truthfulness requires "toning up the muscles of the mind."[28] To the extent that our perceptive faculties are in good shape, our emotional dispositions are more likely to be reliable.[29]

In moving from one period to another, and from one language to another, one must always be cautious about forcing correspondences between words that are far from synonymous. There is less than the usual difficulty, however, in bringing the classical scholar Kierkegaard to terms with the Stoics: in his research notes and his published writings, he often quotes a word or passage in Greek, for the sake of incorporating it into his own Danish. Sometimes he draws direct parallels between the two languages, as when he notes that

Zeno's organization of the passions is a way to distinguish among what in Danish are called *Lidenskaberne*.[30] This word for *pathos* has strongly intentional connotations in Danish, and it is noteworthy that Kierkegaard's direct quotations of the Greek word for passion often occur in the context of discussions that are comprehensible only in light of an understanding of emotions as cognitive phenomena. For instance, in *Two Ages* he speaks of a contemporary Danish literary character as being supported "by the *impetus* of passion" and then aided in making a crucial decision by her *plērophoria eis pathos,* or passionate assurance.[31] And it is in the midst of a discussion of Skepticism that "Johannes Climacus" claims that someone who abstracted from his deepest beliefs would be left with *metriōs pathein,* or moderate affect.[32] Obviously, cognition and emotion are at least interconnected in Kierkegaard's writings. We know that he learned the phrase *eukataphoria eis pathos* (disposition toward passion) from Tennemann's history of philosophy, where it is rightly ascribed to Chrysippus.[33] And the account of Stoicism that he would have learned from this source is generally dependable: Tennemann reports that, according to the Stoics, emotions are a kind of false perception, "always founded on some belief" about their objects which "ought to be . . . eradicated." We also know that Kierkegaard studied Stoic logic in Copenhagen, and may have seen it as an alternative to Hegelian logic.[34] That, from all of his research in ancient philosophy, Kierkegaard also gained a basic understanding of the Stoic theory of emotion, is evident—and unsurprising. As a student and an author he was someone on whom nothing was lost.

Kierkegaard also recognizes the distinction between the primary emotion of love and the subsequent diversity of passions that follow.[35] Although it "can give birth to pain," Kierkegaard believes that love's initial coming into existence is a "wonderful" and "enigmatic" process.[36] He uses the word "passion" to refer to both aspects of this dynamic: the primary care that we identify by saying that I "have a passion" for something, and the later reactive "passions" which this initial care may dispose me toward experiencing. The word can be used, that is, to refer both to my abiding interest in the success of my favorite baseball team and to my happy and sad reactions to its actual wins and losses. One Kierkegaard commentator illustrates the two aspects of passion with the example of a bookshop owner:

> We can know she is passionate about her shop without knowing how she is feeling. If the shop is flourishing, then on the basis of her concern for it, she will be glad (happy, joyful). If it is not quite thriving but she notes

signs of its beginning to do so, she will be hopeful. If business is going badly and she is aware of the prospect of having to close the shop, she will be anxious. If the shop fails and irrevocably closes, but she continues to care about it as before, she will experience grief. If a friend of hers takes difficult or heroic action to keep the shop solvent in time of need, she will feel grateful to him.[37]

At the end of this narrative, the commentator concludes that "virtually any concern (passion, interest, enthusiasm, attachment, involvement) can give rise to any or all of the whole range of emotions." Of course, that is why the Stoics anticipate the whole range of suffering by extirpating concern for anything beyond their control: consider what this person could have saved herself, if she had never had a passion for her shop in the first place! Although his attitude toward the passions is ultimately quite different from that of normative Stoicism, Kierkegaard is aware of the relation between grounding attachment and subsequent response.[38] In Kierkegaard's writings the best measure of how much one cares about something, of how significant it is, is the severity of the grief one would feel if it were lost: "The more grief at the loss of the particular, the more its reality and value in one's life."[39]

Just as this grief could be more or less appropriate to the actual state of the world, other emotions are susceptible to being veridical or groundless for Kierkegaard as for the Stoics. This is why he and his authors continually speak of passion in mental, often specifically epistemological, language. For example, the discussion of ancient and modern drama in *Either/Or* introduces a character with an "almost untrue" passion,[40] explicitly assigning a truth-functional adjective to an affective state. Kierkegaard makes it clear that a certain mood may be necessary for a certain understanding: no one lost in tranquil speculation, for instance, could really conceive of the concept of guilt.[41] His authors speak of the "conclusions of passion" and the "passion of the understanding,"[42] and he himself admits the risk of emotional misapprehension and the possibility that the experience of suddenly perceiving a significant truth could resemble the bodily shock of being struck by lightning.[43] One of the passages in the first part of *Either/Or* even goes so far as to coin a word that means something like "suffering-through" [*gjennemlide*] to denote the mental process of undergoing and working through the meaning of an ongoing emotion.[44] Kierkegaard's commentators have not always linked his theory of passion with the classical sources that stand behind it, but it is only because he understands emotions as cognitive phenomena that he can be accurately described as an advocate of "passionate thought," or "passionate reason."[45]

Earlier it was noted that the normative arguments of the Stoics tend to be framed in epistemological terms. Here again, with Kierkegaard, we are confronted with a philosopher who can accurately be called a "moral episte-mologist" and commended for treating certain moral and epistemological themes together.[46] Prominent among these is the question of what attitude we should have about the moral and rational status of emotion. In some places, it might appear as if Kierkegaard is endorsing a stoical distrust toward the passionate. He denounces people who are "prone to any passing emotional in-fluenza" and, in response to a friend's ill-conceived attempt to offer him romantic advice, claims to "know nothing of these sentimental palpitations."[47] He laments that we are often troubled by unworthy concerns and vexed by "these small provocations that make life so infuriating."[48] In a passage that would be at home in Seneca's discussion of anger, one of his literary charac-ters describes a moment of excessive passion:

> I opened the desk to pull out the money drawer and take what happened to be at hand. But the drawer would not budge. It was a most unfortu-nate situation. . . . The blood rushed to my head; I was enraged. Just as Xerxes had the sea whipped, so I decided to take dreadful revenge. An axe was fetched. With it I gave the desk a terrible blow.[49]

This blow supposedly released the papers that make up *Either/Or*—a lucky outcome, no doubt, but nonetheless the "editor" of those papers demon-strates that greed and haste can lead to a distorted emotional response: in this case, inflated anger. In true Socratic fashion, Kierkegaard implores his audi-ence not to care for the wrong things—for instance, not to worry about earthly concerns to the detriment of the soul.[50] When we care for the wrong things, it is as if we have "put the accent of pathos in the wrong place."[51]

It is because of the "untrustworthiness of human feelings left to their own devices" that Kierkegaard recommends a limited degree of stoical dis-trust.[52] The one confessed Stoic among his authors admits to having "always strongly mistrusted all upheavals," and Kierkegaard himself claims to have met the disdain of his critics with a stoical attitude that kept him from be-coming upset.[53] He accepts the distinction which (as he notes) is drawn by Epictetus, between what is within our power and what is not,[54] but rejects the coldness with which the Stoic detaches himself from everything that falls into the latter category. We should be wary of what we care about, but it would not be good to care about nothing. To some extent, the need for vigilance is based on a distrust of the underlying source of emotion: Kierkegaard shows some sympathy for the "Young Man" in *Stages on Life's Way,* whose outlook on love is that, "if I cannot understand the force to whose power I am surrendering, then I will not surrender to its power."[55] Even without such a fundamental distrust, however, we can believe that emotion may in some cases be flawed—as with the hypochondriac's somatic apprehensiveness, or the "sorrow" that does not yield to any reason.[56] As sharp as Kierkegaard was in his psychological observations, he did not fail to observe the possibility that a strictly physical agitation could make quasi-emotional noise. He also saw that emotions cannot always be taken at face value: he criticizes Sibbern for failing to acknowledge the "disguised passions" in which one emotion takes the form of another.[57] But most of his misgivings about the affective side of human rationality have chiefly stoical grounds. He repeats the Stoic complaint about the triviality of emotion: passion, he says, ought to be linked with significance, yet we often get passionate about insignificant trivialities.[58] And, in line with the Stoics' charge that emotions reveal a weakness in us, he recognizes that we are liable to be "buffeted by the storms of life," suffering at the hands of fate, as long as we are living in the world.[59] In *Philosophical Fragments,* "Johannes Climacus" says that the goal of ancient Skepticism was to avert the risk of being deceived by not drawing any conclusions; in the same way, Stoicism guards against "spurious emotionality and sentimentality" by not having any concerns and, hence, no emotions whatsoever.[60]

But admitting the need for caution does not require absolutely repudiating risk. And just as the Skeptic may decide to venture some belief (say, that he exists as a doubting being), the Stoic might tacitly accept that emotion could be an acceptable kind of cognition in at least some cases (at the very least, in the case of remorse at having failed to maintain her principles). Kierkegaard's limited affinity with Stoicism does not make him a member of that sect, and his vision of human life at its best is quite unlike the Stoic paradigm. He will not accept the notion that happiness is wholly up to us,[61] and he recognizes that some emotions can be unreliable without rejecting all emotions as false. Instead, he maintains that accurate passion can be a uniquely valuable mode of perception. He does not share the bias against the passions that has pervaded so much of Western philosophy and Christian theology, and in a provocative epigraph he invites his reader to question it as well:

> Is reason then alone baptized,
> are the passions pagans?

This passage, adapted from Edward Young's *Night Thoughts*,[62] stands at the front of *Either/Or* and, therefore, at the beginning of Kierkegaard's entire authorship. It poses a challenge that cuts to the heart of normative Stoicism: why couldn't passion be as legitimate as dispassionate rationality?

That Kierkegaard parts company with the Stoics on this point is unmistakable. When he condemns sentimentality, it is in order to contrast it with "true and genuine feeling"; the "sentimental palpitations" which he accuses his friend of glorifying are set, to their discredit, beside a "far more exalted" class of "healthy and powerful" emotions.[63] Kierkegaard's critique of false emotion is a step toward distinguishing what is authentic.[64] Alongside the criticism of fearing what we should not fear is the statement that we are equally wrong not to fear what *is* fearful.[65] Even anger, which admittedly can be "a dark passion," may also (it is suggested) take the noble form of "righteous indignation" that is entirely justified by circumstances.[66] On the topic of "authentic *pathos*," Kierkegaard says that "only great souls are vulnerable to passions."[67] With this idea, we are far from the stoical notion that wisdom is consummated in apathy: Kierkegaard in fact explicitly sets himself against the Stoics, saying that what he wishes to see in a person is exactly the disposition toward emotion that a Stoic must oppose.[68] In spite of the suffering that follows from affirming love, Kierkegaard will not opt for the wretched contentment of those who are past feeling: as he rhetorically asks, when someone has attempted to escape from suffering altogether, is it worse to say that he failed—or that he succeeded?[69]

Bernard Williams argues that the "real question raised by skepticism, for any sane person, is not whether any of what we say about the world is true, or even whether we know any of it to be true, but how we know any of it to be true, and how much."[70] Along the same lines, we could say that (for any sane person) the question raised by Stoicism is not whether emotion could ever be reliable, but how to know when it is and when it isn't. Kierkegaard argues that it would be a bad idea to strive for a norm of dispassionate rationality: it is insanity to talk nonsense, he concedes, but "the person is fully as mad who states a correct opinion if it has absolutely no significance for him."[71] In the *Postscript*, this is depicted with a story which comes "directly from a madhouse":

A patient in such an institution wants to run away and actually carries out his plan by jumping through a window. He now finds himself in the garden of the institution and wants to take to the road of freedom. Then it occurs to him . . . when you arrive in the city, you will be recognized and will very likely be taken back right away. What you need to do, therefore, is to convince everyone completely, by the objective truth of what you say, that all is well as far as your sanity is concerned. As he is walking around and pondering this, he sees a ball lying on the ground. He picks it up and puts it into the tail pocket of his coat. At every step, this ball bumps him, to put it nicely, on the rump, and every time it bumps him he says, "Bam! The earth is round." He arrives in the capital city and immediately goes to visit a friend. He wants to convince this friend that he is not insane, and so he paces up and down the floor exclaiming, "Bam! The earth is round." But is the earth not round?[72]

Of course, the earth is not flat, and the human world is not devoid of significance, either: the way to attain sanity is not to go around flatly asserting impertinent facts, but to gain clarity in discerning significant truth.

All talk of the possibility of emotion takes for granted, of course, that we can indeed perceive significance in the world.[73] For Kierkegaard, we can affirm meaning in life over the bleak prospect of "atoms and void" only if we do not reject the possibility of perceiving value through emotion.[74] If perceptions of significance are fundamentally illusory, then we must accept a terrifying view of the universe:

> If underlying everything there were only a wild, fermenting power that, writhing in dark passions, produced everything, be it significant or insignificant; if a vast, never appeased emptiness hid beneath everything—what would life be then except despair?[75]

In this part, I will set aside questions about the "underlying" source of emotion; these are reserved for Part III. The sequence of Kierkegaard's works invites us to begin with an analysis of the many ways in which emotions can be unsound, and then to move on to the question of whether they are fundamentally grounded.

To sum up, Kierkegaard's writings encourage us to regard passion as "the main thing . . . the real dynamometer" for human beings; at the same time, they point toward an ideal of passionate integrity.[76] Kierkegaard cautions his reader not to misunderstand him as indiscriminately approving of *every* emotion.[77] Yet if we work with vigilant persistence toward the goal of "integrated passion" or "sharpened pathos," we might succeed at extirpating false emotion without becoming apathetic.[78] We then would have replaced the Stoic ideal of an invulnerable soul with a very different model, of a person whose soundness of character arises from perceiving value in the world.[79] We would have shown that emotions *can* be justified, opening up a view of life that admits deeper experiences of meaning than Stoicism.[80]

These are admirable ideals. But unless we have a method of investigating what it would take for passion to be as reliable as other modes of rational activity, there is no reason to abandon the distrust of emotion that we have been given plenty of reason to maintain. It is one thing to argue for the importance of emotion in human life, but it is quite another to work out how we might cultivate truthful, and avoid false, emotion. Kierkegaard's works, however, give us a configuration within which an answer to this question may be worked out: the three spheres of existence.[81] The aesthetic, ethical, and religious forms of life provide us with the structure of an "ascent of love" that proceeds from the immediacy of feeling all the way to a religiousness that essentially consists in truthful passion.[82] This ascent is not the sort of ladder that one climbs in order to leave earlier stages behind entirely, but a means of identifying, step by step, the necessary conditions of reliable emotion.

CHAPTER 6

Aesthetics and Sentimentality

The air is so warm, yet the whole city seems deserted.—Then I remember my youth and my first love—then I was filled with longing; now I long only for my first longing.[1]

In one of his fragments, the young man known as "A" shows us a portrait of his own soul, cast upon the outward landscape—and what we see is a strange combination of passion and apathy. He seems to be aware of this paradox, describing his own condition as one of tormented sterility: he longs for emotion, "to have the viscera of both anger and sympathy shaken."[2] Yet he finds himself impassive, and says that he feels like a chess piece when it cannot be moved.[3] Capable as he is of momentary emotional sensitivity, even to the point of being "painfully moved" sometimes, at other times he drifts listlessly in an unemotional void.[4] In his letters to the troubled young man, Judge William pays attention to these drastic fluctuations, adding his own favorite imagery. Right away, he compliments "A" for the intensity of his passions, comparing him to a wild horse; later in the same letter, he adds that the aesthete also knows how to keep his soul as motionless as a hovering bird of prey.[5] *Either/Or*, the two-volume narrative that inaugurated Kierkegaard's authorship like a lightning bolt out of a clear sky (in the words of a contemporary reviewer), begins in the moment of emotion as it is reflected in the temperament of a pseudonymous author. The papers of "A" are brilliant but troubling: how can a person slip so quickly from passionate agitation into an immovable state?

As we have seen, emotions are responsive to objects in the world to which one has a relation of care. To be moved and then attempt to preserve the raw feel of one's emotion in abstraction from its grounding conditions is to lose touch with the emotion's meaning. When "A" talks of once having longed and now longing for that old longing, he makes this kind of shift. In the first case, his emotion had an object outside of himself; later, the object of his emotion becomes *his own emotion*. It is one thing to admire another person, and quite another to admire one's own admiring. In the latter case, the emotion has been cut off from its intentional object and become senti-mental.[6] As Kierkegaard writes, "Sentimentality is to true, genuine feeling as the sparrow to the swallow. The sparrow lets the swallow build its nest and get everything ready and then lays its young there."[7] The sentimental person, in other words, wants to have the effect without the cause; that is, he wishes to have an affective experience without having to deal with its grounding conditions. So we find "A" rejoicing in the moment of emotion (say, of falling in love) by taking his emotion home like a treasure, which is no longer a response to value but something valued in itself.[8] Once this shift has taken place, the sentimentalist can dispense with whatever was moving—so he kicks away the ladder he has used to climb up into his emotional state.

This is the sense in which, as the judge points out, "A" demonstrates that "sentimentality and callousness are one and the same."[9] His life is a constant oscillation between responsiveness and disengagement:

> You let everything pass you by; nothing makes any impact. But then something suddenly comes along that grips you, an idea, a situation, a young girl's smile, and now you are "involved."[10]

He is not involved, only "involved," because the passions arising out of his participation in concrete reality are kept separate from their original objects. And once they are deprived of the reason for their existence, they tend to lose their substance, become vapid, and evaporate, leaving the aesthete with apathetic exhaustion in the wake of his passion. He wants to have the luxury of an emotion without paying for it, and this short-lived excitement followed by emptiness is what he must suffer for taking the easy way out, rather than attending to the intentional referent of his emotion. Take, for instance, an episode of grief: this supposedly involves attitudes about a valued person that one has lost. If one really feels this way, one will continue to live in accordance with the idea that this uniquely and immeasurably valuable person is gone forever. But to live with this awareness, Kierkegaard says, is too much for most of us: we prefer a "momentary upsurge" of grief, followed by "spineless nonsense"—letting the emotion register and accepting its consequences would make life too strenuous.[11] So it can be said of the sentimentalist that his evaluative responses never truly get hold of him, or that he always remains a cynic at heart.[12] It is logically impossible to have detachment from contingent externals and authentic emotion at the same time.

Here, in the momentary upsurge and the spineless nonsense—that is, the passion whose meaning is lost on the aesthete and its abstract aftermath in which he lives oblivious to this meaning—lie the two major mistakes of this pattern of emotional existence. If we take emotions seriously as perceptions of significance, we should try to appreciate their significance by understanding whatever is being perceived. But "aesthetic pathos," as Johannes Climacus says, has these structural flaws: it either distances itself from existence or else is present in it through an illusion.[13] In other words, it either assumes an inappropriately detached point of view, or else it takes part in the surrounding environment but does so on false terms. Later on, I will offer a more charitable reading of what might motivate the aesthete's reluctance to participate; for now, I intend to focus on the problems that follow from his negative attitude toward moral engagement.

Emotional responses, for Kierkegaard, are "a kind of immediate impression of the way things are," that is, a kind of intentional perception.[14] In using the term "aesthetic," he is alluding to the Greek word *aisthēsis* and its association with perception in a broad sense, not simply referring to the philosophy of art.[15] The "aesthete" is someone whose emotional responses tend to be sensationalized, as the objects that aroused them are forgotten:

> What a strange, sad mood came over me on seeing a poor wretch shuffling through the streets in a somewhat worn pale green coat flecked with yellow. I felt sorry for him, but nevertheless what affected me most was that the color of this coat so vividly reminded me of my childhood's first productions in the noble art of painting. This particular color was one of my favorite colors.[16]

What begins as an intentional perception with moral significance (i.e., it involves pity) shifts to a mere color-perception, and soon the aesthete is basking in an after-image, as he forgets the coat and contemplates a merely sensational color-phenomenon. If his emotion is about anything, by the end of the passage, it is about himself, as he mixes in a nostalgic memory. For the most part, it appears to have been emptied of meaning and turned from a perception into an objectless sensation. Sometimes "A" notices certain qualities of the object, but not others, as when he hears the sighs and cries of anguished unhappiness as beautiful music.[17] These may sound beautiful, but they are also the expression of a meaning which is not beautiful: to be moved only by their beauty, one must be blind (in this case, deaf) to other properties of the object to which one is ostensibly responding. This is how emotion frequently becomes sentimental: one falsifies the world in order to feel the way one wants to, noticing only those details that justify the desired response.[18] This kind of selective attention is a form of emotional self-deception. It is at least an epistemic fault, and may take forms that are morally deplorable as well: if we shield ourselves from perceiving whatever does not appeal to our taste, then we will be limited to "aesthetic" emotion in the pejorative sense. For a person in this mode of existence, reality can have significance only as superficially and temporarily stimulating, not as the source of deep or abiding value. The aesthete is a kind of emotional gourmet, who pays no attention to the significance of his or her passions but relishes them as a kind of delicacy—which, like salmon, ought to be enjoyed in small quantities.[19]

This merely quantitative attitude toward emotion gives a person no reason to care about whether the basis of a given passion is solid or shaky, clear or confused. Anyone who is unconcerned about the truthfulness of his emotions might as well be satisfied with an indefinite "longing gazing into an eternity"— that is, if the sentimental thought is "to cast a twilight glow over existence, like the blue mountains on the distant horizon, if the unclarity of the soul's condition is to be satisfied with the greatest possible ambiguity."[20] The aesthete is not interested in perceiving things accurately: his romantic soul refuses to come to terms with the mundane world, and searches for some ideal object instead.[21] It does not matter how vaguely conceived the object may be, as long as it gives rise to some emotion or other that can animate one's experience with affective intensity. If the sentimentalist is in touch with reality at all, he sees it only through the colored lenses and shifting mists of illusory belief.[22] But when we ignore the reason for the existence of our emotions, we cannot tell when they are well-founded phenomena and when they are weighing us down with their stupidity.

If what the aesthete seeks is nothing more specific than "momentary passion," then it doesn't matter whether he is focusing on the most sublime or the most trivial object: why not give one's birthright for a bowl of cereal, as "A" at one point nostalgically feels like doing?[23] If his goal is only to regard *something* as highly significant, then a bowl of cereal will serve as well as anything else; likewise, if one's goal is to have sweet and tender emotions only, it is necessary that, instead of seeing things as they are, one see only such properties as cuteness and innocence. This may, unfortunately, require the simplification of ignoring other properties, or the distortion of projecting the desired properties onto the object.[24] When we seek to be equally passionate about everything, we lose sight of the boundary between the significant and the insignificant. This, according to Kierkegaard, is the problem with salt-of-the-earth theologian Nikolaj Grundtvig: he has the capacity to become intensely emotional, but lacks the ability to judge "whether it is something great or something empty" that has moved him.[25] He cannot make the distinction, and as a result his passions are of indefinite significance.

Emotions that involve a mistaken relation to reality, which dissolve when the facts come to light, are not worth having. The emotions that we avoid by shielding ourselves from unhappy facts, on the other hand, are the ones that we should have the courage to experience, not because of their unpleasantness but because of their truth. One of Kierkegaard's authors laments how, in his "courageous age," people often lack the courage to admit a simple fact— for instance, when "we dare not tell a patient that he is about to die," even if we would show this person more respect by being honest about his condition.[26] Is it worth lying, is it worth a fantastic misunderstanding, to save ourselves and others from unpleasant truths? The sentimentalist answers "yes" and maintains an asinine happiness by projecting false qualities onto the world, or by cultivating a selective attention and seeing only what he or she wants to see. We may not be able to sustain an awareness of every disturbing truth at every moment, but a life lived in deliberate ignorance of all such truths is incompatible with emotional integrity.

Anyone who does not take her emotions seriously in the first place is unlikely to follow them up with a sustained awareness of the ways in which she has been moved. She will merely enjoy the momentary upsurge, then follow it with spineless nonsense, acting as if nothing significant had happened. So, after being momentarily affected, the aesthete suddenly becomes a Cynic and cuts away the ties that bind him to life "in order to rejoice in his lightness"[27]— in this way, his sentimentality feeds upon itself, adding moral evasion to mental distortion and entailing a wholly corrupt relation to the world. To focus on "subjective pleasure" merely, and to "kick over the traces" that connect one's passionate reaction with its outward grounds, is to free oneself from the limitations of temporal existence.[28] It is to introduce a gap between the object (that tree, my beloved) and the qualitative phenomenon (the color green, my feeling of being in love) which one experiences in perceiving it. And this refusal to acknowledge the external source of one's own emotional responses closes a person off from any honest involvement in moral life.

As we have seen, both Kierkegaard and the Stoics argue that to acknowledge a proposition fully is to live with an embodied sense of its truth. So when "A" states that he lacks the courage to acknowledge anything, and that he continually views his life from the standpoint of eternity, we can see these remarks as evidence of the aesthete's tendency to detach himself from the passions he experiences when he does "swoop down into actuality" from his remote emotional fortress:

> My sorrow is my baronial castle, which lies like an eagle's nest high up on the mountain peak among the clouds. No one can take it by storm. From it I swoop down into actuality and snatch my prey, but I do not stay down there. I bring my booty home, and this booty is a picture I weave into the tapestries at my castle. Then I live as one already dead. Everything I have experienced I immerse in a baptism of oblivion unto an eternity of recollection. Everything temporal and fortuitous is forgotten and blotted out.[29]

The sorrow of young "A" is not really sorrow, once he has lifted it out of its context. He dips into a world in which he has no intention of consistently participating, only to snatch a bit of prey—some fragment of passionate experience—and then take flight, returning to his isolation. Like Proust's narrator, "Marcel," toward the end of *Remembrance of Things Past*, "A" then adopts an aesthetic attitude toward his own life.[30] Only two days after his mind was heaving "like a turbulent sea in the storms of passion," the author of the "Seducer's Diary" has made a similar shift: "How beautiful it is to be in love; how interesting it is to know that one is in love. This, you see, is the difference."[31] To regard his passion as the object of a higher-order mental state with such clinical detachment, he must withdraw from the challenge of being present *in* his passionate experience.

It should be possible to be aware of one's emotional state without abstracting oneself from it, but for the seducer it seems that the shift from being in love to knowing *that* one is in love is a step from inhabiting a state of emotion to observing it from a spectator's point of view. This is one way in which "aesthetic" has a similar meaning for Kierkegaard as it does for the philosophy of art. But what is wrong with viewing one's own life in the same way that one would look upon a work of art? Basically, the error lies in taking the perspective of a spectator where one is in fact a participant: from the aesthetic standpoint one avoids being personally implicated, contemplating beauty and ugliness, good and evil, from a position of detachment. With regard to artworks, there is nothing wrong with this; it may even help to educate our emotional dispositions when we observe possible situations and consider how we *would* react to them if they were real. Unless I believe that Desdemona is an actual person, I do not experience fear but only "fear" for her when she is threatened. The difference is that I accept the hypothetical nature of her situation: I do not believe that she is in danger (as if it would make sense to rush the stage and rescue her), but that if a nonfictional person were in such a situation, then she would be endangered. As Stanislavski points out, aesthetic truth involves reference to ethical possibility: what matters is how a person would act in Othello's circumstances, not whether or not the dagger held by the actor playing this role is made of real metal.[32] A good way to characterize our cognitive relation to such fictions is to say that our "aesthetic" emotions are not founded on belief, but on the entertaining of propositions unasserted.[33] Moral problems arise, however, when one merely entertains propositions having to do with actual matters of concern. According to T. S. Eliot, Othello in his final speech is trying to escape from reality, and it is "by adopting an *aesthetic* rather than a moral attitude" that he becomes sentimental.[34] He suddenly becomes a spectator who is feeling sorry for Othello, instead of taking responsibility for his involvement in the tragic situation.

Kierkegaard never tires of emphasizing how wrong it is to abstract from existence in this way, as when "participants would shrewdly transform themselves into a crowd of spectators," and attain a kind of abstract sentimentality.[35] Emotionally, there is an important difference between the actor on the stage and the agent in the realm of actuality.[36] When we observe our own lives as the objects of aesthetic response, we forget that we ourselves are involved in the drama and that our comportment should be informed by an awareness of our role as participants. Indeed, the thinker who forgets himself in his satisfying abstraction is an aesthete in relation to existential concerns, and much of Kierkegaard's opposition to systematic philosophy can be seen as primarily a rejection of this kind of detachment. He would agree that it is a dangerous mistake to translate moral concepts into unnecessary jargon while shying away from the idea that we human beings are responsible "in any real political or practical world."[37] We are already involved and therefore responsible—to take an aesthetic attitude toward one's own life is deplorable, regardless of whether one adopts the style of Don Juan or Faust.[38] The judge sums up the relation between mental abstraction and emotional aestheticism when he complains in his first letter that "A" is all too adept at talking in generalities about everything without ever letting himself be personally affected.[39] Intellectual contemplation can be just another version of the aesthetic attitude, if it serves as a way to evade moral life; speculation can turn the world into a mere spectacle, from which the thoughtful spectator is disengaged.

By now it should be clear that the aesthete, who resists any virtues that require consistency and commitment, will be incapable of future-oriented emotion for the same reason that he cannot live in accordance with the ways he has been affected in the past. By "future-oriented emotion" I mean not only emotions such as hope and worry that refer to the future, but also those that require some kind of action in the future. For instance, if I regret having teased you, I ought to refrain from doing so again; if I feel pity for someone whose company I have forced into bankruptcy, I should amend my business practices or maybe get out of the banking profession altogether.[40] But the sentimental aesthete, unbound as he is from any temporal sequence of cause and effect, is a creature incapable of making promises: "Sure," he says, "I will say something, but I will not be bound by my words."[41] Such a person is disintegrated, that is, lacking integrity (the word used by Kierkegaard is *opløst*, meaning "dissolved").[42] Lacking any continuity in time, he or she lives in a world of fleeting and abbreviated passions. The progress from emotional response to ethical resolution, which sometimes requires little more than a series of imperceptible transitions,[43] is not going to be made by the aesthete.

Kierkegaard has characterized a mode of existence in which a person remains unattached to the episodes of his or her life, never becoming grounded in his or her situated being in time.[44] When such a person encounters other human beings, his aestheticism can have a pernicious effect on those unfortunate enough to interact with him. In *Notes from Underground*, after Liza responds to Dostoevsky's paradoxalist with genuine affection, he scornfully repudiates his former emotion:

> "I'll tell you why you came, my dear. You came because of the *pathetic words* I used with you then. So you went all soft, and you wanted more 'pathetic words.' Know, then, know that I was laughing at you that time. And I'm laughing now."[45]

Upon hearing this, Liza tries to utter something, and then sinks down shuddering, crushed by his cynicism. Only a spectator, never a participant, the aesthete acts without identifying fully with his embodied particularity. As we have seen, two of his main traits are his agility in moving from one superficial passion to another and his inability to follow up his emotions with appropriate behavior. What is unethical about this is that one person's practice of drifting through situations can easily lead to suffering for another whose life is not merely a series of either boring or interesting spectacles. Another literary character, John Barth's "Jacob Horner," who feels a "plurality of selves" and cannot identify with his own recent actions, comes to recognize that "I was not so consistently the same person . . . that I could involve myself seriously in the lives of others without doing damage all around."[46]

In Kierkegaard's own commentary on a biblical example, before the good Samaritan came along and was moved with compassion, a priest walked past the severely beaten man on the roadside: "He perhaps was momentarily moved but went on his usual light-minded way, given to a momentary impression but without depth."[47] The priest's reaction to seeing the beaten man lasts only an instant; it does not take hold of him, and he is not moved to act in accordance with the emotion that he quickly forgets. Here, we might once again be reminded of Meursault in *The Stranger*, who reacts to Raymond's brutal beating of his girlfriend by stating: "I didn't think anything but that it was interesting," and who also gets bored easily, even at his own murder trial.[48] Most closely related to Kierkegaard's primary example, though, is Meursault's belief that nothing follows from love: he regards a romantic affair as something that can be taken up lightly and lightly dropped, without even conferring the status of "girlfriend" on Marie, and certainly not implying that he will continue to care about her in the future.

I refer to Camus's narrator as the closest example to Kierkegaard's, because his best demonstration of the effect that an aesthete may have on another person is the "Seducer's Diary" in *Either/Or*. Late in the "Rotation of Crops" section which precedes the diary, "A" takes a phrase by Marcus Aurelius about seeing things afresh and turns it into a method of recollection that involves forgetting everything painful in one's past experience, while making sure that one is not affected too strongly by any new emotion. It is a way of playing lightly with life, entering into passionate experience while maintaining a detached perspective at the same time. And, "A" claims, once a person has perfected this method, "he is then able to play shuttlecock with all existence."[49] The author of the seducer's diary, for instance, is someone who "did not belong to reality yet had much to do with it."[50] As his "editor" goes on to inform us, the seducer "Johannes" always floats lightly over the human world. Even as he lays plans and carries them out, he does not wholeheartedly identify with his own role in the drama he is orchestrating. As a manipulative observer, he is "incapable of genuine relationships,"[51] unable to keep a promise or to commit himself to another person.

In the chronicle of his sentimental flirtation with reality, Johannes records some moments of measured feigning and others of rapturous transport, all oriented toward the unfortunate girl who is the victim of his seduction. He not only knows devotion when he sees it, but is appreciative of Cordelia's evident affection:

> She embraces me encompassingly, as the cloud embraces the transfigured one, lightly as a breeze, softly as one cups a flower; she kisses me as vaguely as the sky kisses the sea, as gently and quietly as the dew kisses the flower, as solemnly as the sea kisses the image of the moon.[52]

Yet he only plays and does not become engaged, resisting the idea that the beginnings of love which he is observing are meaningful except as a prelude to his conquest. Throughout the course of his deliberations and calculations, his attentive rendering of every interaction, and his beautiful metaphors of the sprouting of flowers and the capriciousness of the wind, Johannes enacts in masterly fashion the aesthetic method described in "The Rotation of Crops." Every tentative passion is balanced by an abstract examination of the seduction, as if from a distance. In the end, when he finally gains his prize, he suddenly loses interest:

> Why cannot such a night last longer? If Alectryon could forget himself, why cannot the sun be sympathetic enough to do so? But now it is finished, and I never want to see her again. . . . I have loved her, but from now on she can no longer engage my soul.[53]

Once his pleasant entertainment is complete, the aesthete coldly goes his way, leaving Cordelia to lament that he has never been "hers" except as her betrayer, the murderer of her joy, and the source of her most profound unhappiness.[54]

Because of the boundary he imposes between the intentional objects of his passion and their phenomenological manifestation,[55] the aesthete experiences

his emotions as nothing more than meaningless sensations. When the titilla-
tion wears off, he is left with bodily exhaustion to show for his experience
rather than any lasting appreciation of its significance. To the extent that he
does retain awareness of the objects of his emotions, he sees them only as the
puppet-objects of a safe fantasy world that is fully under his control. But, as
Epictetus continually reminds us, every emotion necessarily involves some
uncontrol, by virtue of its relation to some feature of the world over which we
are not omnipotent. By distorting or refusing to acknowledge the content of
our emotions, we do violence to the concrete engagement that emotion depends upon in the first place.

After his amusement dies away the aesthete can only be bored, since he
has not allowed anything to take on more than momentary importance. But
what if the seducer had been paying such close attention to the particularities
of the situation, yet without regarding the actual world as if it were unreal?
His emotional awareness is obviously alive to "such things as may happen" in
concrete existence.[56] His problem is not obtuseness, but deliberate coldheartedness: his descriptions are remarkably acute, but none of this matters to him
except as material for his shrewd game. He knows exactly how Cordelia is
being affected every moment, and uses this knowledge to his own manipulative advantage, lacking any sympathy for her emotions. He stands as an exception to the Aristotelian idea endorsed by a character in *Stages on Life's Way,*
that the image of another person's suffering ought to induce pity and fear:

> The ability to be affected on the part of the spectator is presupposed, and
> tragedy assists here by awakening *phobos* and *eleos,* but then it takes away
> the egotism in the affected spectator in such a way that he loses himself
> in the hero's suffering, forgetting himself in him. Without fear and pity,
> he will sit in the theater like a clod, but if all he gathers within himself is
> selfish fear, then he sits there as an unworthy spectator.[57]

Unlike the unworthy spectator, the one who views a narrative that is *not* his
own with an awareness that it is something that *might* actually happen gains
from his poetic experience an emotional wisdom that is attuned to the specific properties of things, an awareness of the particularities of the human
world.

As the aesthete knows, it is more comfortable to sustain the "lascivious-
ness of spectatorship" than to enter into the tension of actuality.[58] Here, the
etymological proximity between "theory" and "theater" makes sense: disen-

gaged theorizing appears to be the activity of the theatrical spectator who does not want to gain insight into the human condition, but simply to escape from reality. The judge entreats "A" to attend such plays as "would horrify you until in the world of actuality you learn to believe in that which you want to believe in only in poetry," but the young man prefers to watch melodrama from a remote corner of the theater.[59] His spectating is evidently not meant to drag his heart through the whole significance of life,[60] but to take him away from the messiness of contingent existence. Like Joyce's young artist, he is unable to merge his life in the tide of other lives, and can only be moved by ambiguous inner feelings.[61]

As long as he holds himself apart from emotional engagement, regarding everything with an ironic attitude, the aesthete will continue to be a moral zombie, a dead man in life. He may live in physical proximity to others, but he cannot share their world. Unhappy in himself and poisonous to anyone else, he ends up rooting out his own passions due to a mistaken way of thinking— as if cutting a flower from its roots would preserve its beauty, rather than killing it. Such a person watches time fly past without becoming a self in any morally significant way. "It is a life adrift," as Mooney says, with "no underlying cares or projects to define its integrity."[62] In Kierkegaard's portrait, the aesthete has a sense of how things strike him, but not of how they have struck—he does not carry around an awareness of whatever has affected him in the past, nor does he carry any resolution into the future. Like the mouse in the poem by Burns, or the skylark envied by Shelley, he does not suffer from forward-looking or retrospective emotions. But this blissful forgetfulness also ensures that his quest for momentary enjoyment will come to grief: after kicking over the traces, he will not even be able to enjoy the pleasant memory of his indulgence.[63] With an ironic stance toward life on earth, he stays free of care, scorning the world as unworthy of concern, with a point of view that is "abstract to the point of vanishing,"[64] until one day he realizes that his life has come to nothing.

The unhappiest person is the one who discovers too late the significance of what has already happened.[65] The consequence of the aesthete's habitual distancing, his incapacitating fear of life, his habit of letting his emotions pass without taking them seriously, is that he ends up discovering that he has not lived. The aesthete has no coherent view of life, no place where he feels at home in the world—he (or she) is threatened by friendship and seeks an unqualified freedom from any commitment.[66] Recoiling from responsibility and shuddering away from love, the aesthete drifts like a phantom through the ruins of a foreign world.[67] Unless he accepts the conditions of finite existence, he is doomed to be, like the main character in James's "The Beast in the Jungle," the man to whom nothing on earth ever happens. After the person whose love he never acknowledged is gone forever from his life, the sight of a grief-stricken stranger awakens in this character a terrible awareness. "No passion had ever touched him," he realizes, "for this was what passion meant":

> The sight that had just met his eyes named to him, as in letters of quick flame, something he had utterly, insanely missed, and what he had missed made these things a train of fire, made them mark themselves in an anguish of inward throbs. He had seen *outside* of his life, not learned it within, the way a woman was mourned when she had been loved for herself; such was the force of his conviction of the meaning of the stranger's face, which still flared for him like a smoky torch. . . . Now that the illumination had begun, however, it blazed to the zenith, and what he presently stood there gazing at was the sounded void of his life.[68]

Broken by this insight into what he has missed, James's character crumples to the ground, and his story ends in utter devastation. Such a person grows accustomed to "hovering above" his own life, so that his participation is "always a falsehood"[69]—that is, until he is brought to his senses with the impact of an unbearable self-awareness. The reader can only wonder what would happen if the aesthete *did* appreciate the significance of his emotions: how might his life be different?

CHAPTER 7

Virtues of Ethical Resolution

When we trace the aesthete's lack of emotional integrity back to its roots, we find that his error does not lie in the mere fact of being affected. The problems begin when he misses the significance of this initial world-oriented perception; then, he escapes the claim of becoming (or remaining) engaged in temporal existence. But what if his sense of beauty could have led him to develop a consistent moral awareness, instead of a fragmentary series of fleeting passions?[1] Kierkegaard hopes that some who have been "moved by the aesthetic" will "decide to follow along" in the right way.[2] The judge who addresses "A" in the second volume of *Either/Or* attempts to persuade the aesthete to do exactly this—that is, to adopt an "ethical" way of life, which would enable him to gain coherence as an emotional and historical being.[3] In his first letter to the younger man, he argues that moral engagement can be justified in terms of its aesthetic validity—as if "following along" means being led away from the aesthetic attitude. Without denouncing the young man's basic passionate nature (indeed, as we have seen, he admires it), Judge William adds only that if "the energy that kindles you in such moments could take shape in you, distribute itself coherently over your life," then the aesthete would surely become something great.[4] The judge seems to be promising to show "A" how to lead a moral life that unfolds in accordance with his most intense moments of emotion; a life that does not compromise, but consistently follows from, those passionate moments. To use one of Kierkegaard's own images, this would convert the "mighty blast of enthusiastic breeze that fills the sails as you set out" into "the steady wind that uniformly fills the sails so that you continuously move forward."[5] We respond to significance in the context of our particular experience, and it is only by virtue of taking such responses seriously that we find ourselves living in a world of sustained value as moral agents.[6] And it makes sense that a corrective meant to apply to the disengaged spectator should begin, as it were, by appealing to him on terms he can appreciate from his theater seat.

Kierkegaard understands catharsis as having an "ennobling" effect upon the sympathies of the spectator, who is drawn out beyond himself into the unreal but plausible world of the drama.[7] Many of the emotions that we have in response to narrative works of art involve entertaining propositions which, if asserted as non-hypothetically true, would affect the way we act. It would be inconsistent for a reader who sincerely admires the romantic devotion expressed in Dante's *Vita Nuova* to recoil scornfully from any similar love in her own life. The way that we respond to art may lead directly into ethical considerations. In responding to possible situations we engage our actual dispositions, and this inward clarification is itself a valuable kind of moral activity.[8] Many of the attitudes that we implicitly endorse in being moved by beauty are evaluative judgments that cannot easily be isolated from the rest of life.[9] Or, as Judge William writes in his first letter to "A": "There is something treasonable in wanting to be merely an observer."[10] He suggests that, instead of being a mere spectator who views the world from an aesthetic standpoint, the aesthete should allow himself to be transformed as a participant.[11] Heroism should not be displayed only on the stage, Kierkegaard suggests, but too often the moral evaluations we experience in the theater are not brought home into our actual lives.[12] Someone who is ostensibly affected by an artistic portrayal of a neglected child, thinking that it would be bad for a child to be neglected, involves herself in a kind of contradiction if she proceeds to demonstrate insensitive neglect toward her own children.[13] If she affirms that *if* such a child existed *then* one should respond to him in a sympathetic way, then a real encounter with such a child should cause her to react with sympathy and to do anything she could to improve his situation. It is a form of emotional dishonesty to ignore the ethical implications of taking one's emotional responses seriously.[14]

The aesthete resists the transition from inspiration to resolution, from being affected to taking responsibility. It is necessary to have the impetus of passion in order to arrive at any decision, according to the judge,[15] but this is not sufficient: even the passion of falling in love cannot move a person to make a commitment without his willing consent. In this consent, this assent to a perception of significance, a person makes the movement from the "me" who experiences an emotion to the "I" who actively embraces its moral significance.[16] The paradigmatic example of a movement from aesthetic response to ethical resolution is the transition from falling in love to getting married. The structure of the emotional promise made in a wedding vow is that a passion which originally "happened," not by virtue of my willing it,[17] now becomes the basis for a commitment that I affirm in saying "I do." What has passively happened to me is transformed into an act for which I willingly take responsibility.[18] Why should Kierkegaard's judge introduce an attitude of "thus I willed it" into a process of finding significance in what is not within one's own control? Since the judge's formal account of moral decision is meant to be a development of what is implicit in the moment of passion, what he means by moral choice cannot be a domineering assertiveness that is opposed to emotion. It must be a willing (that is, consenting) receptivity,[19] an endorsement of particular emotions that have shaped me as a moral agent, and a commitment to living in accordance with them in the future.

This is what it means, Kierkegaard says, to "renounce sentimentality" along with momentariness and falsehood and subject oneself to "the rigorous upbringing of resolution."[20] It is to abandon dabbling and plunge into passionate experience, to become thoroughly immersed where one had been only partially involved. The decision to take this plunge does not come out of nowhere, since it is prompted by one's own emotional responses, but it is free in the sense that it is something that one might not have done.[21] Even weak, incipient passions reveal that we are already beginning to take an interest in significant features of existence, though we have been only intermittently and conditionally engaged so far. To identify with such emotions, to integrate them into one's temporal existence, is to accept the terms of responsible selfhood. One becomes ethical by virtue of having a character defined by the set of evaluative dispositions that have already started to become embodied insofar as one has been suffering in person.[22] Taking things seriously in this way, assenting to the self as it is formed in and through its particular emotions, is the principal condition of becoming an earnest person. Transforming lightness into weight, the aesthete who makes this transition into ethical life begins to develop intimate human relationships and deeply felt convictions, to orient his or her life in accordance with definite goals. He or she begins to experience such authentic passions as can only exist for someone who is leading a meaningful life and is therefore vulnerable to disappointment.

Apart from being occasionally entertaining, the aesthete is not a *character* at all. With an irony that will not be reconciled to concrete reality, he (or she) remains opposed to any earnest immersion in the moral world. Preserving a fantasy of abstract freedom, "will" in the sense of *liberum arbitrium*,[23] the aesthete reduces the faculty of moral choice to a vanishing point of unlimited liberty. Being "free" in this arbitrary and unqualified sense, a person never gains any momentum as a moral agent: this is why the aesthete has no clear identity. He plays a variety of roles without identifying with any of them, tentatively entering into relationships in order to enjoy the experience of emotion. The aesthete is trapped in a fantasy which, though oriented toward existence, does not decisively come to terms with it; he "has thought everything possible, and yet he has not existed at all."[24] He avoids taking anything seriously, and thereby guards himself against the emotional risk of being more than ironically involved. And the fragmentary nature of his temporal experience also keeps him from occupying any role that requires sustained care: he can be a dilettante but not a devoted artist, a temporary acquaintance but not a loyal friend.

This emotionally uncommitted lifestyle would limit the aesthete from becoming even a true sports fan. By this I mean someone who is passionate about certain contingent events: for a Yankee fan, the events in question are the baseball games played by the Yankees, other games which bear some relation to these (those played by rival teams, for instance), and other associated events (ranging from a major injury to a star player to an impressive performance by a minor-league prospect). A true fan cares consistently about these events (she does not shift from one allegiance to another, or from enthusiasm to disinterest), and her care is the basis for her liability to be moved one way or another as the events unfold. Hence, it may be said of someone that she lives and dies with the Yankees: that is, her abiding care for this particular team is the disposition that underlies many episodes of emotion in her life. One day she may be pleased by an extra-inning victory, but at a different time she may be worrying that a change in the dimensions of the ballpark will lead to more home runs by visiting batters. The "diehard" fan faithfully suffers through all of this, for better or worse. But for the aesthete, everything is measured in terms of its momentary entertainment value;[25] so he hedges his bets, cheering for the team only when its record is a source of pleasant emotion. He "rejoices" when the Yankees win the division, but he quickly abandons ship when they suffer a disappointing loss in the playoffs—that is, a loss disappointing to anyone who really cared in the first place.

As the reference to the true fan's suffering "for better or worse" shows, the example could be extended to other concerns: we could equally speak of fair-weather spouses, friends, or citizens. It is "a wonderful thing," as one philosopher has remarked, that a sports fan or any other human being can be moved by good or bad fortune that is not his own.[26] But the aesthete's unwillingness to be resolute and faithful in his emotional dispositions, his adoration of whatever is immediately convenient, limits him severely: when the team wins the pennant, he cannot celebrate as deeply as the person who is condemned to be affected by every one of the team's wins and losses. Likewise, the friend who enjoys my company on some occasions, but shrugs and walks away when I am unhappy, is not much of a friend at all: a true friend has a loyalty that shows itself not only in happy times but also in others. The emotions that are a part of genuine friendship go beyond the sensations of pleasure and pain, since they depend upon a consistently maintained ethical disposition.[27] Without any such concern defining the framework of a person's engagement with the world,[28] he or she is left with a narrow emotional range and prevented from taking on any distinct identity. The life of someone for whom everything remains indefinite easily deteriorates into a game of charades, an inane masquerade:

> At times he walks around with the proud air of a Roman patrician wrapped in a bordered toga, or he sits in the *sella curulis* with imposing Roman earnestness; at times he conceals himself in the humble costume of a penitent pilgrim; then again he sits with his legs crossed like a Turkish pasha in his harem; at times he flutters about as light and free as a bird in the role of an amorous zither player.[29]

This is what happens to someone whose heart is like a birdhouse, where one momentary passion flutters in and another flutters out without either having a lasting effect on him. He may take the form of the stunted recluse who cannot even become an insect, or of the smiling ironist who cannot take anything seriously;[30] in either case, the joke is on him: his life goes by without acquiring any definite content. And, as Judge William asks the aesthetic young man, isn't it sad that this should happen?[31]

Along with his lack of identity and purpose, another consequence of the aesthete's failure to appreciate the meaning of his emotions is that he suffers from chronic discontinuity of character. Instead, his amorphous self drifts along, always trying to capture the fullness of the moment, but forgetting that the moment gets its full significance from what is not immediately present. This is why Judge William says that "A" is "in fact fighting for the moment against time," and that his way of living "at all times only in the moment," by turns sentimental and heartless, renders his life disintegrated and inexplicable.[32] As we have seen, the aesthete's passionate attachments are never more than tentative, and can be abandoned easily. Trying to indulge in the immediate intensity of passion while scorning the wholehearted care on which passions are based, he condemns himself to a procession of passing fancies, nothing more. In order to know the fullness of the emotional moment, it is necessary to be aware of the significance of the whole progress of time: but the way that "A" was affected yesterday means nothing to him today, and whatever significance his life might acquire in this way is lost through his dubious power of going forward and forgetting.[33] This is why, as the judge says, "the one who lives aesthetically is only superficially moved."[34] By inhabiting the vanishing instant, with a hypothetical and subjunctive relation to the beliefs that he tacitly affirms in his emotional responses, he renders himself incapable of distinguishing between emotions that arise from a lasting disposition and those that are superficial and temporary.

Becoming ethical involves thickening the moment with an awareness of how our loves and cares have shaped us, from long ago until now. This cumulative history allows a life to be shaped over time by passions that were important enough that we held onto them, brought their significance along with us, and were not distracted by something else a moment later. By allowing every emotion to flame up and burn out quickly, the aesthete gets trapped in a fragmented sequence of sufferings, bound "by a chain formed of gloomy fancies, of alarming dreams, of troubled thoughts, of fearful presentiments, of inexplicable anxieties."[35] His life, he says, "is utterly meaningless. When I consider its various epochs, my life is like the word *Schnur* in the dictionary, which first of all means a string, and second a daughter-in-law."[36] All that is lacking, he adds, is that the word should mean, third, a camel, and fourth, a whisk broom. Since he does not understand his momentary affections as meaningful, his self lacks integrity and he collapses into an absurd ambiguity. As the judge points out, the aesthete does not remain faithful to what he has loved, does not allow himself to be shaped by the cares he has formed toward objects in the world: if he has any shape at all, it is that of the jellyfish, which lacks form and is always taking on one shape after another.[37] Defined only by his indefiniteness, the aesthete does not represent a unified way of life so much as total fragmentation.[38] Since he lacks a temporally extended self, he is condemned to undergo erratic fluctuations in his passions.

What has affected us has made us what we are, and if it is not brought forward as part of our awareness then we obliterate not only the past but also ourselves: this is the principle behind the preservation of identity over time. Preserving a narrow horizon of experience by continuously erasing the past, we divorce ourselves from anything we might have learned by living. Whatever remains of our emotions is likely to be a confused sentimentality. "We cross our bridges when we come to them and burn them behind us," says Tom Stoppard's characterless character Guildenstern, "with nothing to show for our progress except a memory of the smell of smoke, and a presumption that once our eyes watered."[39] We can tell a whim from a significant inspiration only if an understanding gained over time is activated in the momentary response. As Kierkegaard writes, sentimentality is characterized by its exclusion of this kind of understanding, which must be a part of sound passion.[40] Because he finds fault with novelists whose characters never attain any coherent self-understanding (or "life-view"), it is clear which of these two characters Kierkegaard might admire, and which he would find contemptible:

> He longed to hit her over the head with the big glass ashtray on the coffee table between them and take away his letters.
> . . . He wanted to efface her from the photograph of his life not because he had not loved her but because he had.

> She knows, of course, that there are also quite a few unpleasant things in the notebooks, days of dissatisfaction, arguments, and even boredom, but that is not what matters. She does not want to give back to the past its poetry. She wants to give back to it its lost body. What is urging her on is not a desire for beauty. It is a desire for life.[41]

"He" resembles the Communist party, trying to rewrite the past, even if this requires him to use violence as well as dishonesty. She, on the other hand, is on the side of the truth that he finds so repellent. While he wants to destroy his letters, she wants to recover her notebooks. She recognizes that without the memory of her formative history she will be stranded in an empty present tense. Isolating an instant from the narrative progress of time will literally make nothing of it.

Whatever else they are about, our emotions are also about the past; and one way of distorting our present emotions is by selectively remembering only certain aspects of the past. This kind of sentimentality, often called "nostalgia," involves revising one's own memories in order to blot out whatever does not correspond with the emotions presently desired. But if we care at all about the authenticity of our emotions, then having only fond memories of (for instance) a horrible war would have to count as a false and potentially dangerous sort of forgetfulness. Apart from the basic untruth of not believing that war also involves pain, there is the added deficiency of not having learned from one's own passionate experience. If our emotional experiences are not allowed to register in our memory, then we will be deprived of any moral awareness that we might have gained from them.[42] Without accurate memory, we may end up replicating our personal and social mistakes like children who keep burning their hands in the same fire. If "accurate, clear, decisive, impassioned understanding" is the basis of moral agency, as Kierkegaard suggests,[43] then any failure to educate one's emotions is an indefensible kind of ignorance.

Emotional attunement to particular situations is, in the eyes of the judge, an essential part of moral agency, and it allows a person to live in a moment filled with meaning instead of a thin, enervating instant.[44] He feels the weight of his cares as a blessing rather than a burden, and describes them as the many bonds that hold him fast in his life, just as a tree is held to the earth by its many branching roots.[45] This is an undisguised celebration of heaviness, significance, and meaning: emotional ties faithfully maintained are not entanglements to be cut away, but necessary threads that enable us to be at home in the world. The heavier the weight of our cares, in other words, the more truthful and close to the earth our lives become.[46] The cares that dispose an ethical person toward emotion also bring him down to earth, as shown by William's tale of a textual scholar whose wife saved him from going crazy by pointing out that an inexplicable diacritical mark was nothing but a speck of dirt on the manuscript.[47] Passionate existence for such a person becomes less spasmodic; he does not flail all over the place but is bound and anchored on the spot.

This concrete emotional awareness is the kind of moral perception in which a person is alert to the significant features of the world.[48] What counts as a significant feature depends upon what one has in fact been affected by, in the context of one's particular history. One's responses to these features are not spontaneously willed into being, but one can take responsibility for the states of character from which they arise.[49] Using the example of the Yankee fan, we can predict from her emotional dispositions that a loss by the Yankees will make her sad. The virtue of her consistent, grounded care is not that it mitigates her suffering, but that it enables her to suffer in truth—that is, even in the agony of defeat she knows that this is what it's like to lead a resolute and truthful emotional life. Because of her emotional integrity, she has a coherent moral identity which is defined by the network of relations that connect her with a world in which some things stand out more prominently while others appear insignificant.[50] If she cannot say that the sharp contours of such a world are easier to tolerate than the flat colors of the Stoic's world or the hazy, shifting reality seen by the aesthete, she can at least point out that she is clearly able to discern what is axiologically relevant in one way or another: it is an unhappy fact that the Yankees lost, and her reaction (given her premises) is unmistakably justified.

This is the kind of stability available to the truly ethical person described by the judge: not the steady temperament of the Stoic, but the security of knowing that one's passions are grounded in consistent dispositions. To someone who asks rhetorically how anyone could be responsible for having appropriate emotions,[51] the plain answer is: by developing trustworthy evaluative dispositions over time. Ideally, just as a skilled musician is pleased by a good tune and offended by a bad one, the virtuous person will have an embodied sense of what is better and what is worse.[52] Of course, this ideal is not likely to be perfectly achieved by anyone: we have seen many ways in which emotions can be corrupted. But we have also seen that, given a plausible moral psychology that recognizes the cognitive aspect of emotion, it is often possible to identify emotions as more or less accurate. And one of the recommendations made by the ethicist to the aesthete is that he should not be afraid to know what he loves in all possible detail, to tie his moods to concrete reality.[53] The idea behind this advice is that our emotions will be more truthful if they are based on a precise awareness of how things actually are. If we feel depressed, we will have a sense of what might be wrong and whether or not the mood is justified. If we are angry about some remark that we overheard, then we will be angry at the right person, for a good reason, and to a suitable extent.[54] At its best, this kind of emotional clarity would allow us to have an "authentic interpretation" of everything.[55] As long as we make some progress in our emotional "consciousness raising" and become more adept at paying attention to moral situations, we also develop a better self-understanding, since the self is defined by its emotional comportment.[56] As we form more reliable emotions, we gain a deeper and more concrete understanding of ourselves as moral agents, always approaching (if never reaching) the optimal condition of absolute transparency. This ideal resembles the epistemic goal of having nothing but true beliefs: although it is impossible to achieve, it can function as a target that guides us in the right direction.

The extent to which we embody this ideal state of awareness will depend upon our history of giving or withholding assent to immediate emotional impressions. If I have for years given my assent to false beliefs about members of a certain ethnic group, then these beliefs will inform my response to someone of this ethnicity whom I meet for the first time today. But even such an entrenched disposition can gradually be altered, if I open myself to new evidence or hear an argument that makes me recognize my racist attitude as mistaken. In short, right responses can be cultivated through critical awareness of the judgments that are implicit in a given emotion. Passions arise out of states of character for which we are responsible, even though we are not in control of how we respond at every moment.[57] Kierkegaard's ethical person recognizes that "passions must be slowly cultivated and constantly renewed."[58] Such a person takes responsibility for himself as a distinct individual with specific passions, habits, and influences; a self, in other words, that is aware of its place in a greater network of significance.[59] When we identify with our concrete particularity, we become more than momentarily and randomly passionate, aligning ourselves with an entire history of evaluative perception.

In order to gain unity and continuity in life, we must occupy a certain space in a network of intersubjective relationships. Inwardness is essentially related to the external world: the attachments that extend beyond us give a life that is more intensely our own. They enable us to experience the human world as a network of caring relations, in which it does not make sense to abstract the moral agent from the bonds of love that make him who he is. It is emphatically as *this* concrete person, with *these* passions and commitments, that I exist as a moral agent.[60] And when I take responsibility for this particular identity, it is in a distinct social world that I do so. For Kierkegaard's ethicist, society and its institutions provide the outward grounding for emotional integrity. Even the sacred wonder of falling in love, as the judge writes in his treatise on marriage, becomes a matter of civic duty when by taking public vows we also affirm our place in the community.[61] From the perspective of a person who resolutely occupies a certain role in society, life is seen in terms of definite tasks rather than unlimited possibilities, and he or she identifies emotionally with the duties of his or her social role. Whereas the aesthete hovers in a state of fantastic sentimentality, without taking the pains of becoming and staying alert to any concrete moral demands, the ethical person sees himself as answerable to these demands and responsible for being attentive to them. The mundane details of life thus take on multifaceted significance, and give the mature person a discerning sense of what is significant in his or her contingent, historical situation. The judge speaks knowingly of "a sense of meaning and also the weight of a responsibility that cannot be sophistically argued away, because one loves."[62] He is someone who plays his role among other human beings as properly as any musical note ever played its role in a Bach fugue,[63] infinitely well attuned to his place in the world.

We should keep in mind that the ethical person need not be a pious, patriotic, workaholic family man. Judge William outlines the structure of ethical life, no matter what its content may be: what matters, he says, is the passion of the resolution—not so much the identity of what is resolved.[64] So the ethical can also be represented by the repentant aesthete who has moved from stupid impulsiveness to educated spontaneity: his emotions gain clarity without ever being toned down to fit the business world.[65] Speaking of a time when he lacked self-understanding, Rilke says that back then everything was vaguely felt: since then, he claims to have become "more conscious in all these feelings," so that he can trust himself in being more spontaneously emotional.[66] He still guides himself by intuition, but now is confident in the validity of what he feels. Critical sensitivity makes all the difference between a sentimental poet and a great one, a difference which is evident when Rilke's earliest poems are compared with his later work, but which is even more pronounced in the poetic development of Keats. From the nauseating complacency of "I stood tip-toe upon a little hill" to the hard-won awareness expressed in the ode "To Autumn" lies the path from sentimental ignorance to emotional wisdom.[67] Even the alter egos of Joyce and Proust realize that the serious artist must be austerely committed to his mode of life (Stephen), obedient in following a rule of life and patient in finishing his work (Marcel), if his impressions are to be worth expressing: and these, even if they are made in the name of aesthetic values, are ethical commitments.[68] The artist cannot trust his judgment unless he replaces his momentary transports with reliable emotions.

Of course, *always* to perceive the true significance of things is a perfectionistic moral and epistemological goal; but, as Kierkegaard reminds us, with regard to our ethical ideals we ought to strive for nothing less than perfection.[69] This means paying attention to oneself as an evaluator in a world of values, who is continually being reshaped in having impressions that are either accepted or rejected. It means sustaining a critical vigilance over one's emotions, being aware of what one seems to feel and whether it is something one really means, and by degrees refining one's dispositions toward emotion so that they are more worthy of trust. Just as anyone who makes an impersonal truth claim can be in a better or worse position to know that X is the case, the person who suffers an emotional response could be drawing upon more or less reliable dispositions.[70] This is why Kierkegaard says that the earnest person will always maintain an "honest distrust" of himself:[71] the goal is to refine one's fallible capacity to perceive what is ethically relevant.[72] Moral perception thus becomes an exercise in attunement: the virtuous person must pay attention to both internal and external circumstances, and be ready to respond to situations in appropriate ways.[73] Emotional reliability can then be seen as a matter of being suitably affected by things, having what T. S. Eliot would call an "objective correlative" to every passion.[74] The ethical person, on this view, would have his or her emotional life firmly grounded in his or her axiological premises.

When we step back and assess the depiction of ethical life that arises from these writings, we can see that Kierkegaard has drawn an outline of the formal structure of a coherent emotional existence.[75] Although the ethicist's motive for becoming earnest is not simply to develop his acuity in perceiving significance, this development is one outcome of his practical commitment to a set of meaningful roles within a moral world. To accept the roles of husband, judge, and friend (or mother, author, and confidante) is to accept certain beliefs about what is of value. And these beliefs, in many cases, are the kind that ascribe significance to contingent externals, establishing in the virtuous person so many dispositions toward emotion.[76] The price that an ethical person pays for having a life that makes sense is to suffer through the highs and lows of the stories of which he or she is a part.[77] The narrative coherence of the ethical life is therefore tied to particular situations—and it shows itself in virtuous dispositions toward appropriate emotions. This link between passion and virtue in Kierkegaard's ethical writings is summarized nicely by Johannes Sløk:

> Underlying all of this, however, is the fundamental concept, passion. It was the aesthete who discovered passion as the deepest part of a human being; but for him passion was wild and unruly . . . because it did not have any definite aim. That is what the ethicist has given it. . . . Passion's goal is to arrive at an existence where one is well-defined and entirely present, and where therefore all things, people, and relationships are real.[78]

The only place where this kind of existence can be found, as the judge believes, is within a local framework of significance, a set of evaluative practices that are not open to any drastic revision. For the Kierkegaardian ethicist, agency is located within the concrete life of a society, not in any cosmopolitan morality.[79] Context-sensitive perception, on this view, takes shape within a coherent system of ethical beliefs which define what is right and what is good.[80] These ethical premises, then, "must be interrelated so as to form a single cohesive unit, whose very cohesiveness acts to exclude other possibilities."[81] Judge William, in his letters to the aesthete, pays tribute to the beauty and order of his own particular system, making it sound like a cozy and well-kept garden, and asks: why wouldn't you want to live in a place like this?

CHAPTER 8

The Romantic Imagination

The moral implications of the aesthetic way of life may justify disapproval on the part of someone looking upon it from the outside; but it is important to understand it from an internal point of view as well. The striking fragments that "A" has written to himself are not the meditations of a happy person, by any means. They are predominantly cries of despair—beginning with the epigraph proclaiming that all is vanity.[1] Although the aesthetic perspective may overvalue youth, what we witness in these fragments is not a young man rejoicing in his youth but someone who already sounds like quite a burnt-out case:

> I lie stretched out, inert; all I see is emptiness, all I live on is emptiness, all I move in is emptiness. I do not even suffer pain. At least the vulture kept on pecking at Prometheus's liver, and Loki had the poison constantly dripping down onto him; at least there was an interruption, however monotonous. But even pain has lost its power to refresh me. Were I offered all the world's glories or all its torments, they would affect me indifferently; I would not turn over on the other side either to reach for or to escape them. I die death itself. Is there anything that could divert me? Yes, if I caught sight of a fidelity that stood every trial, an enthusiasm that sus-

tained everything, a faith that moved mountains; if I came by a thought that bound together the finite and the infinite. But my soul's poisonous doubt is all-consuming.[2]

Living, moving, and having his being in a climate of emptiness, the aesthete sees everything under the aspect of vanity. Clearly, "A" does not speak as a person who has come to terms with the world through emotional relations with significant elements of his environment. He doesn't identify with his situated perspective, and yet value is imperceptible from a position of absolute detachment; consequently, he cannot perceive anything as consistently meaningful.

When our concerns weigh too heavily on us, aesthetic detachment promises to make all difficulties vanish.[3] But although we may dream of complete freedom from responsibility, we should also recognize that our lives become more weighty, more fraught with significance, as our emotional bonds with the world are strengthened and extended. By contrast to this fulfillment, the aesthete must suffer what Kundera has called the "unbearable lightness" of a care-free existence.[4] Rather than letting his episodic emotions grow into longstanding attitudes, the aesthete lets them weightlessly pass away, so that both joy and torment end up meaning nothing. This positive loss of experience shows why the lighthearted, though they may laugh down from the balcony of their aristocratic detachment, are also likely to be jealous of those who are able to embrace the world unreservedly.[5] While they may escape the pain of many earthly sufferings, they find that it is also painful to be unable to reconcile oneself to the particular conditions of existence. Unlike the Stoic, whose laughter is predicated upon a sustained commitment to viewing contingencies as insignificant, "A" wishes to eat his cake by partaking in temporal experience and to keep it by preserving abstract detachment as an available sanctuary. So it is no wonder that he comes up empty, that he is left with an unbearable lightness after having loved.

Imagination [*Phantasien*], for Kierkegaard, might be defined as the faculty of access to unrealized possibilities.[6] It draws us out into reality by offering provocative ideas that we wish to live out—and only then do we truly begin to exist.[7] To confine oneself to the imagination, then, in the name of repudiating an imperfect existence, would set the stage for the later discovery that one had not lived. This is the end that Judge William fears "A" will come to, if his exacting imagination has the unfortunate effect of holding him back from moral agency.[8] There is a difference between a dissatisfaction with the particular limitations of a given state of affairs and the obstinate refusal to accept *any* concrete limits. If the aesthete will not come to terms with the world under any circumstances, then he is condemned to remain "a stranger and an alien" to actuality.[9] Estrangement may be based on a revolt against surrounding values, but it can also be caused by a refusal to accept human existence as such.

The essay "Rotation of Crops" shows this refusal taken to the extreme. Its author understands the terms of moral life, and will not yield to them: accepting a definite identity means not only limiting oneself to certain concerns, but rendering oneself vulnerable to suffering by virtue of those concerns.[10] We should refuse this limitation and avoid this risk, he maintains, by not developing friendships, getting married, or entering a profession.[11] He even suggests that two people who fall in love ought to break off the relationship immediately, since they have nothing to gain. The emotions that might ensue from this lifestyle are shown when another "young man" laments that he no longer sees his beloved for what she is, and cannot give any actual expression to his love:

> The actuality in which she is meant to have her significance remains but a shadow for me, a shadow that runs alongside my spiritual actuality, a shadow that sometimes makes me laugh and sometimes wants to enter disturbingly into my existence. It would end with my fumbling for her as if I were grabbing at a shadow or as if I stretched out my hand after a shadow.[12]

This character in *Repetition* has lost contact with finite existence, and is unable to find his way back to the object of his emotion. However idealistic it may sound, his romantic imagination was not always out of touch with his beloved in her particularity: earlier in the novella, when he "perceived that he had made her unhappy," this "wrought up his passion to the wildest agitation."[13] Nevertheless, he somehow loses his attunement to the world.

How could such hopeless romanticism lead a person to suffer from such etiolated passion? The premises of aestheticism appear to be antithetical to those of Stoicism: the aesthete does not seek to minimize his emotions toward the goal of apathy, but to maximize them in the direction of affective intensity. All that interests him is the sheer force of emotion, apart from its significance.[14] Yet this is precisely why his passions are susceptible to diminishing quickly: since an emotion depends for its existence on particular significant objects, to isolate its raw force from its grounding conditions is like depriving a plant of its native soil and expecting it to survive. When Hamann sought to include sensuous impressions as an element of rational understanding, it was because he wanted philosophy to be aware of the particular, not simply to increase the magnitude of emotion.[15] Just as the native language of a culture embodies and shapes its ongoing experience, each human being ought to have his or her own peculiar emotional vocabulary: the more thoroughly we register and remember our emotional impressions, the more acutely we should be aware of what we care about and who we are.[16] The aesthete, however, is romantically infatuated with the idea of infinity to the point that he cannot accept even the "limitation" of being a concrete individual with specific interests.

In order to understand why anyone would want this, we should consider whether this estrangement—especially if it is not a prejudice against contingent existence but, perhaps, a plausible response to surrounding values— might have some kind of merit. One advantage of hovering above the finite is that this gives free rein to the imagination: like a child, the aesthete is free of any life-defining obligations.[17] Though he may be caught in a bad infinity of possibilities, he is not tied down by any mundane entanglements. And one motive for seeing only the pleasant facets of the world is that, without rose-colored glasses, one does not like what one sees. The ability to recoil from what seems unacceptable, far from being an immature weakness, shows a demanding imagination which envisions how things could be different and expects something better. It prevents a person from complacently accepting everything just the way it is, whether good or evil.[18] Just as it is an epistemic virtue to question one's beliefs and get rid of any that are false, it is morally praiseworthy to ask oneself whether or not certain values and commitments are worth affirming. How astonishing it is, Kierkegaard says, to witness how people can become passionate about such negligible trivialities; and the aesthete agrees:

> The most ludicrous of all ludicrous things, it seems to me, is to be busy in the world, to be a man who is brisk at his meals and brisk at his work. . . . What, after all, do these busy bustlers achieve?[19]

Here, one might be reminded of a passage from a letter by Keats:

I go among the Fields and catch a glimpse of a stoat or a fieldmouse peeping out of the withered grass—the creature hath a purpose and its eyes are bright with it—I go amongst the buildings of a city and I see a Man hurrying along—to what?[20]

It has been said that neurosis, the dissatisfaction with reality as it is, can be nothing other than the response of an especially sensitive individual who has not yet found a context in which to realize his or her highest aspirations.[21] The ignoble goals with reference to which entire societies guide themselves— obtaining and displaying hollow symbols of wealth, shooting themselves to the moon only for the sake of hitting golf balls—do not appeal to the aesthete's need for meaning.[22] Surveying his own age, "A" complains that most of his contemporaries are dull, their activities trivial, their passions lethargic; their most heartfelt thoughts, he concludes, would be unworthy of a worm.[23] He sees no reason to lower himself into a charade of quiet desperation. As Kierkegaard says, it is sad to let the soul be damaged by trivialities; so, rather than getting into a life that is not worth living, the aesthete saves his integrity by holding back from moral engagement.[24]

Does this simply represent a failure to "grow up" and realize the universal? Kierkegaard writes in his first book, *From the Papers of One Still Living*, of the present generation which is still making up its mind about the world.[25] As he sees it, the youth are not being obstinate so much as deliberate in figuring out what to do with their lives. They may in some cases be inspired with the same sense of urgency that Kierkegaard felt on a trip to Gilleleje during the life-defining crisis that was burning him up in his early twenties: "What I really need is to get clear about *what I must do* . . . to find *the idea for which I am willing to live and die.*"[26] This kind of idealism is not merely a negative way of shrinking from moral participation; as Hannay comments, what distinguishes a human being from a plant "is, among other things, the person's consciousness of an 'infinite' disparity between familiar finite nature and the unspecified infinite aspiration."[27] Judge William shows a conspicuous lack of this aspiration, along with an inability to conceive of the possibility of living differently. He says what there is to be said for bringing order into the chaos of one's life, and (as we have seen) this correction is necessary for the attainment of emotional integrity. Yet when "A" speaks of "that happy Greek view of the world" that uses the word *kosmos* to praise the well-ordered universe in which the moral agent dwells, we see that the obstacle that prevents him from viewing his own life in those terms is not any failure to appreciate the value of order.[28] Rather, he doesn't perceive things as transparently meaningful—he cannot find his way into a context of action in which the meaning of life is not (or, no longer) at issue. He has the primitive ability, as Kierkegaard calls it,[29] to assess the prevailing values of his society and, if necessary, to oppose them. On a charitable reading, his hesitancy in coming to terms with public standards of evaluation is based upon a refusal to reduce himself to trivial conformity. The judge, in his attempt to reconcile "A" with the world as it is, does not consider the possible validity of the young man's wish for something different than the present state of things.

This is the virtue of the romantic imagination, which Kierkegaard associates with the exuberant overflowing of all boundaries.[30] At best, it is capable of making a person refuse to adapt himself to a situation that strikes him as morally unacceptable. Clearly, the aesthete is not someone who can simply get used to anything: if he is to be denounced for his inability to form relationships, he should also be praised for criticizing his contemporaries in Socratic fashion, for caring about the wrong things.[31] He may not know what way of life would satisfy his need for meaning, but he will not abandon the heroic search for it:

> there is a fire
> And motion of the soul which will not dwell
> In its own narrow being, but aspire
> Beyond the fitting medium of desire . . .[32]

This fiery striving is too easily dismissed by smug judges and businessmen: it may be called naïve, but it could equally be described as uncompromising. And when the Romantic poet looks around and sees the "dreary intercourse of daily life,"[33] he does not want any part of it. Far from a scornful misanthropy, this reaction might come from a lofty conception of human dignity, according to which we have a demanding moral imagination "so that we may not be content with mean things but may aspire to the highest things."[34] There are human capacities higher than "a sense for insignificant matters" and "a memory for trifles," the qualities that would equip the aesthete for an ethical life on the judge's terms,[35] in which one "marries, takes a job and so forth," and accepts the evaluative standards of prevailing social practices and institutions.[36] Like Aristotle, Judge William is "extremely complacent about the existing order";[37] it is only as a virtuous servant in the Hegelian state that he attains his integrity.[38] Although he shows us how to cultivate the virtues within a given context of action, he does not justify the conventional values upon which his own lifestyle is based. There are other ways of being virtuous, in accordance with different conceptions of how one ought to live. As Kierkegaard laments, people do tend to care for the wrong things, "frittering" or "dribbling" their lives away.[39] Within a culture whose fundamental values are dubious, a life of social conformity is no guarantee of moral integrity.

In short, the ironic detachment of the aesthete may be an expression of a romantic imagination that will not accommodate itself to absurdity and falsehood. Of course, to live *is* to accept some compromise and limitation, and there is nothing good about an ironic detachment that will not come to terms with any concrete circumstances. But not every ironist is so crass: Socrates was capable of opposing his society in many ways without finding all of human existence to be unworthy of concern. Although romanticism is often guilty of a comprehensive rejection of the finite world, this is not always the case. Kierkegaard notes in *The Concept of Irony* that Solger sometimes describes "true irony" as proceeding from the awareness that our highest destiny can be realized only in this world, that striving for the infinite only leads to indefinite emptiness.[40] It is at least conceivable that the aesthete is hindered not by a resistance to actuality as such, but by doubts about the values of a particular civilization. One may consistently believe that the individual is not free to "create his own values" in a vacuum while acknowledging that public opinion is not so authoritative that one is deprived of a standpoint from which it is legitimate to oppose fashionable prejudices.[41] This leaves open the possibility of becoming oneself while also letting others be themselves in a way that makes room for intersubjective recognition but does not require of self or other an uncritical allegiance to social norms.

Kierkegaard suggests that the "romantic fire" within a person could cause him to be disaffected with the world. At an early age, he writes, "I saw through people"; he says in another journal entry that he was never able to run with the herd.[42] What he cannot tolerate about the empty courtesy of social gatherings and the noise of cocktail-party chatter, he says, is that it abolishes the distinction between what is and what isn't significant.[43] Suave urbanity can easily degenerate into mere triviality, as we become lost in a meaningless illusion of meaning, mechanically respecting norms out of dead habit instead of any sense of their respectability. There is danger in joining the conformists who "go whichever way the wind blows because they are more concerned with feeling comfortable than with the grounds of the principles they accept."[44] Again and again, the aesthete emotionally revolts against all that the ethicist slavishly takes for granted:

> When I opened my eyes and saw reality, then I began to laugh and since that time I haven't stopped. I saw that the meaning of life was to get an income, its goal to become a counselor-at-law, that the rich desire of love was to catch a well-off girl, that the blessedness of friendship was to help each other in financial difficulties, that wisdom was whatever the majority assumed it to be, that enthusiasm was to make a speech, that courage was to risk losing ten dollars, that kindness was saying "You're welcome" after dinner, and that piety was going to communion once a year. This I saw, and I laughed.[45]

Throughout this litany of what he finds ridiculous, the aesthete relies upon a tacit belief that love, friendship, wisdom, courage, and so on, could be something greater than what they are commonly taken to be. According to the ethicist, every human being should be able to find a place in "the rational order of things" in such a way as to express both "the universally human and the individual."[46] Like the Danish Hegelians, he believes that "the more each individual self-consciously develops his own individuality, the more representative he becomes of general humanity."[47] But when societal norms are "not particularly inspiring," why should anyone want to take his or her place in the body politic?[48]

The fact that local practices can be challenged suggests that it is possible for the individual to be related to a nonlocal source of value.[49] In going along with or opposing the ethical conventions of his or her community, a person must rely upon some evaluative sensibility that is not derived exclusively from those conventions. Training in virtue is only as good as the principles it instills in us;[50] if we reject the values of our society, then we must find other evaluative premises if we are to develop reliable emotions. It is morally valuable to be able to criticize a given situation, to feel that something is wrong. To judge that something is rotten in Denmark is to compare the status quo with some inward sense of how things ought to be. What enables one to make such a judgment is a vivid moral imagination.[51] By now it ought to be clear that this is not a capacity that the aesthete should want to sacrifice:

[There] are people in whom the lack of a sense of reality is a real deficiency. But the possible includes not only the fantasies of people with
weak nerves but also the as yet unawakened intentions of God. A possible experience or truth is not the same as an actual experience or truth
minus its "reality value" but has—according to its partisans, at least—
something quite divine about it, a fire, a soaring, a readiness to build and
a conscious utopianism that does not shrink from reality but sees it as a
project, something yet to be invented. After all, the earth is not that old,
and was apparently never so ready as now to give birth to its full potential.[52]

Not only will our emotions be corrupt if we go along with what others are
wrongfully applauding, but we may thereby do violence to our own sense of
value.

Speaking in favor of accepting one's ethical task, Judge William says that
such a choice can bring a person into an immediate relationship with the
power that pervades all of existence.[53] This grounding power is elsewhere
identified by Kierkegaard as love; the same basic emotional force that constitutes our individual distinctiveness is the condition of our ability to be
morally involved with one another.[54] But is the unromantic judge in a position
to say anything on this topic, or is he out of his depth? He does suggest at one
point that a human being is nothing without love,[55] as if to acknowledge the
formative influence of emotion in the history of the individual. And he admits
that ethical self-choice is not a matter of spontaneously creating oneself:

> When around one everything has become silent, solemn as a clear, starlit
> night, when the soul comes to be alone in the whole world, then before
> one there appears . . . the eternal power itself, then the heavens seem to
> open, and the *I* chooses itself or, more correctly, accepts itself.[56]

It is more accurate to say that the self "accepts" or "receives" itself than that it
"chooses" itself: to speak only in terms of voluntary decision would imply too
much self-fabrication, when in fact individuality crystallizes amid conditions
that are largely beyond one's own control.[57] Appropriately enough, the judge
tends to use language that gives priority to receptivity as opposed to volition.
Some of the time, however, it seems that he would like to describe the ethical
life as free of any uncontrolled element, as he shifts from a vocabulary of emotional openness to one of self-sufficiency.[58] What allows the judge to become
so caught up in automatic patterns of activity, to lapse into such complacency,

that he needs to be upbraided at the end of *Either/Or* by a minister who proclaims that it is "cowardly and dismal" to trust that one's life "may proceed in tranquillity"?[59] It is for the sake of unsettling the ethicist's contentment that Kierkegaard places the parson's jolting "Ultimatum" at the end of the judge's second letter and its undue moral certainty. If there are any issues to be raised about the legitimacy of apparent value, they are not likely to find an answer in the judge, who is quite satisfied to say that his life and work must have some meaning, even if he cannot identify what it is.[60] What must he implicitly believe about the nature of value and evaluation in order to know that he is not mistaken in his basic ethical comportment? Judge William himself cannot say: like the barbarians who unreflectively inhabit their assumptions, he does not question the premises of his traditional morality.[61]

The achievement of Kierkegaard's ethicist is to show us how passion can be transformed into habit, how the cognition involved in an emotional response can take on lasting moral significance. But he lays so much emphasis on decision that the will threatens to replace emotional openness altogether. It is unfortunate, Kierkegaard says, that the heart should grow cold as a person gets older, becoming less affectionate and closed to new attachments.[62] What, then, are we to think of Judge William? He admits that significant interruptions are not often allowed in the humdrum routine of married life, and confesses himself unable to imagine being in love more than once.[63] Apparently the judge has allowed his earlier emotions to form his character so rigidly that he is no longer open to perceptions of significance. But if those emotions that formed him were valid, there is no reason to think that all possible discoveries of value have been made; and if they were mistaken, then his present character has no validity. In other words, the self that is defined by its emotions must be open to the possibility of being moved again when it is presented with unforeseen significance. Since one is not self-consciously "cultivating a style" but living with what has been established in one's experience, there is no warrant for becoming closed to new experience after a certain point. The aesthete's main epistemological flaw lies in never assenting to an emotional impression; to borrow an image from Stoic epistemology, the ethical person might be described as grasping an early impression and then keeping his or her fist tightly clenched.[64] This resolution is necessary for emotional truthfulness; but so is the passionate receptivity that the aesthete exemplifies.

We can understand why Kierkegaard says that the aesthetic is not meant to be left behind entirely.[65] Its immediate responsiveness, its uncompromising romanticism that can imagine a better world, is an essential prerequisite to emotional authenticity. With help from the Stoic theory of emotion, we are able to see that this is not merely a taste for competing ideals: the logical structure of this tension is that (1) the aesthete should assent to the proposition that is implicit in his momentary emotion; and (2) the ethicist, since his life is built upon having taken some evaluative responses seriously, should believe that it is possible to be affected by new axiological discoveries. Aesthetic perception at the most basic level involves the revelation of value; by giving our assent to such a perception, we accept the premise that our emotions can provide us with significant insight: ethical, and perhaps even religious. When the aesthete gives wholehearted endorsement to the propositions embodied in his nascent passions, he takes the first step toward attaining emotional integrity. But, although this structural correction is necessary for coherent and sincere emotion, the romantic inability to come to terms with the world has introduced another legitimate concern. How is radical estrangement to be overcome, once we are in doubt about our basic emotional orientation? A nonsentimental romanticism could exist only if the moral agent could find sanction for his or her highest values in something other than local authority— "something which is bound up with the deepest roots of my existence," as Kierkegaard says.[66] In order to finish this inquiry into the possibility of emotion, we must look past the virtues of social conformity and identify a more reliable source that could ground our perceptions of significance.

PART III

FUNDAMENTAL QUESTIONS

And this one Love becomes and is many loves. . . .

—Plotinus

Be ahead of all parting, then, as if
it lay behind you like a passing season.
Among the winters, one (so endless) winter
will leave your over-wintering heart unbeaten.

Be always dead in your love—arise and sing,
return and praise the absolute relation.
Amid these fading and decaying things,
be the glass that rings out as it's breaking.

Be. But know the terms and limitations
of not-being, ground of your intimate vibration,
so that you fully fulfil it just this once.

Jubilantly with all that is dumb or empty,
the innumerable whole of nature's plenty,
number yourself as well—and annul the sum.

—Rainer Maria Rilke

CHAPTER 9

Love as Necessary Premise

Why should our perceptions of significance be traced to something other than local moral authority? With this question we run up against the boundary between aesthetic/ethical and ethical/religious issues. To begin answering it, we need to shift our focus from the cultivation of emotional virtue within a particular context of action to the nature of value in a more general sense. As we have seen, the Stoics put forward a weaker and a stronger version of their normative thesis about the falsity of the passions. The weaker or "structural" version involves a qualified critique of the ways in which emotions are liable to be cognitively flawed (unstable, excessive, distorted, and so on) due to some particular kind of error.[1] The stronger or "fundamental" argument is that the passions are categorically wrong about value, because they one and all endorse the tacit premise that something external to our moral control is of value—and this premise, according to the Stoics, is false.[2] On their view, the notion that any contingency could affect us for better or worse arises from a basic mistake about the nature of reality. Emotion is a mode of experience in which significance, or value, is allegedly perceived. This invites the metaphysical (or axiological) question: upon what interpretation of reality as a whole does passionate cognition rely? That is, what must one implicitly believe about being and value in order to believe in the possible validity of emotional perception?

Ultimately, every passion has to do with the value, or the significance, of what is not up to us. Resolving the "structural" problems of emotion is a necessary but not sufficient condition of proving that the passions can be rationally legitimate: not only must they be internally consistent, but they must also be outwardly grounded. What must be true about the intentional referent of an emotion, in order for it not to be guilty of falsifying its object? What must be the case in order for emotions to be truthful, rather than false, perceptions of significance? This is the fundamental (or "transcendental") question in the philosophy of emotion, and it demands a distinct type of reply. When asked why I am angry at a certain person, I may provide a detailed explanation of what this person has recently done to me. Perhaps he or she has deprived me of some possession that I care about—this is a coherent explanation, as long as my premises are not questioned. But what if I am asked why I believe that it is right in the first place to care about something that is liable to be stolen and therefore out of my control? This question goes deeper, and forces me to admit that the *coherence* of my self-explanation would be undermined if it were shown that my response did not *correspond* to this sort of object, since it is not really important.[3] It would be foolish to accept our affective experiences at face value without questioning their validity, because although we are able to "express human values and elicit relevant emotional responses" within a familiar moral framework, it does not follow that we know "whether anything of the sort is justified by objective conditions in the universe."[4]

Kierkegaard does not imply that such a question can be answered only after one has moved through the aesthetic and ethical spheres of existence. But he does point out the difference in kind between those problems of the self that arise in the midst of life and the question of whether or not the self is ultimately justified in its moral and emotional comportment. In *Either/Or,* the judge promises his young correspondent a richer and more consistent emotional life, but his voice does not offer the last word for anyone who is moved by the aesthetic to seek "a higher meaningfulness than that of immediate passion."[5] It is not until the "Ultimatum" at the end of *Either/Or* that the cracks in Judge William's rock-solid common sense are split open by the words of another character, different from the aesthete and the ethicist.[6] Although the judge has continually used religious language in order to put the stamp of absolute sanction on his undoubtedly serious commitments, it now appears that he has been taking the name of God in vain. He is entirely certain, for instance, that his profession has some kind of divine endorsement, as if God's sacred role for him is to serve as a judge in the local courts.[7] But the "pastor" who speaks in the closing pages of *Either/Or* takes the complacent judge to task by pointing out that a person's own plans, and what others regard as his duty, could be "in the wrong" in a religious sense. In other words, a person's ethical habits are not necessarily in line with "the longing with which he seeks" and "the love in which he finds" his true, sacred vocation.[8] Without knowing how such nonparochial meaning could be discerned, we can recognize that the parson is raising a question that is revisited in *Fear and Trembling* by another pseudonymous author: "Is he justified? . . . How does the single individual reassure himself that he is legitimate?"[9]

And how *does* the individual gain this assurance, if not from the "obvious" norms and values of his society? When Kierkegaard chastises the "insignificant concern" of those who care about the wrong things,[10] or when he worries about the possibility that a passion might not correspond to its object (e.g., when a trifling object provokes a powerful response),[11] he is speaking as a thinker who is willing to raise abstract questions about what is valuable and what is not, apart from all empirical questions about what is in fact valued. When the aesthete revolts against misplaced ethical seriousness, he is likewise raising what he takes to be a legitimate question—about whether all that is hallowed is therefore holy.[12] Axiology, the philosophy of value, can be defined as the study of what is worthwhile and what isn't. If wisdom regarding what is valuable or significant were defined as "whatever the majority assumed it to be," then there could be no possible contradiction between ethical conformity and personal integrity.[13] And yet the majority can be wrong in its prevailing judgments of value, regarding as morally wrong whatever is at odds with its current biases. We learn from Thoreau that abolitionist John Brown was considered "insane" due to his uncivil indignation at the institution of slavery.[14] If we believe that he was right to respond with anger at this state-sanctioned practice, then we cannot accept the Hegelian idea that "what counts as an accurate report of experience is a matter of what a community will let you get away with."[15] From another perspective, the emotions of the reformer may appear to have been appropriate—but they could only be regarded as irrational by the law-abiding citizens of the day.

In his state of estrangement, the aesthete challenges us to consider that it might be the situation, not the individual, that is infirm or unsound.[16] When shared values are specious, the person who simply becomes "adjusted" to a socially acceptable way of life is not thereby vindicated as a person whose values are in order—nor is he thereby saved from the awareness that he is living badly or that his life is absurd. "A" cannot make himself get used to just *anything* because he is too acutely aware of the needs of his soul. Our "emotional orientation to the world," says Jonathan Lear, "demands that the world present itself to us as worthy of our love."[17] The crisis of legitimacy that the aesthete is experiencing is directly related to this passionate demand, and it raises the question of how *any* context of moral action can be meaningful. This is the kind of question that the advocate for ethical commitment, Judge William, is utterly unable to answer. He can only become defensive in response to the young man's conviction "that there is meaning in the world if only [he] could find it"; the judge distrusts anyone who exempts himself from the standard pattern of having a wife and a job in society as it is.[18] He does not entertain the possibility that this rebel without a cause could be "seeking, without knowing it, a moral philosophy or a religion."[19] In talking past his listener, the judge reveals himself as a person whose morality of popular slogans is not up for debate, who does not know what it is like to experience alienation, or "the profundity which is rooted in being nothing at all."[20] He is unable to say *why* a socially acceptable life is good, or why it is worth living. And yet, as the narrator of *Repetition* states, if you cannot explain the exception, you have explained nothing—that is, if your theory of social meaning cannot account for the individual who thinks about "universal" moral norms "with intense passion" and then goes against them, then you have not explained the binding force of those otherwise shared values.[21] Constantin Constantius, the pseudonymous author of *Repetition,* remains hopeful about the prospect of a "legitimate exception" who would refer himself not to established practices for guidance but to an inward source of value that enables one to become engaged in moral life. Such a capacity would perhaps answer Kierkegaard's existential demand to base his involvement with the external world upon "something which is bound up with the deepest roots of my existence."[22] It might also give us some leverage to get "below the social accretions"[23] and down to a more reliable source of emotional discernment.

Kierkegaard challenges us to realize that contemporary etiquette should not be mistaken for a source of normative authority, that it is "philistinism" to believe that the self is shaped only by social forces.[24] Although we are always influenced by the intersubjective context of action, it is sophistry to define truth in terms of solidarity—and not only because the majority can obviously be wrong. In one journal entry, Kierkegaard endorses Schelling's statement that "where the mass is judge of the truth, then it is not long before people resort to deciding matters with their fists."[25] This view is at the furthest possible remove from a social-consensus theory of truth:[26] society may provide the space in which values can be experienced, but it does not have absolute evaluative authority.[27] But if we want to avoid an idolatrous faith in the state, then we must be able to attain a practical wisdom that is not in line with local standards. Consistent virtuous commitments are necessary for emotional integrity, but must themselves be justified with reference to something other than a particular normative framework.[28] By taking seriously our sometimes frustrating love affair with the world, we may be able to gain some insight into the process of forming emotional bonds between self and world—even in non-problematic cases. The human being's capacity for estrangement from shared values need not be regarded merely as a threat to social order; it might be a key to the discovery of what it is that could ground a wholehearted moral engagement.

What is inauthentic about the aesthetic mode of existence is its "carefree" attitude, in which a person lacks "any concern for reality" and resists emotional commitment; what is valuable about it is the way in which it "seeks to detach itself from any limited perspective" and "to explore every possibility it can."[29] There is an infinite sense of possibility in the romantic imagination, an overflowing movement of the heart that longs for involvement in a life worth living just as vehemently as it resists a compromised existence.

> Only in the instant when there awakens in his soul a concern about what significance the world has for him and he for the world, about what significance everything within him through which he belongs to the world has for him and he therein for the world, only then does the inner being announce itself in this *concern*.[30]

The inward "concern" that Kierkegaard describes could arise from an awareness of "the nothingness which pervades reality" such as the aesthete possesses.[31] Between the inward need for meaning and the perceived lack of meaning in the external world, we have what might be called a nihilistic impasse. This predicament is perhaps more readily attained at a time when faith in sustaining values is precarious, but there is a perennial philosophical possibility of experiencing doubt about whether one's life makes sense.[32] This doubt can be experienced as a "dizziness" which is "infinite," engulfing a person's world of concern with an emotion similar to "that which comes from looking down into a bottomless abyss."[33] And yet this obliterating dizziness is uniquely capable of making a person realize his or her primitive ability to care (that is, to become concerned), which itself is an impetus toward moral participation.

By contrast, the person who has never caught a glimpse of the abyss does not know what it would mean to be engaged with the world on authentic emotional terms. Judge William venerates the social institution of marriage with all the enthusiasm of a zealot, as if a legal contract were able to infuse a relationship with significance *from the outside*.[34] He undermines his own argument, however, by admitting that married life is meaningful only insofar as its "real constituting element" is the emotion that animates it from within. "To a talented but wayward aesthete," writes Mooney, "a stuffy municipal judge might recommend marriage as a timber of identity. But in the Kierkegaardian long run, such civic virtue . . . can't count as *the* absolute."[35] The power that gives meaning to human existence, and which indicates how *I* should orient my life, does not have its origin in established social practices. We are closer to it when we focus on the individual's primordial concern—without which, Kierkegaard argues, moral life would be hollow.[36] Like Hegel, Kierkegaard tends to use religious language when talking about the underlying principle of spiritual life: it is a sacred agency that gives significance to the things of this world. But he does not agree that the Spirit of God is objectively present in Our Civilization; for him, divinity is a subjective influence available only to the individual *qua* individual.[37]

"In this concern, the inner being announces itself and craves an explanation," Kierkegaard writes, and nothing is more difficult to explain than the finitude of human life.[38] Death itself "explains nothing," and yet it can teach the earnest living person that there is no serious meaning in life "unless the external is ennobled" by virtue of the sincere concern that "lies in the inner being."[39] It is an enigma which "gives life force as nothing else does," inviting us to think about our values in light of first and last things.[40] But if the end of life as we know it does not explain life's meaning, then what about its beginning? We find ourselves in the midst of existence, having been thrown into an uncertain world from an unknown source, and like the first person on earth we wonder: if anything in this world is of value, then where does it come from?[41] Not everything that exists "is something man himself produces"; indeed, our own being is not something that Epictetus would classify as simply "up to us."[42] All human experience is predicated on the division between a finite subject and the rest of what comes to be known as objective reality: this division exists prior to anything that we ourselves create, or anything that we can comprehend.[43] We do not require a "special revelation" in order to recognize that our moral and emotional life is grounded in something not constituted by us.[44] And, if "what a person most fundamentally is" cannot be traced to the realm of what is up to us, then we ought to acknowledge what might be called "the ultimate givenness of the self."[45] And this acknowledgment leads us to ask: what gives? By virtue of what do we inhabit a significant world, in which so much that we value is not up to us?

The answer, in a word, is: *love*. "Love," Kierkegaard writes, "is the source of all things and, in the spiritual sense, love is the deepest ground of mental life."[46] This sacred force which moves the human soul is the ground of all significance in life as we know it:

> There is a place in a person's innermost being; from this place flows the life of love, for "from the heart flows life." But you cannot see this place; however deeply you penetrate, the origin eludes you in remoteness and hiddenness. Even when you have penetrated furthest in, the origin is always still a bit further in, like the source of the spring that is further away just when you are closest to it. . . . Love's hidden life is in the innermost being, unfathomable, and then in turn is in an unfathomable connectedness with all existence. Just as the quiet lake originates deep down in hidden springs no eye has ever seen, so also does a person's love originate even more deeply in God's love. If there were no gushing spring at the bottom, if God were not love, then there would be neither the little lake nor a human being's love. Just as the quiet lake originates darkly in the deep spring, so a human being's love originates mysteriously in God's love.[47]

Love is the enigmatic power at the base of the psyche, and the deepest ground of human existence. This, Kierkegaard says, is the explanation that we crave in our inner being, which explains the meaning of life "in the God who holds everything together in his eternal wisdom."[48] This God of infinite wisdom, manifest in the experience of love, is the "source of all love" so that, as emotional beings, we are what we are only by virtue of being *in* love.[49] Kierkegaard traces all significant existence to the primary love upon which the self is ontologically dependent, and interprets this fundamental emotion in religious terms:

> What is it that makes a person great, admired by creation, well pleasing in the eyes of God? . . . What is it that makes a person unwavering, more unwavering than a rock; what is it that makes him soft, softer than wax?—It is love! What is it that is older than everything? It is love. . . . What is it that cannot be given but itself gives all? It is love. What is it that perseveres when everything falls away? It is love. What is it that comforts when all comfort fails? It is love. What is it that endures when everything is changed? It is love. What is it that remains when the imperfect is abolished? It is love. . . . What is it that sheds light when the dark saying ends? It is love. What is it that gives blessing to the abundance of the gift? It is love.[50]

That upon which we are inevitably dependent is not of our own making; love is the creative source from which all things proceed as well as the ground in which they subsist. Instead of declaring with Protagoras that "man is the measure of everything," we ought to follow Heraclitus in granting that we cannot fathom the limits of the psyche, "so deep a measure does it possess."[51]

But why should we apply a sacred name to such an enigmatic factor, and how can it explain so many things? Kierkegaard's answer is that the phenomenon of love gives us a direct insight into the basic nature of existence: "God is Love, and therefore we can be like God only in loving."[52] It does not make sense to speak of divinity as if it could be encountered as an object; it is understood only in the experience of loving.[53] Kierkegaard's view that love is fundamental to the self informs his reading of the New Testament idea that our being is "rooted and grounded in love":[54] in loving others unselfishly, we also define our own individuality. From an oceanic primordial unity,[55] each of us develops as a distinct self by forming bonds of love, or care, with the external world.[56] Love may begin as "a pre-individual and pre-moral force," but this initially unreliable impetus can be refined and developed into the religious virtue of neighborly love.[57] This conception of a loving God as the enabling condition of all meaningful existence ties in directly with an account of what it would mean to live morally. To describe love as the ground of existence is to make "an ontological claim of the most fundamental kind, about the dynamic energy which founds all things,"[58] and this sacred agency is present in each person "in such a way that it demands that I recognize and affirm this same validity and dignity in every other human being."[59] Since love not only "proceeds from the heart," but also *forms* the heart," a person's moral identity is defined by love in such a way that only the person who loves knows who he is and what he must do.[60] And because each of us owes his or her distinctive singularity to the fundamental influence of love, moral goodness can only take the form of affirming each person's existence as the unique loving individual whom he or she is. This means valuing her well-being for its own sake—that is, caring about whatever she cares about only for that reason—and being aware that her sphere of concern both defines her identity and affects her happiness.

Love is the "passion of the emotions," or the "emotional passion," that connects the one who loves with the second-person beloved, thereby constituting the middle term in the relation.[61] On Kierkegaard's trinitarian view, "The love-relationship requires threeness: the lover, the beloved, the love—but the love is God."[62] Ferreira explains, "God is not the 'middle term' by being the direct object of our love in such a way as to marginalize the beloved; God is the 'middle term' by being the center of the relationship because 'the love is God.'"[63] Love is the sacred power that connects us to the finite realm in which our concrete duty is to love the person we see. By loving others not *as* gods, but *through* God, we become subject to existential imperatives and susceptible to moral emotions. Situations that merit our perceptive attention are made salient by our love, since we are emotionally affected one way or another as what we care about is affected for better or worse. In taking a selfless interest in whatever is in the interests of the beloved, the loving person forms a specific moral orientation in the world, finding that selfhood depends upon intersubjectivity.[64] Human life would be empty and vain if nothing were valued for its own sake, and so we must love unselfishly (at least in some cases) in order to avoid a nihilistic predicament. It makes sense, then, to characterize love as the divinity that shapes our ends.[65] Going a step further, we could say that to practice Christianity means, above all else, to live in accordance with the conviction that God is love; that is, to follow the promptings of a religious influence which one does not necessarily understand but to which one is comprehensively indebted. To admit one's radical dependence upon a God of love, without whom one would be capable of nothing, is not to debase oneself but to make an ennobling concession. If we are ontologically dependent upon love, then we have the choice either to affirm this fundamental dependency or else to live in a state of denial. In the name of truthfulness, Kierkegaard invites us to make a wholehearted affirmation of the ground of our being.

When we see things with loving eyes, every aspect of the world is enriched.[66] If we believe that God is love, then we ought to find that life is meaningful and good—not because a loving attitude projectively endows objects with value, but because it disposes us toward a charitable interpretation of external reality. In other words, with a loving disposition we appreciate things for being what they are: love is not an objective entity, but a subjective mode of comportment which enables objects to appear significant. Our given emotional world is one in which ordinary things are weighted with significance (a corpse is revolting, a living room soothing); but these value-rich features would be perceived as neutral facts by anyone other than an emotionally responsive subject.[67] Describing what it would be like to be completely indifferent to everything under the sun, Dostoevsky's "Ridiculous Man" writes:

All of a sudden, I realized that it *would not matter* to me whether the world existed or whether there was nothing at all anywhere. I began to intuit and sense with all my being, that *there was nothing around me*. At first I was inclined to think that in the past there had been a great deal, but later on I divined that formerly too there had been nothing, it had merely seemed otherwise for some reason. I gradually became convinced that there would be nothing in the future either. It was then that I suddenly stopped being angry at other people and almost ceased to notice them. Indeed this became apparent even in the most trivial matters: for example, I would bump into people as I was walking along the street.[68]

Except for a bit of Cartesian certainty about his own existence, this narrator has lost everything to axiological skepticism: he is so indifferent to the palpable objects he bumps into that they might as well not exist. He does not have the loving mode of awareness that is required in order to be able to perceive the significance of things. "If you yourself have never been in love, you do not know whether anyone has ever been loved in this world, although you do know how many have affirmed that they have loved": it is only "if you yourself have loved," Kierkegaard claims, that you know what it is like to perceive the world this way.[69] "The blind person cannot know color differences; he must be content that others have assured him that they do exist and that they are thus and so." Likewise, the person who is not blind does not spawn the world of light and color out of his own mind: he must be constituted in a certain way in order to perceive what is there. In any case, it does not make sense to talk about preexisting subjects actively bestowing significance onto objects, since moral perception cannot occur at all unless we are already involved in life as persons to whom things matter. It is not an incidental fact about us that we are loving or caring beings—rather, it is "a structuring condition of the universe of our possibilities."[70] Along the same lines, Heidegger writes: "It is not the case that objects are first present as bare realities, as objects in some natural state, and that they then in the course of our experience receive the garb of a value-character, so they do not have to run around naked."[71] From the point of view of an unloving observer, it would not even be self-evident that the external world exists.

To the apathetic person, it will never be *obvious* that anything *deserves* to be loved. But what is at issue here is not objective warrant: it is a basic disposition to see things in the best possible light.[72] Just as love is unasked for by us, it is uncalled for by the world—and yet it is only by virtue of its gratuitous "infinitude, inexhaustibility, immeasurability" that love can summon the romantic soul into a caring engagement with contingent reality.[73] It is therefore appropriate that the edifying discourse which begins with the litany of love's various capabilities should have as its epigraph the biblical enjoinment to the early Christians to *be sober,* and to maintain a heartfelt love for one another.[74] Becoming sober, as Kierkegaard says in a later meditation on the same phrase, means accepting that one is nothing without God and yet not becoming piously detached but, rather, "infinitely, unconditionally engaged."[75] If we have a religious understanding of the love that sustains our world of cares and obligations, then we ought to be committed to them in a wholehearted way. It may be that the "pagan" also extolled love, but only in a selfish way: for him, Kierkegaard argues, nothing was as sweet as revenge.[76] The "pagan" may have loved up to a point, but not selflessly or unconditionally; on Kierkegaard's view, the Greek conception of love is hedged with reservations, qualified by a concern for objective worthiness and for getting what one deserves in return. But wait—who is this ancient pagan, and what is the univocal notion of love that "he" supposedly extols?

Kierkegaard's emphasis on the idea that loving is a spontaneous activity which affirms *beyond reason* the value of whatever is loved—rather than simply responding to the lovable qualities of the object—explains why he might be read as an advocate of *agapē* as opposed to *erōs*. And it is true that he distinguishes a right way of loving, which is quite difficult to achieve, from a wrong way, which is closer to our natural tendencies. Yet although he does not prefer *erōs* over *agapē* as a name for divine love, as do some early Neoplatonist Christians (e.g., Dionysius the Areopagite), he is also far from the neo-Manichaean view introduced by Anders Nygren, according to which the two forms of love are incompatible and engaged in "a life-and-death struggle."[77] Like the Greek authors, Kierkegaard uses more than one word to refer to love: *Elskov* and *Kjærlighed* in Danish could be roughly aligned with *erōs* and *agapē*, since *Elskov* indicates specifically a love between two human beings and *Kjærlighed* has broader connotations (not excluding intense, personal affections).[78] The latter term is used by Kierkegaard to indicate an unselfish, neighborly love; the former has more of a romantic tone. But these different shades of meaning do not amount to a technical separation of the two terms: Kierkegaard uses *Kjærlighed* in reference to a Platonic speech in praise of *erōs,* and *Elskov* not only as a specification of *Kjærlighed* but even in speaking of "agapic" love of neighbor.[79] Although he distinguishes between *erōs* and *agapē*—and also uses a third term, *Venskab,* which is closest to *philia*—this lexical range is used in order to point out different aspects or manifestations of love, not to form discrete categories which can only be locked in violent conflict.[80] On the contrary, it is one of Kierkegaard's most important points that diverse forms of love can be traced to a common origin, such that the "truest" kind of love does not need to abolish drives and inclinations but only to refine these crude expressions of the one "fundamental universal love" into a more unselfish kind.[81] The analogies and differences between Kierkegaard's understanding of love and the various ancient views that he assimilated, "pagan" or not, are worthy of a more careful analysis.

"I have now read so much by Plato on love," Kierkegaard writes in a letter to his fiancée, and this would prove to be more than merely a youthful enthusiasm: even his latest religious writings contain overt allusions to the *Symposium* and the *Phaedrus.*[82] It is not without justification that one commentator calls *Works of Love* "a courageous effort to re-introduce eros into philosophy."[83] Although Platonic Eros is not Kierkegaard's ultimate concern, it would be false to say that his writings are not at all concerned about it. Even the non-pagan Judge William commends the classical reverence toward *erōs,* which is indeed "a wonder," and (seen in a different light) is also what inspires ethical life.[84] Kierkegaard himself praises the *Symposium* for its "indescribably wonderful presentation of the power of love to ennoble man,"[85] the *Phaedrus* for its "great picture" of "the madness of love."[86] His admiration is more often extended to Socrates, the passionate existing thinker, than to the speculative Plato; it is even plausible that Kierkegaard's concept of the inward moral conscience might owe something to the Socratic *daimon*.[87] Surely it is no accident that his one citation of the *Theages* refers to the passage where Socrates declares that his "spiritual thing" has "absolute power" after making a strong claim about his knowledge of love.[88] If nothing else, Kierkegaard's works share with these Platonic dialogues an interest in the moral and epistemic development of the self's emotional capacity for love.

Kierkegaard's principal criticism of Plato's notion of love is that it is not adequately a love of the individual. Writing about the progress of speeches in the *Symposium*, he observes that "love is continually disengaged more and more from the accidental concretion in which it appeared"; the abstract reflection "mounts higher and higher above the atmospheric air until breathing almost stops in the pure ether of the abstract."[89] It is wrong to begin with the concrete only to become lost in abstraction; but this is what happens when love is defined only negatively, as a yearning for the eternal which is mistakenly focused on one or another specific object. The secret of earthly love is that it bears the imprint of divine love, Kierkegaard claims, and this idea of the beloved as the stimulus for the lover's spiritual ascent is certainly reminiscent of Plato's *Symposium*.[90] Yet, for Kierkegaard, the earthly love relationship is not merely a step on the way to the eternal, just as it is not justified in merely romantic or humanistic terms: rather, it is the sacred process by which contingent existence is infused with divinity. He insists upon the unique individuality of the person who is loved, as opposed to a flight toward "that great sea of beauty" and away from the love of the concrete individual.[91] In the "Young Man" of his own "Symposium," the dialogue on love at the beginning of *Stages on Life's Way*, he creates a character who believes that "the lovable" is untrustworthy if it has no abstract rational essence that could be explained in a way that would compel objective consensus.[92] It is a selfish lover, Kierkegaard suggests, who must independently define "the lovable" so that he can be guided by an abstract idea in seeking an object that suits him.

Because he considers it "a sad but all too common inversion to go on talking continually about how the object of love must be so that it can be loveworthy," Kierkegaard's vision of love is even more strongly opposed to the Stoics than it is to Plato.[93] The Stoic wise man knows what is and is not deserving of his so-called love: whether it is defined as a rationalistic version of *erōs*, or as a form of *philia* which excludes *erōs*, Stoic "love" is meted out selectively, and with a strict preservation of apathy.[94] When its authority is too potent, the Stoic argues, love is untrustworthy; besides, it is unjustified in any case, because if there were any object that truly warranted such a strong response, then it would be loved by everyone.[95] The Stoics do not assent to any apparent value "unless we get a convincing impression," and "the nature of things is not such as to compel our judgments of them."[96] On the Kierke- gaardian view, by contrast, "There is a way of caring for a patch of earth, for a philosophical text, for those we hold dear, which sustains identity and world."[97] If you are erotically drawn to appearances of beauty, but you are committed to believing that nothing is truly significant except your own ra- tional will, then of course your "love" will not extend to the point of opening with reverence and gratitude to the unpredictable emergence of meaning be- tween self and other. With its guarded self-sufficiency and its love based in reason alone, the Stoic's self "is the most isolated self" of all.[98] For Kierke- gaard, on the other hand, divinity "may in no way be considered a-pathetic," since God "is such pure passion and pathos" as to be known only in loving and being loved.[99] Needless to say, this is not what Epictetus has in mind when he talks about the sacred principle in the human psyche.

Still, the emotion which can sometimes be a threat to other-regarding love may also serve as a motive toward the development of genuine intersub- jectivity; and the ancient philosophers who believe that *erōs* can lead to *philia* are somewhat closer to the Kierkegaardian conception of love.[100] This is be- cause Christian love, as he sees it, is not a vague "love of humanity" in general (as in the ideal city where no one cares too much about anyone in particular); it is a love of the human being *nearest* to me, each person I see, as a distinct individual.[101] What it means to love one's neighbor is "essentially to will to exist equally for unconditionally every human being."[102] To say that I love you is to say that I want you to be. And nothing else in "pagan" Greek thought ap- proaches this idea so closely as Aristotle's conception of the friendship which consists "more in loving than in being loved," since it involves affirming the existence of the friend and wishing him good things *for his own sake*.[103] "Love," points out Vlastos, is the only English word "robust and versatile enough" to cover the range of emotions denoted by *philia* in Aristotle;[104] Nussbaum con- curs, adding that Aristotelian *philia* refers to many affective relationships other than what we call "friendship," including some of the most intense loves that human beings are capable of forming.[105] There are elements of Aristotle's ac- count of love which are not compatible with Kierkegaard's, of course.[106] Still, it does introduce the idea of loving another person for his or her own sake, as well as the corollary notion that such a love can only be directed toward a being which has a distinct principle of individuality: I cannot wish good on behalf of the other *herself* unless it means something for her to *be* herself.[107]

If it is corrupted by an egoistic concern for one's own ends, then love cannot fulfil its role as a world-forming force. The creative agency that gives weight to things, allowing a world of value to emerge for the loving person, is meant to express itself not as a "being-for-itself" quality but as "a quality by which or in which you are for others."[108] Self-seeking egotism is bound to be an empty quest—when we love nothing unselfishly, we do not find ourselves with a robust self-made self. Instead, we suffer the unbearable emptiness of a life in which there are no final ends, because nothing is cared about for its own sake. Moral integrity is not attained by asserting a secular self-determined life plan: it requires a receptive acceptance of the loving engagement in which I become myself.[109] There is no definite self, nor any significant world, in abstraction from the "engagements in which we find ourselves," i.e., the concrete, other-centered loves that bring us into being in relation to the values that surround us.[110] Anyone who "seeks his own" with a selfish love is never happy, but always worried about losing whatever good he may "possess."[111] To love in this "pagan" way is to be capable of great anger, to respond with violent rage whenever one does not get what one covets. Christianity, on the other hand, commands us to love in such a way that we do not enviously begrudge what has been given to others.

Our natural tendency is to love selfishly, to measure our own good against the good of others, grasping at what we ourselves want. We draw our circles of concern too narrowly, and what does fall within them is too often regarded as an extension of the ego, not as a separate center of agency and care.[112] Love of the neighbor does not need to be at odds with love of individuals, but sometimes it is those closest to us who are most difficult to love as ends in themselves. When we think only of ourselves, we find plenty of reasons to complain about our circumstances. But "what one sees depends upon how one sees," and through love we may be able to overcome this ingrained mistrust.[113] The loving gaze, which does not merely seek its own good, sees a divine hand in what might otherwise appear to be an unhappy state of affairs. Selfish jealousy may doubt the value of life, but a loving person will trust that there is some benign significance to everything—whether or not this is immediately evident. Kierkegaard does not advise a facile smiley-faced attitude: what he recommends is the grim comfort of trusting in love *in spite of all doubt* as a fundamental spiritual disposition.[114] If we believe that God is love even when life seems disappointing or absurd, then we will never fail to interpret reality in the best possible light—instead of allowing its positive value to be lost on us.

When we concede that there would be no meaningful existence without love, we confess our existential reliance upon this emotional force which is "an absolute gratuity, for which it is perfectly appropriate for us to feel grateful and indebted."[115] The way we receive this gift, however, is up to us to decide: it is quite possible to resist aligning oneself wholeheartedly with the passionate basis of one's identity. We do not have the option of turning into inhuman beings who are not rooted and grounded in love, but we can attempt either to deny its influence or to set ourselves against it. Cognitive assent, even to a powerful impetus or impression, is a voluntary act that can be resisted; and the kind of consent that allows the self to have its world grounded in love is not a matter of being coerced but of saying "yes" to an unchosen dependency.[116] The values that ground our moral existence are not spawned out of our own minds, even if a loving subjectivity is a necessary condition of perceiving them. Love itself is not initiated by an act of will, and the course taken by our emotional life is not entirely within our control. It *is* "up to us," nevertheless, to adopt one or another attitude toward our fundamental capacity for emotion. The unchosen influence of love is what brings "absolute meaning" to human life, even though this primary emotion needs to be affirmed and then refined.[117]

On Kierkegaard's view, the person who "does not want to accept love as a gift" is taking a problematic stance toward the ground of his or her own being.[118] Authentic emotional life requires an honest acknowledgment of the power upon which the self is ontologically dependent. It is simply ungrateful to imagine that we are the makers of ourselves, since we are thrown into a world that we did not fabricate by a force that is prior to any intention of our own. Anyone who denies this is living on false terms: "the whole meaning of his life" is founded on "something else," he knows not what.[119] Yet without love as the edifying ground of the self and the foundation of significance in human life, where would we be? It is a question of giving credit where credit is due: Kierkegaard's aim is not to prove that God exists, but to respond appropriately to the empirical truth that it would be "phenomenologically false" to describe ourselves as masterfully constructing the value of people, places, and things that matter in our life.[120] Rorty's ideal of "giving birth to oneself" is the pipe dream of a defiant pride, a goal predicated upon an untenable belief in the absolute freedom of the will; "passionate acceptance" of one's received individuality, on the other hand, is based on a more realistic appreciation of what is *not* up to us.[121] Recommending an attitude of reverent acceptance toward love, Kierkegaard situates himself within the tradition of Augustinian Christianity, arguing that from a benign source only goodness can flow.[122] Love is the necessary premise of human existence: our need to love and be loved, our lack of metaphysical self-sufficiency, is the condition of our dignity as the expression of something greater than ourselves.

CHAPTER 10

Suffering as Logical Consequence

The affirmation of love's divinity goes hand in hand with a belief in the overall goodness of existence.[1] At the very least, if God is love, then the value of life is not in question—however, this is not because the sum of all pleasures and pains shows that it is mostly enjoyable to exist. On the contrary, there is a nonaccidental connection between love's ontological status as a creative power and the vulnerability which it induces in the person who loves.[2] We have seen how the spontaneous movement of love arises in a human being, as the wellspring of his or her concern for other beings. And we have come to understand the self as defined by love, that is, by the inward basis of *one's own loving* and the outward bonds to *what one loves*. We have also seen why Kierkegaard interprets the self-defining role of love as evidence that "love builds up," serving as the ground of both practical reason and moral agency. To sum up with another philosopher's image, "the multiform history of our loves, with all their complications and incidents, lives finally from that elemental, cosmic force, which our psyche . . . merely administers and models in various ways. The differently styled turbines and engines which we submerge in the torrent should not make us forget that it is the primary force of the torrent itself which mysteriously moves us."[3]

Does it follow that we should be ready to join in unequivocal praise of this sacred force, for making every thing the way it is? Not yet; and, it may be, not at all. We have yet to consider why Kierkegaard not only concedes that love "can give birth to pain," as if it were a possibility, but even goes so far as to claim that "suffering is the very token of God's love," as if suffering were essentially correlated with love.[4] In other words, we have not yet considered the darker consequences of following love's influence wherever it may lead, like the mystics who "feel within them something better than themselves," and hence "simply open their souls to the oncoming wave."[5] A poem by Philip Larkin begins with a celebration of this oceanic feeling:

> And the wave sings because it is moving;
> Caught in its clear side, we also sing.

However, the flux and undulation of emotional existence will not always make us feel like singing: only a few lines further on, Larkin suggests that we may be "so devised as to make ourselves unhappy."[6] The joy expressed in the poem's opening lines now appears to have been naïve: "If the waves began to reflect, they would suppose that they were advancing, that they had a goal, . . . that they were working for the Sea's good, and they would not fail to elaborate a philosophy as stupid as their zeal."[7] But what is the nature of this connection between love and suffering?

In other words, why is it that a person who is "moved in love" must "suffer in love"?[8] This "unfathomable conflict" at the heart of love is not foreign to the Stoic, nor is it inexplicable. Epictetus, who at one point shows reverence toward love's coercive influence, is generally concerned about its capacity to attach us to precarious things and hence to dispose us toward suffering.[9] Every bond of love is a bond to possible sorrow: even the most unselfish love of another human being is a vulnerable attachment to another center of agency. We are captivated, both by the subjective experience and by the intentional objects of our love. Unless we manage to stifle or resist this overwhelming experience, we are decisively *bound* by it.[10] As opposed to the "isolated self" of the Stoic, the Kierkegaardian self is open and engaged in a network of caring relationships which define its identity. This is why we betray ourselves when we resist love's influence: we are who we are by virtue of what we love. And this fabric of attachments can also be described as a web of care that places us at risk of being affected directly by, and empathetically for, whatever stands at the other end of these fibers of connective tissue. Insofar as a person loves, he or she is at the mercy of a world in which value may dawn unexpectedly and what is valued may be taken away. The life lived on these terms is always difficult—it is vulnerable to passionate suffering in so many ways—but this is the price we must pay for a meaningful existence, in which significance is not nihilistically projected by the will but in which it almost forces itself upon us.

It may be an edifying observation that faith in love is one of the conditions of "a life that is truly worth living," but it is by way of this great blessedness that we experience the heaviest suffering.[11] A self that is built up by love is *thereby* rendered susceptible to *pathos;*[12] nonetheless, to wish to be rid of one's emotional self is a form of despair, in which one denies that God is love and attempts to tear the self away from the power on which its existence depends.[13] To trust in the sacred agency of love is not to be assured that one will be granted whatever is wished for: no such guarantee is available to us as finite creatures. There may be times when what we happen to receive fits our conception of what is good, but it would be wrong in these cases to think that we have been treated preferentially in a providential sense. What appears to be happy fortune does not bring any assurance of favored standing, just as tragedy is not necessarily merited. Reverential trust is not a conclusion drawn from favorable circumstances; it is an inward disposition through which we perceive every external state of affairs. A person with this trust will not assume that he must somehow deserve whatever good he may have been given, nor will he assume that it will not be taken away. Faith in love is neither a calculated arrangement nor an exchange in which one receives tit for tat: it is an acceptance of whatever may proceed from an enigmatic, unpredictable source. A cost-benefit analysis of all the emotional highs and lows that follow from this venture would not necessarily show that it is a wise investment.[14]

In the edifying discourse entitled "To Need God Is a Human Being's Highest Perfection," Kierkegaard argues that an awareness of one's reliance on this self-grounding power, although it "makes life more difficult," is needed if one is to know oneself.[15] When the erotic self covets objects in the external world and then has its wishes luckily fulfilled, it imagines that it can count on a happy fate from now on.[16] In a deeper sense, the passionate human being ought to be aware that circumstances may change; however, "the surrounding world can actually be so favorable, so tangibly trustworthy," that a person is seduced into a superficial feeling of secure well-being.[17] When its good fortune is threatened, the covetous self clings more tightly to its probabilistic hopes; but it is precisely at such times that one is in a position to learn the deeper truth that, with regard to valued externals, a person is not in a position of ultimate control. To accept this uncontrol is to open oneself to a gratitude which is not based upon the false belief that one is securely in possession of the good. To trust in love with an unconditional faith that no contingent experience could shake is to cultivate a different way of perceiving things, according to which even the most difficult experiences are seen as meaningful. When Paul says "Rejoice, and again I say, rejoice," Kierkegaard suggests that he is pausing to listen "to everything terrible that may be uttered," and then, in spite of everything, repeating his conviction that one must nevertheless rejoice.[18] This is the assurance of a faith that preserves its spirit of gratitude even "in the maelstrom of spiritual trial"; it does not follow that one's life becomes easy—on the contrary, "it can become very hard."[19] But it is simply not possible to prohibit hardship from a life that contains deeper meaning, beauty, and truth, in which one traces everything to a God of love. Love "does not secure against despair by means of feeble, lukewarm comfort," and faith is not a recipe for tranquillity: indeed, the "magnitude of the terrifying" is proportionate to the influence of this grounding and edifying power.[20] The essential connection between love and suffering does not imply that passion ought to be sought as an end in itself: the point is that by virtue of loving, a person is liable to be affected in many different ways by contingent events. This vulnerability is a consequence of caring about aspects of the world that one cannot predict and does not control.

As a matter of logical implication, it is because the self is built up by love in such a way as to be susceptible to passion that our well-being is bound up with our vulnerability. The religious sensibility of the true Christian is an orientation toward what is loved, not a belief in God as a very large bird, an elderly uncle, a fluffy marshmallow, or any other objective entity that can be imagined to exist on a cloud somewhere, apart from human inwardness.[21] Suffering that arises from a faith in the divinity of love is not egoless or illusory, but is grounded in the reality of the individual subject and its relations of care with objects outside of itself.[22] If we are committed to believing in the possibility of love, and in the significance of the threads by which it connects us to the world, then we must accept the possibility of suffering.[23] What others do to me is not my responsibility: to care about them *is*, even if they hurt me in return.[24] Schopenhauer is aware that "the thousand threads" which hold us emotionally "bound to the world" are precisely what lead us to suffer, but he also realizes that a life without any susceptibility to passion would not be that of an individual.[25] Although some of Kierkegaard's late religious writings turn to Schopenhauer and advocate an immolation of the self,[26] *Works of*

Love and the earlier discourses affirm individuality and passion.[27] The philosophical anthropology developed in these works leaves us with a choice between individuality-and-suffering or neither/nor: and the latter alternative cannot be acceptable to anyone who believes that, since a divine agency "has *created* and *sustains* this world," we ought to avoid the "ascetic fanaticism" that "hates it."[28] The heavier the burden of our concerns, the more value we experience in life; but the weight of our cares can also lead to seemingly unbearable suffering. This is the predicament that every loving person must live with: authentic passions cannot be turned on and off like a water faucet, since they arise from a basic emotional engagement which subsequent emotional responses presuppose. This basic engagement enables a person to be a moral agent, but it is not itself a moral evaluation—it is better described as a religious acceptance of the conditions of human existence. Either one loves or one does not love, and this fundamental commitment is not made from an ideally rational standpoint. It is made without any knowledge of what will ensue. Of course, one may theoretically preclude suffering by resisting or revolting against this initial commitment, and withdrawing one's care from the world.[29] But is it perhaps better for this project not to succeed? We are tempted to resent whatever threatens our security, hardening ourselves against the external world,[30] but we can also trust in the incarnation of "the divine-human love that *freely chooses avoidable suffering*."[31] The idea of a suffering God who makes a passionate sacrifice exemplifies the commitment to love and suffer in an uncertain world, instead of stoically avoiding unhappiness and frustration (together with happiness and fulfillment). Love is not predicated upon anything but itself—one might say, as with nihilism so also with love: "Why?" finds no answer.[32]

In the face of this unasked-for and inexplicable givenness, Kierkegaard suggests that we should not ask why, but rather give thanks for whatever has been given, even when it seems that we have been dealt a bad hand. With an annoying persistence, he asks:

> And when your allotted portion was little, did you thank God? And when your allotted portion was sufferings, did you thank God? And when your wish was denied, did you thank God? . . . And when people wronged and insulted you, did you thank God?[33]

To these questions, the reader might answer: no, of course not. After all, the concept of thankfulness does tend to imply that one is happy with what has been given. But Kierkegaard insists that gratitude should not be contingent upon the quality of the gift in the eyes of the recipient: instead, it ought to take the form of unconditional acceptance. Along with the risk of being disappointed, wronged, and insulted, he acknowledges two general kinds of unhappiness. Sometimes our allotted portion is little: this grounds the nihilistic complaint of *too little significance*. At other times, the world is too much with us: this is the basis for the pessimistic complaint of *too much suffering*.[34] Kierkegaard is aware of both emotional possibilities, and of the immense obstacle they represent for any grateful affirmation that God is love. When we are tempted not to affirm this proposition, it may be because we simply cannot comprehend it.[35] Our concrete experience may lead us to wonder whether the view from nowhere is more truthful (or at least more tolerable) than the perspective of a loving person.

It is possible, not only by virtue of a lack of effort, to experience a comprehensive sense of desecration, like the concerned person whose soul was worn out by cares to the point that everything seemed confused, as if "the wild pandemonium of life" could not be resolved into any overall harmony. Looking at "the anarchy into which everything seemed to have disintegrated," such a person may have given in to despair. Or, Kierkegaard writes, perhaps he simply became alien to everything: "He saw what others saw, but his eyes continually read an invisible handwriting in everything, that it was emptiness and illusion."[36] This nihilistic vision may be the result of having loved and suffered, and seen too much: the tragic consequences that often follow from trusting in love can make us incapable of believing that it is fundamentally worthy of trust.[37] As Thomas Hardy points out, our passionate experience is sometimes of the "incapacitating kind" that does not leave us wiser but only "unfits us for further travel."[38] After suffering her tragic fate, his character Tess laments:

> It wears me out to think of it,
> To think of it;
> I cannot bear my fate as writ,
> I'd have my life unbe.[39]

It may be admirable for the subject of an apparently meaningless suffering to avoid utter despair, but it is not easy to maintain a faith in love that believes all things. When "despondency wants to make everything empty for you," to transform all of existence until "you do indeed see all of it, but with such indifference" that it seems as if God has withdrawn from the world, "far away from all this triviality that is scarcely worth living for"—this, Kierkegaard says, is precisely when it is most important to have faith in love. "If for one moment, one single moment, it were to be absent, [then] everything would be confused."[40] Still, the fact that we are both the instruments and the victims of this dynamic force does not by any means require us to endorse it with joyful reverence, and thus to embrace the risk of suffering.[41] If Kierkegaard still believes in "a benign and love-impregnated cosmic order," this cannot be a facile belief which is blind to the many legitimate reasons for thinking differently.[42] Faith does not consist in an asinine confidence that, in the scheme of things, everything works out nicely for those who love with a proper religious understanding: it is a matter of accepting one's place in the whole unknown process.

The standard example of a character who faithfully embraces his fate in spite of all sufferings, not merely in the Judeo-Christian tradition but arguably in all of world literature, is Job. He is introduced as a *blameless* and *upright* man, who lives a flourishing existence as a friend of God, appreciative of his many contingent goods: animals, pastures, family, and health.[43] But when the work animals are stolen and the livestock struck by lightning, when the house is blown down onto the heads of the children, and when Job's own body is covered with painful and disfiguring sores, he refuses to curse God or to give up on life. Surveying the ruins of his former happiness, he does not self-deceptively comfort himself by denying the loss that he has suffered, "as if there were strength in falsehood."[44] Instead, he feels and acknowledges the full extent of his loss, recognizing (as Kierkegaard comments) that "if God is love, then he is also love in everything, love in what you can understand and love in what you cannot understand."[45] This is not a rationalization of the ways of God, simply a recognition that our attitude toward what is out of our hands must ultimately be either acceptance or distrust—and a refusal to admit the limits of our own power and knowledge is one of the more perverse forms of distrust.[46] The "young man" in *Repetition,* in a dumbstruck apostrophe to Job, asks: "When all of life collapsed upon you and lay like broken pottery at your feet . . . did you immediately have this interpretation of love, this joyful boldness of trust and faith?"[47] This character, who is initially unconvinced by Job's "miserable worldly wisdom" and the reverence that accompanies it, eventually takes heart in his story.[48] Job's witness, as Kierkegaard suggests, is addressed not to the happy but to the troubled, who will listen only to the voice of someone who has suffered miserably. Job does not lecture on the perfection of life: he never accepts the idea that his suffering must be *for the best* from some viewpoint. Neither misrepresenting his present wretchedness, nor forgetting the significance of what he formerly loved, Job throws himself on the ground and cries out with the words that Kierkegaard cites as the title of his discourse: "the Lord gave, and the Lord took away; blessed be the name of the Lord."[49] Because of this affirmation in the midst of the blackest plight, Job strikes a chord with those to whom optimism seems ludicrous or stupid: he demonstrates that "all the joy proclaimed in the world in which sorrow is not heard along with it is but sounding brass and a tinkling cymbal."[50]

It is not as if Job suffered once and for all something that would never be experienced again. As Kierkegaard points out, only a light-minded person could wish not to be reminded of the story of Job and his incomprehensible distress.[51] This narrative reminds us that the source of human suffering is impossible to fathom, in any case. This is why an exemplary truth is illustrated by "someone in the world who lost everything," for whom "the whole thing remained inexplicable and obscure."[52]

> How would he not understand that when the sea is raging wildly, when it heaves itself toward heaven, people and their fragile buildings are then flung about as in a game; that when the storm rages in its fury, human projects are but child's play; that when the earth quakes in the anguish of the elements and when the mountains sigh, men and their glorious works then sink as a nothingness into the abyss.[53]

How, indeed? Yet faced with the same evidence, Job does not yield to despair: singing out with absurd praises, he traces everything to God. Confessing that he was born naked into the world and does not know what is going on, Job responds to his profound loss with gratitude for all the blessings that he must have been given, if he was in a position to have them taken away.[54] Those who take themselves to be immune to suffering are asked to think about how they might respond when similar trials arrive at their doors, and are advised to learn from Job how to be honest with themselves about the source of whatever good fortune they may enjoy. Whatever is of value in human life is a contingent gift, and ought to be appreciated as such; as Kierkegaard writes at the end of the discourse, "no one knows the time and the hour when the messages will come to him, the one more terrible than the other."[55]

But, Mooney asks, "how can a man as afflicted as Job is, nevertheless affirm the inexhaustible meaning of the particulars around him, or of the particular he is?"[56] The answer comes from the voice of God that speaks from out of the storm to call Job's attention to all the wonders of the world that Job did not create and does not comprehend. The givenness of love itself has much in common with the contingent givenness of all things: Job gives credit where credit is due when he praises the sacred agency that has made him what he is and given him everything that he is in a position to lose. Only love can suffer and yet maintain this perspective of acceptance, in spite of all objective grounds for nihilistic doubt and all pessimism about the connection between emotion and vulnerability.[57] No doubt, it takes audacity to affirm this "interpretation of love" even in the worst of circumstances: Job violates Ockham's razor, going beyond empirical facts to conclude that his children were given and then taken away, when a far less extravagant explanation would be that they were simply born and raised, and then unfortunately buried by a storm from the desert.[58] Visible evidence does not compel trust in love: indeed, it is possible to go on for a long time "in the agonizing suffering of getting no impression *in concreto* that God is love."[59] When a person maintains faith in love after surveying the range of human suffering, he or she is not making a "scientific" observation but stating a basic principle of interpretation.[60] Because love alone is able to give significance to existence, our life as value-perceiving moral agents is predicated upon an implicitly religious affirmation. For Kierkegaard, this is the real either/or: "Either God is love: and then it is absolutely valid absolutely to stake absolutely everything on this . . . or God is not love: and then, yes, then the loss is so infinite that any other loss is of no consequence whatsoever."[61]

It requires courage to say *thy will be done in me,* to identify one's highest perfection with one's most abject dependency, and it may also require a belief that love is more than a blind striving. But Kierkegaard seems to have an answer even for those who argue that existence erupts from an abyss and is otherwise groundless.[62] He speaks in one letter about how "the *blind* god of love always finds a way," as if teleology could supervene upon an intrinsically meaningless process; in another, he makes reference to "accident, Governance, or whatever it may be" that governs contingent events.[63] And in a suggestive journal entry that aims to explain how suffering can be accounted for without reference to "the devil," Kierkegaard writes:

> The unconditioned, the being-in-and-for-itself, is so terribly strenuous for a human being, and one would therefore so much like to be rid of it, [to] press a purpose upon God—and in that very second he becomes in

fact dependent upon finitude. . . . This is why I repeat so often that God is pure subjectivity, has nothing of objective being in himself which could lead to his having, or having to have, purposes.[64]

In each of these cases he suggests that we ought to comport ourselves affirmatively, even if significance is merely an emergent property of a process which is incomprehensible only because it is senseless; a force that is basically aimless cannot go wrong, at least.[65] Still, this is hardly a consolatory remark. When Camus takes at face value the question from *Fear and Trembling*—

if at the basis of everything there were only a wild ferment, a power that writhing in dark passions gave rise to everything significant or insignificant, if a voracious and unfathomable emptiness were hidden under everything, what would life be then except despair?[66]

—he answers that despair may indeed be the appropriate response.[67] Of course, Kierkegaard will not be reconciled to absurdity so easily; instead, he suggests an "absurd" religious perspective from which even tragic frustration can be traced to the origin of all significance in life. And he reminds us that the way we perceive things always depends upon how we are disposed: a charitable gaze regards everything in the best possible light.[68] This may be more of an ideal hope than an achieved state of being, but he agrees with Simone Weil that the self needs to "go on loving in the emptiness, or at least to go on wanting to love, though it may only be with an infinitesimal part of itself."[69] It is only faith in love, not a rejection of emotion, that can save us from despair.

Perhaps there is not only a human need at stake in this, but also a truth about the nature of reality which can be understood only in a spirit of gratitude. Circumstances may provoke us to say, "it was somewhat unkind of love to let it happen," but it is not good to allow this response to expand into a comprehensive ingratitude for existence.[70] Rather than being so petty as to keep track of every single way in which we have been hurt, we ought to place trust in the eternal power in which our being is rooted. Even the person who has "passionately experienced" that "hope disappoints" should not for this reason cease to believe that God is love, since this belief is not susceptible to circumstantial disproof.[71] It is something that must be accepted or rejected as an axiomatic premise. And the religious conviction which it brings has little in common with the sentimental idea of God as "an old fussbudget who sits in heaven and humors us"—it requires submitting to the terms of an uncertain world in which value is precarious and impermanent, and in which there is no assurance of a happy ending.[72] In support of his thesis that life is not "decidedly preferable" to nonexistence, Schopenhauer asserts that only a blind life-force could be responsible for placing us in a predicament which is "so precarious, obscure, anxious, and painful."[73] By virtue of existing, however, we have already been tacitly accepting and relying upon the influence of this force: we are always already living as emotional creatures whose being is rooted and grounded in love, and a consistent nihilism toward the ground of our being would require us to commit suicide.[74] Kierkegaard urges us to make the best of our dependency by interpreting the source of all things as a sacred power. What he offers us is an understanding of self and world which stipulates what is most worthy of the reverence that we often find ourselves directing at patriotic causes, fashionable habits, symbols of prestige, lecture audiences, and television celebrities. To identify the hidden basis of existence as worthy of reverence is not to introduce an optional attitude but to reorient our religious tendencies so that they take a less ridiculous form.[75] It is to view religious faith not merely as a set of positive assertions but as an existential comportment that is informed by intelligent convictions about an unavoidable topic.

Our life as emotional agents does not follow from a reasoned conclusion that such a life is unambiguously worth living, but from a commitment that is not exactly rational. This is the sense in which emotion cannot simply be reduced to rationality: our capacity for emotional reason could not be realized if we did not, at least implicitly, affirm our existence as loving beings. In making this affirmation, we thereby open the door to suffering. But to have no such reverence, to be closed to the possibility of experiencing significance in life, is not simply to be liberated from a superfluous belief. It is to watch significance withdraw from the world, and to do violence to the sacred basis of the self. Love is a pre-moral force, whose visible results are so chaotic as to justify ambivalence if not outright distrust; nonetheless, Kierkegaard suggests that a truthful human being must affirm the mystery at the heart of its existence, calling an unknown source by the name of God.[76] Whether or not we can bear the weight of this affirmation is another question. The point is that faith in love is a necessary condition of meaningful existence, even if it is terrifying for us to accept that what builds us up is also what makes us suffer.

CHAPTER 11

Value on the Other Side of Nihilism

It has been remarked that the philosophical study of emotion leads to a tragic view of life.[1] The preceding two chapters demonstrate why this might be the case: to identify love as the source of all meaning in existence is to accept that a life of wisdom cannot be either care-free or invulnerable to suffering. It would be naïve to suggest, then, that the tragic sense could be explained away, or that an authentic emotional life will be compatible with absolute happiness. However, I will suggest that faith in love can be justified as a basic attitude, even if from an unloving standpoint it does not appear to be warranted or worthwhile. A positive belief in love as the sacred ground of being gives ontological backing to the idea that mental integrity might consist in something other than apathy. It makes possible an alternative (nonstoical) resolution of the moral-psychological problems with which this inquiry began, including the problem of defining how a passionate life could be both legitimate and worth living.

Since love is the creative ground of each human being, it is impossible to look back upon one's life and find a time at which its influence was not yet felt. The Stoic considers love an enemy and guards himself against it;[2] the aesthete yields to its influence only intermittently

and with partial trust. The Kierkegaardian ethicist describes the formal structure of a less hesitant, more internally consistent way of being affected. However, he overvalues stability in life at the cost of losing his emotional openness
and the ability to perceive value anew; and he fails to appreciate the claim of
the romantic imagination, in its exacting demands and its difficulty in coming
to terms with the world. Just as being reasonable is not simply a matter of
attaining consistency in one's beliefs regardless of what they may be, emotional virtue is worth cultivating only if the source of passionate attachment is
fundamentally trustworthy.[3] If love is unreliable, then there is no reason to get
one's passions in order: one must simply get rid of them altogether. On the
other hand, by dwelling on the heart that longs to be involved in moral life, we
can recognize this overflowing source of yearning and concern as precisely
what must animate any genuine engagement with the world. The name we
give to the fundamental restlessness at the core of our being will color our experience of it. By calling it "love," we affirm that the primary emotional force
that forms the heart can be developed toward the ideal of unselfishness and
giving. The secondary passions that arise from our love-based engagement
with the world are sanctioned insofar as our capacity to love is good. The interdependence of these two aspects of emotion can now be understood, not
merely as a curious psychological fact, but as a basic premise of life as we
know it. Emotion is "the innermost and sustaining element in human life,"
and what structures the world, guaranteeing its significance.[4] In the emotional space between mind and world, between the loving subject and the
beloved other, there is a delicate balance which makes all questions about
value subjectivism or objectivism collapse.

To "believe in love," one scholar writes, means "to 'see' from the standpoint of love rather than mistrust."[5] To see things from a loving perspective is
to allow oneself to respond to the full weight of their significance, to experience the force of perceptions that apathetic rationality does not know. Love is
not a product of the will, and the mode of receptivity in which value is perceived is not one in which the self projects value outward; but passionate impressions are not so coercive that we are entirely passive in yielding to them,
either. Without the right kind of emotional openness, a person will not be
able to perceive anything as weighty or convincing:

> On the whole, a reason is a curious thing. If I regard it with all my pas-
> sion, it develops into an enormous necessity that can set heaven and
> earth in motion; if I am devoid of passion, I look down on it derisively.[6]

What he is talking about, and what he calls passion, is the impassioned, the inward, which is exactly what a firm conviction is. Just as a rooster cannot lay an egg—at most, a wind egg—"reasons" can neither beget nor give birth to a conviction, no matter how much intercourse they may have with one another. Conviction arises elsewhere. . . . This is the positive saturation point, just as when a lover says: "she is the one I love," and he says . . . nothing about reasons.[7]

Practical reason is a kind of weighing,[8] and we weigh or evaluate things accurately only when we see them from a loving standpoint. Our passions are meaningful because their intentional objects are valuable in themselves, apart from what we might want them to be; but only if we are loving (not guarded or untrusting) can we apprehend their value as it is revealed to us.[9] This mode of perception is utterly unlike the sentimental consciousness in which one sees only what one wants to see or else takes flight from concrete reality into a fantastic realm. The gaze of love is not a wishful evasion, but a way of seeing things as they are in the best light.[10] It does not overlook tragedy, but includes it in an ambivalent yet unconditional embrace. Although it refuses to explain away negative emotions, it also does not use mixed feelings as an excuse for halfhearted affirmation: love's "yes" must be prior to any other judgment.

As love draws us into a "difficult flight along the ground," we not only realize our own need for meaning but also do justice to others, by presupposing that they must be loving beings and understanding them in light of this principle.[11] The "love that sustains all existence" must be at the ground of every existing being, establishing the particular cares that define the self in time.[12] This is the sense in which, in being passionate, we are implicitly being religious: since humanity is essentially passionate, to adopt an attitude of reverent acceptance toward the "basis of all religiousness" in "emotional inwardness" is to make an explicit affirmation of what is shared by all human beings.[13] When our capacity to love is made into the basis of our moral life, it gains "enduring continuance" and our participation in finite existence is shaped by an eternal power.[14] As Dante's *Purgatorio* shows, this primary emotion is by no means immune to perversion: "Love is the seed in you of every virtue / and of all acts deserving punishment."[15] But if love is cultivated into a caring, unselfish disposition as Kierkegaard prescribes in his religious ethics— if it embraces the distinctive being of the beloved without attempting to possess or control—then its influence is likely to be benign, even ennobling: I enable you to be yourself when I affirm you in your own temporal progress of love and suffering.

It is a virtue "to be truly in love," but simply to call it a virtue is to risk missing the moral-psychological point: without love, it would be impossible for the self to gain access to the values that orient its moral existence.[16] Our emotional capacity to perceive things as meaningful is a necessary condition of both our continuity as persons and our awareness of the external world. Meaningful spiritual existence arises from the recognition that "to be edified we must be open to love."[17] In the art of human life, we are not the artists but the works of art; to live in accordance with this truth is to believe in the infinite significance of each unique loving person and of his or her self-defining passions.[18] In philosophical terms, what this means is to be committed to a kind of axiological realism: that is, to subscribe to the doctrine that "reality is a meaningful, structured whole in which human life (for Kierkegaard each human life) plays a significant part."[19] Because love is fundamental to existence, it is reasonable to conclude that passionate cognition is ontologically vindicated as a mode of knowing which is consistent with the nature of things.

This conclusion is radically different from those at the heart of Stoicism, according to which "what is best in us" is rational volition.[20] In either case, however, moral psychology is grounded in broader religious principles: for Kierkegaard as for Epictetus, authentic perception relies upon acknowledgement of a transcendent power that is active within the self. And, just as Epictetus does, Kierkegaard wishes to follow Socrates in learning "the true nature of each reality."[21] They differ not in their Socratic commitment to truthfulness but in their conception of what rationality *is*. If love is a fundamental category through which we perceive and conceptualize the world, then we are forced to reconsider what it would mean to be aware of the true nature of each thing that exists. There is no reason for us to believe that external reality is more accurately perceived without emotion, or that we would see things more clearly from a "scientific" viewpoint according to which love is not a part of "objective" nature.[22] Such a belief reveals a basic philosophical mistake about both subject *and* object in a sense that we are only now in a position to understand.

As opposed to dispassionate rationality, passionate reason is a way of seeing that opens us to the significance of particularity in existence. Moral life involves the activation of this kind of awareness, without which we could not navigate our way in the world—that is, unless (like the Stoics) we believe that it would be better to see things from a perspective so far removed from the human world that emotion and value are left behind altogether.[23] But this ambition is dubious if love is a key to the inner nature of things, for the same reason that living human beings are not most accurately regarded as dead bodies. Although I am outside of you, I can see you either as an animate being or as a corpse. The former way of seeing is the caring awareness which an executioner must omit; the latter might be defended as more "rational" or "objective" by an observer who is committed to stoical principles.[24] But naturalistic description should not characterize things as empty of meaning, if love is a basic component of the natural world. Instead, we should perceive each object of knowledge in "the distinctiveness and intensity of its specific being," as part of "the rightly ordered ecology of the whole universe" in which being reveals itself as love.[25] This is why, as Kierkegaard argues, rationality does not consist in unemotionally holding oneself apart from what is known: "To love and to know are essentially synonymous, and just as to love signifies that the other becomes manifest, so it naturally also means that one is revealed oneself."[26]

In other words, love is essential to my awareness of what is not myself, and also to the realization of my own distinctive identity. Things exist for us only insofar as we are not indifferent to them; when we see them with an unselfishly loving gaze, we are in the best position to appreciate their significance. As Jean-Luc Marion says, "only love opens up knowledge of the other as such."[27] This, of course, depends upon the nature of "the other" in question: if what we are perceiving is not a lifeless object, then Stoic rationality is unfit to see it as what it truly is. With a loving consciousness, we encounter the object on its own terms, with a sense of its realized distinctiveness and of its mysterious ground.[28] The mind's subjective capacity to find value in objects is therefore not a falsification of a reality that ought to be seen in a different way, but a constructive process that ought to be seen as reliable. Emotional involvement is a necessary condition of moral awareness—and, perhaps, of "objective" knowledge in the best sense. Defining the criteria of existential wisdom, Kierkegaard writes: "an objectivity which takes shape in a corresponding subjectivity, that is the goal."[29]

In an irony that would not have been lost on Socrates, it is only when we abandon the goal of absolute rational sovereignty that we open ourselves to the sort of insight that is bound up with the deepest roots of our being.[30] Such pertinent truth is not the sort of thing we actively procure, but something that becomes manifest only if we are emotionally receptive. What we perceive in this mode of knowing is neither "queer" in itself nor foreign to our nature;[31] it is the empirical particularity of the world, seen through the lens of an appreciative perceiver. In a "scientific" sense, the loving subjectivity of a human being is not the center of anything—but it *is* the center of the world, in the only sense in which a world can exist for each of us.[32] The "impassioned understanding" of which Kierkegaard speaks is the form of moral awareness without which nothing makes sense: each of us strives to develop an "authentic interpretation" of phenomena in our inspiring and frustrating love affair with the external world.[33] Each of us has a different axiological consciousness, in which the world appears radiant with significance insofar as we have seen it with loving eyes. Through your prescription lenses, some things may appear larger than they do to me; but the "fact and meaning" of your vantage point is part of the emotional truth that my impassioned understanding ought to acknowledge.[34] When I feel empathy for your point of view, I do not add a needless quantity of suffering to the universe, but broaden my own moral awareness.

At the basis of whatever "knowledge" may be available through this way of seeing is an emotion that can transform both self and world. It only makes sense that, to skeptical eyes, this evidence will never be compelling: trust in love cannot be based on objectively evident trustworthiness or lovability. For the same reason, there can be no hard empirical interpretation of the facts that refutes the premises of a religious existence.[35] Either we love or else we don't, and this fundamental premise then conditions our experience, for better or worse. To hold oneself back from the loving embrace in which the self accepts life in all of its ambiguous detail is not intellectual virtue, but weakness. So much for Ockham's razor: as Kierkegaard points out, we "can be deceived by believing what is untrue, but we certainly are also deceived by not believing what is true," by hardening ourselves against the possibility of being deceived.[36] Which of these is the more dangerous risk?

> To defraud oneself of love is the most terrible, is an eternal loss, for which there is no compensation either in time or in eternity. Ordinarily, when it is a matter of being deceived in love, however different the case may be, the one deceived is still related to love . . . but the self-deceived person has locked and is locking himself out of love. There is also talk about being deceived by life or in life, but the one who in his self-deception deceived himself out of living—his loss is irreparable.[37]

Nothing does more violence to a person than defensively cutting oneself off from love: if the potential skeptic would surrender his or her doubt, he or she could regain the world that had been obfuscated. "It is in my gratitude for life that I may come to love the world," says Rush Rhees.[38] Such a shift in perspective could bring the once blinded moral agent back into the light of a passionate engagement with others.

Through the stimulus of love, the skeptical attitude gives way to an acceptance of life that is comprehensive, even if it is uncomprehending. Nihilistic, halfhearted, and stoical doubts are abandoned in favor of a belief in the "infinitely compelling subjectivity" of love.[39] When I affirm this primary emotion, it illuminates the world that I inhabit with others, each of whom I also affirm as a distinct passionate being at the same time that I realize my own unique individuality. Accepting my dependence on the unknowable ground of my existence, I open my heart to an appreciation of other beings, enabling them to be what they are in their singularity—not seeing them as the instruments of my selfish ends.[40] The difference between this emotional perspective and that of the Stoic is the difference between eyes that see things in all of their colorful reality and those that refrain from awe even when faced with the extraordinary; Kierkegaard encourages us to consider that only a loving person attains an accurate view of things.[41] The upshot of this is that achieving emotional integrity "does not require taking an objective, impersonal point of view," as Cheshire Calhoun would agree.[42] What it does require is the cultivation of a mode of consciousness in which one does not extirpate the passions but remains aware of love, and of the patterns of significance that it has revealed.

This emotional consciousness is not compatible with the idea that I am essentially a disembodied mind, and that truth is to be found in the security of abstract or mathematical knowledge, such as I might imaginably have obtained in a realm of timeless contemplation.[43] Rather, this mode of knowing must arise from my way of being as a situated agent with a particular contingent history of passionate experience. There can be no scheme of meaning that makes sense of human existence, unless it recognizes the validity of perceptions of significance. Moral life is not the unfolding of a logical process, but an uncertain realm of movement, in which "a true conception of life and of oneself" is attainable only for a person who is attuned to his or her environment.[44] Practical reason is a capacity of emotionally involved persons, and has nothing in common with the cool rationality of a radically disengaged (or Platonically self-contained) spectator, who could only be "a stranger in the world."[45]

What philosophy needs, therefore, is an existential category to replace the classical doctrine of recollection: as opposed to the Platonic notion that "all knowing is a recollecting, modern philosophy will teach that all of life is a repetition." Kierkegaard's narrator continues with a rich but cryptic introduction of the concept:

> Repetition and recollection are the same movement, except in opposite directions: what is recollected has been, is repeated backwards, whereas repetition properly so called is recollected forwards. Therefore repetition, if it is possible, makes a person happy, whereas recollection makes him unhappy—assuming, of course, that he gives himself time to live and does not promptly at the moment of birth find an excuse to sneak out of life again, for example, that he has forgotten something.[46]

After this dismissive allusion to the idea that the embodied soul longs to return to a realm of timeless abstraction, he adds that "repetition's love is in truth the only happy love," suggesting that emotional fulfillment can be found only within the realm of temporality. Or, as Eriksen comments:

> We do not relate to the eternal by relating to ourselves. Any retreat from the temporal world is a retreat into the realm of self-projection, rather than a way of encountering the eternal. To believe in repetition means to live in such a way that one seeks the eternal in the temporal rather than behind it. . . . Kierkegaard's critique of the metaphysical tradition, then, is based on his conception of motion as something transcendent by which the eternal appears in the temporal.[47]

This means that, in order to achieve the ideal of repetition, a person must realize an emotional openness toward the future and toward other human beings.

Since love has been identified as the "eternal power" that animates temporal existence, it is easy to see what is at stake in the discussion of repetition. The question is: how can emotionally-perceived significance, and moral identity along with it, be sustained in the midst of finitude? Nihilistic skepticism about value would be overcome only if a human being's loving subjectivity could be legitimately and consistently brought to terms with the actual world.[48] How can the self register the emotional influence which has moved it to become passionately involved in the relationships and creative works that define a life in time? In a journal entry from 1840, Kierkegaard writes:

The unity of the metaphysical and the contingent already resides in self-consciousness, which is the point of departure for personality. I become at the same time conscious in my eternal validity [and] in my contingent finitude (that I am this particular being, born in this country, at this time, under the many-faceted influence of all these changing surroundings). This latter aspect must not be overlooked or rejected; the true life of the individual is its apotheosis. And that does not mean that this empty, contentless *I* steals, as it were, out of this finitude in order to become volatilized and diffused in its heavenly emigration, but rather that the divine inhabits the finite and finds its way in it.[49]

Whatever *repetition* is, it is not a "weak and sentimental sneaking out of the world," in order to preserve a vacuous "I": rather, it must involve allowing one's historical perspective to be shaped, and continually transformed, by the force of emotion.[50]

The blunt outcome of the romantic novella that bears the name *Repetition* (subtitled "A Venture in Experimenting Psychology") is that no one seems to have attained the described ideal. There are two speaking characters, a "young man" who is experiencing an unhappy love affair and an older one who observes this predicament and acts as the young man's analyst or confessor. The older man, whose very name ("Constantin Constantius") indicates his strictly academic interest in the possibility of movement, is manipulative, cynical, and prone to fits of nostalgic sentimentality.[51] We know him as the host of the symposium on love in *Stages on Life's Way*, who throughout the speeches of that dialogue displays a world-weary aversion toward emotion. Meanwhile, the "young man" in *Repetition*, whom we have already encountered in his apostrophes to Job, "advances further" toward the ideal of repetition, but is not much better off in the end.[52] He is guilty of idealizing his beloved, looking beyond her concrete existence, and then looking beyond the present tense altogether in order to bask in the safe haven of imaginative detachment. Although he is initially receptive to the experience of love, he cannot ultimately become and remain himself in relation to another human being.[53] Nonetheless, a negative way can be discerned in the midst of the failures of the two main characters in *Repetition*. In its fragmentary speculations and its conspicuous absences, this narrative points toward the ideal that Constantin still believes in, although he cannot realize it in his own life, and which the young man erroneously believes himself to have achieved.[54] It leaves us with an intimation of how one might cultivate emotional integrity in the highest sense while remaining in the midst of temporal existence.

In order to love the actual people we see, it is first of all necessary to "give up all imaginary and exaggerated ideas about a dreamworld where the object of love should be sought and found"—rather, we must "become sober, gain actuality and truth by finding and remaining in the world of reality."[55] In the words of Robert Frost, "Earth's the right place for love: / I don't know where it's likely to go better."[56] But in *Repetition*, neither Constantius nor the young man meets this criterion with regard to "the girl." The young man believes that she simply *is* the image of his wishful thinking, while Constantin is unimpressed with the girl's "lovableness" and encourages the young man to size her up from a skeptical perspective:

> What especially amazed me was that she could have such great significance for him, for there was no trace of anything really stirring, enrapturing, creative. . . . He idealized her, and now he believed that she was that.[57]

Both of them, however, are mistaken. As we have seen, an understanding of the beloved as she is in her distinctive singularity is not available except from an unselfishly loving point of view. If we are trapped in fantasies which distort reality, or in unloving distrust, then we cannot perceive her both *as she is* and *in the best possible light* at the same time. The young man omits the reality principle, while Constantius neglects the principle of charitable interpretation. Expressing the same point in acoustic imagery, we could say that the young man is only hearing a tune in his head, while the older one has closed his ears to music and is simply not listening anymore.[58] Neither achieves a receptivity to meaning as it emerges within temporal experience to those who have eyes to see, or ears to hear.

Those who are properly disposed, on the other hand, know that unselfish love is not a content-free normative ideal; instead, it demands that each person's concrete historical perspective must be taken seriously: that of the lover as well as that of the beloved. Significance arises between beloved things, which have a future and a past, and loving subjects, who themselves are also contingent beings whose nature is neither unspecific nor eternally fixed. The ideal of repetition stands for the possibility that the perceiving self could sustain a delicate balance between openness and integration—that is, between aesthetic responsiveness and ethical resolution. What I have loved has made an impression on me which has something to do with its qualities and something to do with its identity as what I myself encountered at a certain point in my own life as a passionate being. Based upon my experience up until that point, I was able to respond to *this* object in the way that I did; and the fact *that* I did changes my existence from then on. That which is loved attains a significance in itself, and in relation to my own particular world of concern: it realizes *its* unique value, and conditions my *own* moral agency, by virtue of the same emotional dynamic. Frankfurt writes that love determines what a person "is willing to do, what he cannot help doing, and what he cannot bring himself to do," and that it is therefore unreasonable for a person not to accept "the coherent impetus of a well-formed love," because he or she "has no basis for declining to accept it" and probably "cannot help being moved to do so" anyway.[59] From this conception of love it follows both that we regard its objects as valuable in themselves and that we see them as significant in our own realm of cares. Repetition, if it is possible, would overcome the prospect of absurdity and the phantoms of self-deception at once.[60] It would stand for a perspective unlike either cynical detachment or naïve idealism, from which all things are released to be what they are *and* embraced by a loving subject— not in a way that is secure for all eternity, but in such a way that the lover is open to being continually affected by his or her experience of the beloved.

"If the young man had believed in repetition," Constantius marvels, "what inwardness he might have achieved in this life!"[61] Then, he adds, "everything would have acquired for him religious significance": with "fear and trembling," but also with "faith and trust," the young man would have understood the events which had happened from the start, and what as a consequence he was morally bound to do later, even though this obligation might have "strange results."[62] If only the "young man" had acknowledged his love, abandoning himself to its influence and respecting its self-defining certainties in the midst of his temporal existence. Then he never would have been tempted to write: "I am nauseated by life; it is insipid—without salt and meaning."[63] Even in his darkest hour, life in all of its sound and fury would have been significant. Consenting to finitude, he would have affirmed the metaphysically unnecessary past in its existential impact on his present identity and future bearing. Making sense of his emotional being in time, he would open himself to new perspectives on the past and to new possibilities in the future.[64] By owning up to what he has become in his trajectory of love and suffering, the person who achieves repetition is at home in his distinct temporal existence. He transforms "one damn thing after another" into a passionate sense of being poised between an authentic past and a promising future.

As for Constantin, his chief mistake is attempting to remain in control of the circumstances of emotion, as if by spontaneously deciding to go to a certain place (or to stay at home) one should be able to orchestrate the desired passionate outcome.[65] However, it is impossible to maintain rigid self-sufficiency and to achieve a state of loving openness toward an unpredictable world of value. To the extent that my capacity to love is realized, I become more fully implicated in what I do not control. The ideal of repetition is not one of dispassionate autonomy, but one in which the self consciously accedes to the emotional power by virtue of which it exists. The perspective of age does not need to be one that preserves earlier memories in a hermetically sealed container, seeing everything as if from far away.[66] It could be one in which even an unhappy love becomes the "precondition of a relationship in which the other is not only part of the self, but genuinely other."[67] Although we cannot force the external world to renew itself in our eyes, we can try to keep our eyes open so as not to preclude such an experience. Consenting to the gift of love, we redeem the meaning of the past in a way that flows directly into a future in which we are susceptible to being moved again.

Through its appreciation of uncontrolled externals, the self realizes its distinct character as "a temporal and dynamic process of relating."[68] We do not arbitrarily invent ourselves as passionate beings, but neither are we simply the victims of circumstances. The inward promptings of the romantic imagination are a primitive datum of human experience no less than the force of external situations, and can shape our moral reality ("this is not worth my time") as much as they are shaped by it ("I didn't expect to get drawn into this in the way that I have").[69] Our sense of vocation is worked out in this encounter between emotional inwardness and the external world. When I fully identify with the temporal progress of my love, I can feel a sense of passionate conviction about what I cannot help but care about, what is significant right now, and what I ought to do in the future. Instead of sentimentally preserving the purity of my unfallen soul with its robust sense of possibility, I take responsibility for the way in which I am implicated in time.[70] Becoming more honest with myself, I acknowledge even the most painful elements of my passionate experience as part of my truth—that is, as axiologically salient factors that influence the way I perceive things, for better or worse.

Suffering is the logical consequence of my decision to identify with my perspective as an involved moral agent, which is an identification that I might not have made. To embrace repetition in the sphere of emotional history is therefore something other than to adapt oneself to naturalistic or metaphysical necessity.[71] The affirmation of what I have become in my loving engagement with an unpredictable world is a gesture which transforms the terms of the relationship. Accepting the limiting conditions of my experience, I do my best to steer between the aesthetic temptation of preserving my love in its abstract purity and the "ethical" risk of selling myself short—that is, selling out—by coming to terms with the world in a way that is internally consistent and comprehensible to others, but which is not *my own*. Authentic love does not consist either in a sequence of unconnected intensities or in dispassionate habits of activity, but in allowing one's love to attain integrity over time in such a way that its emotional force is not lost, but is open to being continually renewed. The notion of "repetition" signifies this ideal of moral existence, in which a person works out his or her relation to finite reality by way of an eternal power.[72] To achieve it would be to perceive the passionate equivalent of truth, and to be delivered back to a world that we already "knew" in some sense, yet whose value we can only appreciate insofar as we have fulfilled our own nature as loving beings.

"I by no means regretted sharing in his suffering," Constantin writes, "because in his love the idea was indeed in motion."[73] Love inspires a person with a dizzying sense of possibility, and does not rest in its movement until his or her eyes are fixed on some determinate external reality. This is the beginning of moral life in all of its detail, in which one gains a "steadily deeper and more concrete knowledge of oneself" only in reflecting upon the course taken by this primary emotion through the context in which the self is enmeshed.[74] From the first instant in this process of simultaneous discovery and self-realization, it becomes difficult (if not impossible) to distinguish *love in this subject* from *love for these objects*. Only in its collision with objectivity does the loving subject discover its own emotional possibilities:

> In a mountain region where day in and day out one hears the wind relentlessly play the same invariable theme, one may be tempted for a moment to abstract from the imperfect image and delight in this metaphor of the consistency and assurance of human freedom. One perhaps does not reflect that there was a time when this wind, which for many years has

been at home among these mountains, came as a stranger to this area, and plunged wildly, absurdly through the canyons, producing now a shriek almost startling to itself, then a hollow roar from which it itself fled, then a moan whose source it itself did not know, then from the abyss of anxiety a sigh so deep that the wind itself grew frightened and momentarily wondered if it dared to live in this region, then a happy lyrical waltz: until, having learned to know its instrument, it worked all of this into the melody it renders unaltered day after day. Similarly, the individual's possibility wanders about in its own possibility, discovering first one possibility and then another. But the individual's possibility does not want only to be heard; it is not like the mere passing of the wind. It is also taking shape, and it wants to make itself visible—that is why each of its possibilities is an audible shadow.[75]

From the moment of our birth, we are already moving, sounding out our possibilities and configuring ourselves in a world of change. It is only appropriate, then, that Stoicism ought to "step aside" in favor of the dynamics of passionate existence. Kierkegaard's notion of repetition suggests that in being emotional we are not "running aimlessly," but realizing our particular significance.[76]

As we go forward in time with the momentum of emotion, we are being composed as caring moral agents *and* being truthfully attuned to our place on earth. This is more difficult than taking refuge in an unchanging domain that we ourselves control, but such is the price of being able to experience real emotions. When we allow our "infinitizing" passionate imagination to express itself in the midst of finitude, we are not only vulnerable to being affected, but ambiguously implicated in life.[77] This gift of love brings us to a position in which we feel that life is meaningful and that there are certain things we must do, but it also brings us to the point of tears by situating us in a realm of change with concerns that extend far beyond the domain of what is up to us. By comparison, our lives become more stable, but also more impoverished, when we are ruled by the "passion for eternal preservation" which "separates us from the *event* of the other, of time, of randomness, of luck, of finitude, and of love."[78]

Philosophical discussions of self-deception tend to focus upon the person who *wishes* to be something he or she cannot be.[79] The normative ideal of repetition is not to be mistaken for wishful thinking; it has to do with the acknowledgment of facts so basic to our identity that we must either accept them or else be guilty of self-betrayal. Unless we believe that the world of change is illusory, we should affirm the validity of the concerned truths that reveal to us the significance of our lives. It is unsettling to recognize that "the power that governs human life is love," since to live in accordance with this primitive force is to attain, at best, a precarious stability.[80] It is to embrace what has already been established by love, while remaining open to the disclosure of new values and of new ethico-religious imperatives. Religious existence "is a repetition, at a higher level, of the structural moments of the aesthetic life,"[81] because it recovers emotional receptivity within the horizon of ethical resolution: "It is a mark of childishness to say: *Me wants, me—me;* a mark of adolescence to say: *I*—and *I*—and *I;*" but true maturity, Kierkegaard suggests, is attained only when a person has accepted "that this *I* has no significance unless it becomes the *you* to whom eternity incessantly speaks and says: *You* shall, *you* shall, *you* shall."[82]

To answer this demand is to cultivate a mode of receptivity in which significance is realized in time: you get to be yourself, and to occupy your unique emotional perspective in a world where what you have loved best remains.[83] The meaning of your life must be open to undergoing shifts and revisions in its composition as new revelations of value are taken to heart and integrated into your ongoing framework of interpretation. Truthfulness, on such a view, becomes something other than the exercise of volitional control, and wisdom consists in something other than undisturbed tranquillity. Instead of the "happy life" of secure equanimity, one lives in a dance of passionate understanding, with a kind of joyful acceptance that does not rise above suffering, and does not explain it away as a foolish illusion.[84] "Life is like music; perfect pitch hovers between true and false, and that's where the beauty lies." In the realm of human values, Kierkegaard argues, to grasp at the fixed precision of "logic, ontology, or abstract morality—here the mathematical—would be false."[85] Just as a melody is "something more" than the sum of its isolated notes, the emotional self does not need to be decomposed by stoical reason: it can attain a truly beautiful integrity, always being redefined and refining itself toward a non-mathematical standard of accuracy.

There can be serenity in dissonance, just as there can be happiness, peace, throughout the religious suffering of the moral self. The moral self is complicated, enriched through struggle with its strangely lifting adversities. . . .

> Beethoven's late quartets [for instance] periodically insert persistent not just passing dissonance that nevertheless does not devastate the sense of key completely.[86]

This returns us to an earlier sketch of the passionate integrity of the non-Stoic sage. The difference is that we are now able to understand why it might be that, in order to attain an emotional state "more wonderful than an old man's serenity," a person would have to "learn to accept his suffering as in some mysterious way necessary."[87] Being vulnerable to emotion is the logical consequence of living in accordance with love.

Unlike the absurd world of the Stoic whose heart is hardened against the possibility of being moved, the hazard of being open to this possibility is that one's heart is liable to be broken—the experience of love and suffering can lead a person to another kind of axiological vacuum. Concrete experiences may point to the conclusion, not that one has a native incapacity to love, or that nothing in the world is worthy of love, but that the whole sum of love and suffering that makes up an emotional life is simply not worth going through with—not in one's own case, at least. A virtue of Kierkegaard's vision of religious existence is that it does not force its way to any triumphant rationalizations about the possibility of attaining happiness in some unqualified sense. To be guided by love's unpredictable impetus is to exist with a discomfiting awareness that human suffering can be a legitimate, significant experience. This is quite unlike being comforted either by the belief that passion is based upon a contemptible philosophical mistake or by an idea of providence in which God functions as "a kind elderly uncle who for a sweet word does everything the child wants."[88] Even the "happy love" of repetition is not a fulfillment of existing wishes but an unsolicited gift in which "you get something new, but only at the expense of . . . some nameless loss."[89] This is partly because it is always somewhat frustrating to bring one's "infinite" emotional aspirations to terms with a limited reality.[90] The reconciliation in which we actualize ourselves as loving subjects does not always make us feel that "here it is good to be."[91]

Accordingly, Kierkegaard does not adopt a self-righteously condescending attitude toward those whose experience of love has been unhappy. His writings manifest a deep empathy for those who feel as if they have been misled, those who are on the verge of losing their sanity, those who are tempted to become resentful or to believe that their suffering has been meaningless, and those who simply cannot bring themselves to believe.[92] Kierkegaard tells us that only a love which never gets weary of believing all things can overcome despair in all of its varieties, but he does not give us any reason to expect that this affirmation could be made in a spirit of idiotic optimism.[93] In unpublished drafts of *Repetition,* Constantin wearily goes back to being a Stoic after the young man in his failed experiment kills himself in despair.[94] Even in *Works of Love,* Kierkegaard acknowledges that one who loves is liable to face the "heaviest suffering," and to encounter long periods of time in which "one cannot see the meaning of things and waits in vain for connectedness."[95] It takes less courage to make complaints about the world than to notice the defects in one's own perspective, Kierkegaard maintains, but he adds that this "does not necessarily mean that every full-grown adult infant with his sweet, sentimental smile, his joy-intoxicated eyes, has more courage than the person who yielded to grief and forgot to smile."[96] Even the most refined emotional awareness of which we are capable falls short of the goal of absolute transparency—nevertheless, it is better to live with the imperfect clarity and fragile happiness of a caring agent than to give up on love altogether. A human being is so deeply grounded in love that to renounce its influence would be "to lose the defining, stabilizing center of self and world."[97] This is why the person who cannot become (or remain) open to love is actually the unhappiest of all.

Life takes on its highest value only after a person has moved past the misery of a love that grasps, covets, and wants, and has thereby "penetrated the wretchedness of this existence so deeply" that his or her initially selfish will can be transformed into an appreciative responsiveness toward others, a reverent acceptance of being.[98] Only when we have renounced all of our demands on the beloved, and on life more generally; only when we have experienced the reasons for not believing in love, and have been drawn toward such perspectives as cynicism, skepticism, pessimism and nihilism; only then are we prepared to enact the love which asks for nothing while embracing and remaining mindful of all things.[99] Only after we have begun to cultivate an emotional consciousness that is both purified of egotism and decisively life-embracing can we trust ourselves in becoming passionate.

Unconditional acceptance of one's identity as a loving person makes it possible to develop a kind of emotional integrity which is realized in moral participation. My own comportment is determined by the primitive inward force of love, which is the basis of my caring engagement with the world outside of myself. As Mooney remarks, the "power to receive identity through vision is essential for a life true to itself. My *particular* outlook or vision—and *yours*—is of irreplaceable importance."[100] When I put aside self-interest and charitably give you a space in which to exist, I enable both of our lives to attain the highest value. Belief in the infinite significance of each distinct person is thus one of the basic presuppositions of religious intersubjectivity.[101] Each of us can attain the truth only as an individual, not simply by following the crowd; but if our moral life is grounded in our authentic perceptions of significance, then we can come together in a shared world that both of us experience on our own terms.[102] I may feel sanctioned in my work as a theological author, as you do in your medical practice, although we recognize that the church-affiliated magazine in which my writings appear and the corporation-managed hospital in which your surgeries are performed are not themselves a source of normative authority. This can only come from within: what ought to guide a person's involvement with the social order, the flawed context of virtuous agency, is the sense of vocation that makes itself known in his or her loving subjectivity.[103] To say that I love you is to say that I want you to be, not merely that I want you to be a respectable member of society.[104] Just as I must never lose empathy for you by thinking that my world of concern is the only one that matters, I must also never forget that you are more than the sum of your actualized capacities. To care for you *qua* human being means also to attend to the passionate ground of your individuality—that is, the love that forms the heart as it flows from the heart, and which is always left somewhat unsettled.

CHAPTER 12

Conclusion
The Tragicomedy of Passionate Existence

The philosophy that a person adopts has a lot to do with who he or she is. Such a commitment is influenced by, and influences, the perspective of the person who makes it. Stoic morality will have perennial appeal to some of those who are searching for emotional integrity. When others complain that we human beings are not only points of moral volition, the Stoic will say: you are wrong about what is truly of value, and you will pay the price for your error. Not everyone will find this answer compelling, because to some of us it seems unacceptable to base practical reason on a denial of the fact that we are embodied beings who live in a world where objects threaten and allure, and where other subjects are a significant part of our own existence. The question, then, is how to gain clarity and sanction in a life of passionate rationality; or, in other words, how to answer normative Stoicism in its weaker thesis that many emotions are flawed and in its stronger argument that emotions are comprehensively false. I have argued, first, that an ethics based upon the cultivation of a sustained awareness of one's particular responses is necessary for reliable emotional perception; and, second, that an understanding of love as the basis of moral engagement leads to a view of reality according to which there is no reason to assume that the world is not meaningful in the way that our passions make it appear to be. These conclusions about virtue and value, which together constitute a positive alternative to Stoicism, also meet the Stoics on their own ground by defending the emotional life not hedonistically but in terms of its truthfulness.

When we make the "ethical" commitment of taking responsibility for having been moved, we assent to the significance of the finite world and to our own caring engagement with it as persons who are shaped by our particular concerns and emotional dispositions. The "religious" transition does not invalidate these commitments, but validates them in a nonparochial way by understanding love as the dynamic ground of meaning as it is realized in temporal existence. If we interpret love as *what is best in us,* then we cannot delimit the realm of value simply by making reference to *what is up to us;* rather than classifying the passions as unreliable, we must regard them as well-founded phenomena. The self is defined by virtue of its love, which forms the heart of each distinct moral agent, flowing into the concrete relations of care which are the fabric of moral reality. Axiological truth emerges from the process in which love reaches its fruition: the subject comes to exist as lover and the external world as beloved. Speaking of the mutually determining encounter in which passionate life arises and has its ground, Kierkegaard writes: "We see from this that individuality, this difference of separateness, is the presupposition for loving. . . . The greater the distinctiveness of individuality, the more pronounced the individuality, the more knowers there are, and the more there is to know."[1] A morality of loving the person one sees is justified by a metaphysics of interest, in which emotional truth comes into being in a temporal genesis that implicates both the perceiver and what is perceived.

Apathy, then, is a deficient form of practical reason, since one must develop empathy in order to gain this emotional knowledge which depends upon warmhearted participation in a shared reality.[2] The person who loves finds that the world is charged with awesome, startling, and endlessly unpredictable significance, none of which could be appreciated by a differently-constituted observer.[3] The hateful spectator who is disengaged from a rejected world does not see things in the way that they appear to one who affirms them in their being and embraces their particularity. Emotional openness, then, is a dispositional prerequisite for the recognition of value in the world.[4] This personally meaningful mode of knowing is also perspective-dependent in the sense that what you are aware of is a function of who you are, where and when you have existed, and how life has unfolded itself to you. Because I have walked down these paths in this order, I have seen (and loved) these people—this, at least, has been my task. It may be a "tragic fact" that my own contingent history has not intersected with everyone who is there to be encountered and cared for along some other road, but this is due to the inevitable limitations of a life in time.[5] The tragedy which it makes sense for me to lament is that, within my temporal existence, I have sometimes fallen short of the emotional goals of being alert and remaining aware.

In order to occupy and maintain the point of view of a loving person, to continue feeling the weight of concrete situations and responding to them as adequately as I can, I need to have patience and faith—but I must also have a sense of humor. The premises of an emotional person's existence include accepting what one cannot necessarily comprehend. Due to its axiomatic place at the basis of practical agency, love cannot be explained or justified in terms of anything other than itself. If we accede to its influence nonetheless, we implicitly grant that it has its own reason for being. This could be seen as either a beautiful or a ludicrous conclusion, depending on what one's philosophical attitude may be. The "knowledge" that external reality is not worth our attachment, for instance, could follow from certain legitimate (if rather humorless) principles of interpretation.[6] This attitude cannot have a claim to "objective" authority—but, for the same reason, it would not make sense for us to imagine that it could be decisively refuted:

> Out of the afternoon leans the indescribable woman:
> "Embrace me, and I shall be beautiful"—
> "Be beautiful, and I will embrace you"—
> We argue for hours.[7]

For "woman" read "world," and then you will see what I mean. It is unlikely that anyone could be argued out of such an impasse, although one could perhaps be moved to see things differently. To recognize that another legitimate perspective is available is not therefore to be capable of honestly adopting it. A love that asks for nothing in return sees the value in an existence which is not incontestably satisfying. It laughs at those aspects of life that are difficult to take seriously, acknowledging the possibility of disbelief, but it does not excuse itself from the burden of trying to see everything in the best light.[8] To persist in this attempt, one must have a sense of humor which does not ironically hold back from the world but is reconciled to it in all of its mixed detail.

What follows from this gratitude is a meaningful existence, if not always a transparently happy one. The extent to which life seems like a blessing in the midst of all ambiguity, and in spite of all misfortune, also depends upon one's perspective.[9] The person who remains committed to an attitude of loving trust attempts to root out, not the passions, but whatever *hampers* his or her awareness of love and of the certainties it has established. Such a person lives in a way that is consistent with certain beliefs about what emotion fundamentally is. He or she embraces the unnecessary past in its significance for the present self, and is borne resolutely into the future, acknowledging what is already of value while also remaining aware of what may still be possible. In this condition, one could trust oneself in becoming passionate—even if it would be unreasonable to expect that *everyone* could be convinced that a life on such terms is worth living.

With his "primitive" melancholy and his "tragic" upbringing, an "authentic" love which he himself betrayed and an "involuntary" calling which he faithfully attempted to fulfil, Kierkegaard tried to make the most of his particular affliction.[10] He did his best to accept everything, including his own mistakes, and although his own biographical story was ultimately more tragic than happy—a narrative of unhappy love and much suffering, as he saw it— he has left a sketch of what the ideal passionate vantage point would be like, for those who may be able to appreciate it.[11] The emotional highs and lows of a particular history of love and suffering will inevitably be more intense than the experiences of someone to whom everything appears to be far away. Jubilation and pain are both magnified for the person to whom certain things appear big with significance.[12] To involve oneself in the tragicomedy of passionate existence is to live with all the ambivalent emotions that follow from unconditionally inhabiting a loving perspective on an imperfect world. The complexity of our responses to ever-changing data will only increase to the extent that we are able to include more of life within the scope of our concern.[13] Adjusting the lens of one's passionate subjectivity is a project of ongoing vigilance and continual revision; it brings things into focus in a way that makes sense.[14] Like a person standing on a particular bridge in a particular city and looking through an oversized spyglass, one who loves sees the landscape in a clear and distinct way.[15] As Kierkegaard says in a letter to his fiancée which develops this image, one who sees nothing but subjective projections, or nothing but scientifically measured objects, has failed to develop an affective consciousness which perceives things *as they are* and *with loving eyes*, bringing together both the external and the inward aspects of passionate experience. Loving in truth, one attains a perspective that has its own validity according to premises quite unlike those that lead many philosophers to prefer the view from nowhere, and which does not need to be defended indefinitely against the possibility of stoical opposition—even if the faith that it takes to maintain these premises must constantly prevail over the prospect of despair. At the end of any progress of thought, there is always something else that remains to be said. One could go further in articulating the insights and difficulties that are visible from within a loving perspective. One might revisit some traditional questions in epistemology and metaphysics from an emotional point of view, or move toward more poetic forms of writing in one's continuing exploration of the passions. But these would be the works of a different author altogether—that is, one for whom the present inquiry is finished.

References to Kierkegaard's works give the location of the passage in both Danish and English texts. The titles of the standard editions most frequently cited have been identified by the following abbreviations:

SV	A. B. Drachmann et al., eds. *Samlede Værker.*
PAP	Niels Thulstrup and N. J. Cappelørn, eds. *Søren Kierkegaards Papirer.*
Breve og Aktstykker	Niels Thulstrup, ed. *Breve og Aktstykker vedrørende Søren Kierkegaard.*
KW	Howard V. Hong and Edna Hong, eds. *Kierkegaard's Writings.*
JP	Howard V. Hong and Edna Hong, eds. *Journals and Papers.*

Translations from classical texts are by the author unless otherwise attributed. The following abbreviations for Stoic sources have been employed:

LS	A. A. Long and D. N. Sedley. *The Hellenistic Philosophers.*
SVF	Hans von Arnim, ed. *Stoicorum Veterum Fragmenta.*

For further information concerning these works, refer to the bibliography.

ONE. Making Sense of Emotion

1. Epicurus, quoted by Porphyry in *To Marcella* 31 (*LS* 25–C).

2. Rather than using "emotion" and "passion" as technical terms with discrete meanings, I will use them as near-synonyms, in accordance with ordinary usage. Robert C. Roberts prefers to speak of particular episodes of "emotion" and to associate "passion" with ongoing concern (see *Emotions*, 2–3); but I will use a different vocabulary to make this distinction. In the English language, either "emotion" or "passion" can be used to describe the sort of thing that Aristotle is talking about when he discusses envy, pride, or shame.

3. The identification of intentionality (or "aboutness") as the characteristic trait of emotions and other mental phenomena is made by Franz Brentano in *Psychology from an Empirical Standpoint*, 87–91. No more than a basic understanding of intentionality as directedness is needed to make this initial distinction between perception and sensation: see, e.g., Roger Scruton, *Sexual Desire*, 377–91.

4. This example is borrowed from Anthony Kenny, *Action, Emotion and Will*, 192.

5. Cf. Robert C. Solomon, *The Passions*, 111–19. See also Aristotle, *Nicomachean Ethics* 1109a.

6. Solomon, *Passions*, 100–101. Cf. W. W. Fortenbaugh, *Aristotle on Emotion*, 10–11. It is true that a headache may be caused by anger, nausea by worry, and so on. But the headache and the nausea are *symptoms* of emotion, which must be distinguished from the intentional upheaval that *is* an emotion: I do not have a headache *at* you, even if my anger at you is causing the headache.

7. A helpful survey of this literature, including many references, is John Deigh's "Cognitivism in the Theory of Emotions." For a bibliography that also contains more recent work in the philosophy of emotion, see Martha Nussbaum, *Upheavals of Thought*, 715–34.

8. Aristotle, *Nicomachean Ethics* 1105b. See also *Rhetoric* 1378a, where an angry person is described as responding to what appears to be a big or conspicuous offense. Aristotle defines passions as "enmattered accounts," that is, responses of the whole (fleshly/ensouled) human being to whatever is being perceived: see, e.g., *De Anima* 403a, 408b. Cf. Plato, *Philebus* 40d–e, 47e.

9. SVF III 171, 391, 456–63. Strictly speaking, this judgment involves a conscious assent to the proposition implicit in the appearance of value; see Richard Sorabji, *Emotion and Peace of Mind*, 41.

10. See Josiah B. Gould, *The Philosophy of Chrysippus*, 132–33; Martha Nussbaum, *The Therapy of Desire*, 371–72.

11. As Cicero observes in *Tusculan Disputations* 4.27, although in *De Finibus* 3.35 he (or "Cato") fails to make this distinction. Brad Inwood presents some evidence for a dual-aspect view of emotion, from Arius Didymus and Aulus Gellius, in *Ethics and Human Action in Early Stoicism*, 146, 177.

12. Nussbaum, *Upheavals of Thought*, 87–88.

13. Inwood, *Ethics and Human Action*, 153–54; F. H. Sandbach, *The Stoics*, 165.

14. Of "passion" in the sense of "affection of the mind," the *Oxford English Dictionary* cites an excerpt from Chaucer, dated 1374, as the earliest usage (the "Passion" of Christ appears two centuries earlier). The first cited use of "emotion" meaning "mental affection" does not occur until considerably later.

15. Adriaan Peperzak argues that "'meaning' is nothing like an object" but "more like 'something by means of which'" things are meaningful or significant. *Reason in Faith*, 11. My position is closer to Peperzak's than to the stronger axiological realism expressed by Nicholas Rescher: "Neither the items that have value nor the facts of their

being of value depend on apprehending minds for their reality." "Optimalism and Axiological Metaphysics," 825.

16. Harry G. Frankfurt, *The Importance of What We Care About*, 80.

17. Cf. Jean-Luc Marion, *God Without Being*, 118. On the relation between the book of Ecclesiastes and Hellenistic philosophy see Michael V. Fox, *A Time to Tear Down and a Time to Build Up*, 6–8.

18. *Being and Time*, §69. Aaron Ben-Ze'ev differs by overemphasizing the active side of the dynamic, speaking as if we "bestow" evaluative meanings upon the environment when we perceive someone as attractive or dangerous. *The Subtlety of Emotions*, 169. But some people are attractive, and others are dangerous (and some, unfortunately, are both): these qualities are not entirely in the eye of the beholder. Another way of making this point would be to say that rattlesnakes are dangerous whether or not I "bestow" this property upon them, or whether I even recognize them as such.

19. Ernest Becker, *The Birth and Death of Meaning*, 33–34.

20. Alphonso Lingis, *Dangerous Emotions*, 18.

21. John Bowlby, *The Making and Breaking of Affectional Bonds*, 127.

22. See Cicero, *De Finibus* 3.18; see also Inwood, *Ethics and Human Action*, 139. On the connection between "true" and "good" in Stoic ethics, see Marcus Aurelius, *Meditations* 9.1.

23. Nussbaum, *Upheavals of Thought*, 71.

24. Augustine, *City of God* 14.7.

25. The first version is favored by many translators, but the second also has its adherents. See, e.g., the authorized translation of this passage in the *Catechism of the Catholic Church*, §1766.

26. Miguel de Unamuno, *The Tragic Sense of Life*, 65.

27. Frankfurt realizes this—see, e.g., *What We Care About*, 90—but Cicero does not. In *Tusculan Disputations* 4.76 he argues that if love were not a form of irrational madness, then everyone would necessarily love the same person.

28. Robert C. Roberts indicates the priority of concern by calling emotion a sort of "concern-based" construal. "What an Emotion Is: A Sketch," 184.

29. Max Scheler, "*Ordo Amoris*," 98.

30. Cf. Jonathan Lear, *Love and Its Place in Nature*, 12–13 and passim.

31. *Group Psychology and the Analysis of the Ego*, 29–30.

32. My distinction between the fundamental and the derivative is mirrored in what Richard Wollheim calls the dispositional and the episodic. *On the Emotions*, 9–10.

33. See Epictetus, *Discourses* 1.1.7; Seneca, *De Ira* 2.3.1–2; and Aulus Gellius 19.1.17–18. See also Margret Graver, "Philo of Alexandria and the Origins of the Stoic *Propatheiai*," 300–301.

34. Epictetus, *Discourses* 1.23.5–6.

35. Freud, *Civilization and Its Discontents*, 76.

36. Willa Cather, *My Ántonia*, 238.

37. Joseph LeDoux distinguishes between the "benign" and the "not-so-benign" versions of the cognitive theory of emotion. The former redefines cognition in order to include emotion; the latter just forces emotion into the traditional view of cognition, which is too limited. *The Emotional Brain,* 68.

38. Cf. Ronald de Sousa, *The Rationality of Emotion,* 109: the objects of emotion include "whatever an emotion is *of, at, with, because of,* or *that.*" On emotions as forms of intentional awareness which can be either true or false, see Nussbaum, *Therapy of Desire,* 80–81.

39. de Sousa, *Rationality of Emotion,* 153. See also William Lyons: "To be emotional is to be literally moved, in a bodily sense." *Emotion,* 60.

40. George Graham points out that depression without intentionality is quite different from reasonable sadness. "Melancholic Epistemology," 405–6. One of Kierkegaard's pseudonymous authors speaks of a depression which doesn't respond to objects, but "hurls itself" at them. *Stages on Life's Way, KW* 11.430; *SV* 8.227. Another characterizes depression as inexplicable and unlimited: "If a depressed person is asked what the reason is, what it is that weighs on him, he will answer: I do not know; I cannot explain it." *Either/Or, KW* 4.189; *SV* 3.177. On the distinction between despair and depression in Kierkegaard's writings, see Gordon Marino, *Kierkegaard in the Present Age,* 99–111.

41. Again, I am bracketing all emotion-like sensation which is about nothing, and which therefore cannot be clarified through a philosophical psychology that explains emotions in terms of reasons. Serious psychological complexities enter the picture only when our emotions are recognized as meaningful perceptions.

42. "To be sure, it is not always possible to draw a hard and fast line here, as almost all moods are invested with object-relational implications." Christopher Bollas, *The Shadow of the Object,* 101.

43. The remarks of one humanistic neurologist would justify this kind of bracketing: "If one studies a complex phenomenon, then there are data about it that science may be able to render with some rigor, but it may not be the case that the data reveal its nature." Edison Miyawaki, "Emotional Man," 155–56.

44. Cf. Nussbaum, *Upheavals of Thought,* 5.

45. "A good interpretation represents the end of a developmental process which begins with archaic attempts 'to say the same thing.' The interpretation allows the mind to understand, at the level of a conceptualized judgment, what it has been trying to say all along, in more primitive ways." Lear, *Love and Its Place,* 8.

46. It may be years later that one finds the right word, or words, to describe an emotion that has already been experienced. See Dylan Evans, *Emotion,* 2–3.

47. We can take responsibility for such an unwanted passion if we recognize that it "is due not to the intervention of a mental faculty other than reason but to the malfunctioning of reason itself," as A. A. Long points out. *Epictetus,* 213. Robert C. Roberts, by contrast, gives full credit to a rationalization which is at odds with a

deeper response, and hence can only make excuses for the inadvertent racist. "What an Emotion Is," 195–96.

48. Nussbaum, *Therapy of Desire,* 376–81.

49. Cf. Merleau-Ponty, *Phenomenology of Perception,* 136.

50. See, e.g., Epictetus, *Encheiridion* 1, 5.

51. See *SVF* II 974, III 177; Cicero, *De Fato* 43.1. See also the discussion by Susanne Bobzien in *Determinism and Freedom in Stoic Philosophy,* 240–63.

52. This point is made by Robert M. Gordon in *The Structure of Emotions,* 117–20.

53. As de Sousa points out, the capacity to experience emotion *at all* seems to be "remarkably universal" in spite of cultural variation with regard to which emotions are recognized and how they are regarded. *Rationality of Emotion,* 82.

54. On emotion and distraction see Michael Stocker, *Valuing Emotions,* 96–98. For a discussion of the "force" of emotion in Stoic philosophy see, e.g., Arius Didymus 2.89.2–3.

TWO. The Structural Critique (Stoic Virtue)

1. See, e.g., Diogenes Laertius 7.110 and Epictetus, *Discourses* 4.1.65–69. On "integrity" in Stoic philosophy, see Long, *Epictetus,* 223. Cf. Nancy Sherman, *Making a Necessity of Virtue,* 108: "[A] passion is a false belief; the cure is a discursive method that leads to true and reasoned belief about what is of value or worth in the world."

2. See, e.g., *SVF* II 977; see also Epictetus, *Discourses* 1.4.27.

3. Epictetus, *Discourses* 1.1.14–17.

4. See Epictetus, *Discourses* 1.22.9–11, 2.22.19–20, 3.1.40. In the last of these passages, Epictetus says that volition or will is what a human being essentially is: "*You* are not flesh . . . but volition [*prohairesis*]; therefore, if you make your will beautiful, then *you* will be beautiful." For Aristotle, this term means something like "decision": see, e.g., *Rhetoric* 1355b. Cf. Seneca, *De Ira* 2.2.1–2. In this chapter, "what is truly of value" and "what is truly significant" are phrases that ought to sound contentious. They allude to the Stoic idea that nothing matters (i.e., nothing is of value) other than rational volition.

5. *Meditations* 8.47.

6. Robert Frost, "Birches," lines 43–49.

7. Letters 23, 92. Cf. Plato, *Phaedrus* 242e–256e. Many of the theses of Socrates' speech in praise of madness are directly contradicted by the Stoics. Writing about this dialogue, Martha Nussbaum says that, according to Socrates, certain forms of passion "are not only not incompatible with insight and stability, [but] are actually necessary for the highest sort of insight and the best kind of stability." *The Fragility of Goodness,* 201.

8. Diogenes Laertius 6.44, 7.110.

9. See, e.g., Alvin I. Goldman, *Epistemology and Cognition*, 3: "Clearly, 'justified,' 'warranted,' and 'rational' are evaluative terms; and the advocacy of particular methods is a normative activity." Or, as Linda Zagzebski says, "Epistemic evaluation just *is* a form of moral evaluation." *Virtues of the Mind*, 256. Epictetus frequently speaks of moral judgments as true or false; see, e.g., *Discourses* 3.17.8. In *De Finibus* 3.72, Cicero also hints at a virtue epistemology: if rash judgment is a vice, then the skill which removes it is a virtue.

10. See, e.g., Stobaeus 2.68 and Marcus Aurelius, *Meditations* 11.38.

11. *De Ira* 2.25.1.

12. Ernest Becker, *Birth and Death of Meaning*, 34.

13. *Discourses* 1.6.30–32.

14. Cf. Nussbaum, *Upheavals of Thought*, 2.

15. *SVF* III 480.

16. Chrysippus says that a good reputation is not worth stretching out a finger to obtain. See Cicero, *De Finibus* 3.57. On limiting our desire for wealth, see Seneca, Letter 2. With regard to both of these ideas, see Schopenhauer, *The Wisdom of Life*, 57.

17. *Tusculan Disputations* 5.40–41 (*LS* 63–L). Long and Sedley translation.

18. Cicero contends in *Tusculan Disputations* (4.68) that love "is of such excessive triviality that I see nothing that I believe comparable with it." He doubts (4.72) that in the actual world there is an instance of love free from disquietude, longing, anxiety, and sighing. The treatment that ought to be given to a person in love (4.74) is "to make it clear how trivial, contemptible, and wholly insignificant [*nihili*] is what he loves."

19. Epictetus cites examples from Sophocles and Euripides in *Discourses* 1.24.14–19, 1.28.7–11, 2.17.17–22, and 2.22.13–16. For an overview of Senecan tragedy and its Stoic background, see Thomas G. Rosenmeyer, *Senecan Drama and Stoic Cosmology*.

20. This example is given by Epictetus. *Discourses* III.19.4.

21. Cf. Aristotle, *Nicomachean Ethics* 1147a, 1149a.

22. Lingis, *Dangerous Emotions*, 15.

23. *SVF* III 424.

24. *Ethics*, 112 (Part III, Proposition 14).

25. Marcus Aurelius, *Meditations* 7.2; Epictetus, *Discourses* 1.29.24.

26. Long, *Epictetus*, 28–29. See also Sorabji, *Emotion and Peace of Mind*, 29, 45–46.

27. Sorabji, *Emotion and Peace of Mind*, 2.

28. See, e.g., Epictetus, *Discourses* 1.22.14, 1.27.14.

29. *De Otio* 4.1.

30. See the discussion by Julia Annas in *The Morality of Happiness*, 174–76.

31. Gandhi's repudiation of partisan divisions takes to a greater extreme the position of Marcus Aurelius in *Meditations* 1.5; and his belief that the divinity of the uni-

verse supports an attitude of respect toward all human beings is comparable to the Stoic idea of living in accordance with nature. See, e.g., *The Sayings of Mahātma Gandhi*, 10, 67.

32. Diogenes Laertius 6.35.

33. *Philosophy as a Way of Life*, 83.

34. Seneca, *De Ira* 3.6.1.

35. *Discourses* 1.4.23.

36. See Diogenes Laertius 7.88, 143; Stobaeus 2.75–76; Seneca, Letter 76; and Marcus Aurelius, *Meditations* 4.23.

37. *Meditations* 7.68.

38. That is, whether we are "on the throne or in chains," as Hegel says (alluding to Marcus Aurelius and Epictetus), we can "maintain that lifeless indifference which steadfastly withdraws from the bustle of existence . . . into the simple essentiality of thought." *Phenomenology of Spirit*, §199.

39. See Diogenes Laertius 7.89 and Epictetus, *Encheiridion* 33; see also Diogenes Laertius 7.119.

40. Ralph Waldo Emerson, "Self-Reliance," 48. Cf. Epictetus, *Discourses* 3.24.112.

THREE. The Fundamental Thesis (Stoic Values)

1. Letter 116. See also *SVF* III 443.

2. The problem of absurdity, the emotional integrity of the individual, the intelligibility of the universe, the fear of death, and the possibility of authentic community are themes as prominent in Hellenistic philosophy as they are for Kierkegaard, Heidegger, and Camus. Hadot takes note of these "existential aspects of ancient philosophy" in *Philosophy as a Way of Life*, 271; likewise, Long remarks upon the "distinctively 'existentialist' dimension" of Stoic philosophy in *Epictetus*, 34.

3. As is argued by one of Plato's characters in *Republic* 604b–c.

4. *The World as Will and Representation*, 2:433–34.

5. See *De Ira* 2.7.1–2: "But if the wise man is to be angered by base deeds, if he is to be perturbed and saddened by crimes, surely nothing is more woeful than the wise man's lot; his whole life will be passed in anger and in grief. For what moment will there be when he will not see something to disapprove of?" Basore translation. Cf. Epictetus, *Discourses* 3.24.28–30.

6. *De Tranquillitate Animi* 15.3. Hadas translation (*The Stoic Philosophy of Seneca*, 102).

7. In Diogenes Laertius 7.101–2, life itself is included on the list of things that, according to the Stoics, have no intrinsic worth.

8. *Discourses* 4.1.111–12. Here we begin to see why it can be said of Epictetus: "His is a love that suffereth all things, but hardly one that is warm and outgoing." F. H. Sandbach, *The Stoics*, 169.

9. Letter 13. In outlining this "milder" view, Seneca adds that the Stoic position is true, even if some are not "manly" enough to accept it.

10. *Discourses* 2.16.29.

11. Nel Noddings, *Caring*, 51.

12. Rainer Maria Rilke, *The Notebooks of Malte Laurids Brigge*, 51.

13. Cf. Scheler, "*Ordo Amoris*," 120.

14. Robert C. Solomon argues that the self "is defined not by its defensive boundaries but by its expansion in *caring*." *About Love*, 256.

15. *The Fall*, 80.

16. Camus, *The Stranger*, 3.

17. *Encheiridion* 3.

18. See, e.g., Epictetus, *Discourses* 1.4.27, 1.25.1, 2.10.1–2, 3.3.6–8.

19. Pierre Hadot, *The Inner Citadel*, 277. Jonathan Ellsworth cites the fawning correspondence with Fronto as evidence of a more passionate side to Marcus Aurelius. Personal communication. See also "Apophasis and Askēsis," 218–21.

20. *SVF* III 486.

21. See Camus, *The Stranger*, 23 (Meursault's indifference toward the soccer fans); 35–36 (his indifference toward both love and domestic violence); 64 ("it all seemed like a game to me"); 84 (where he calls himself "a kind of intruder"). According to Marcus Aurelius, the "stranger in the universe" is not the apathetic spectator but, instead, the person who is affected by any unexpected happening: *Meditations* 12.13. On learning not to cheer for either team at the races, see *Meditations* 1.5.

22. *Don Juan*, 5.25.

23. Letter 9.

24. Cf. Lawrence Blum, *Moral Perception and Particularity*, 31–37; See also Nancy Sherman, *The Fabric of Character*, 45: "To see dispassionately without engaging the emotions is often to be at peril of missing what is relevant."

25. This phrase comes from Michael Frede, as does the example I have adapted involving Socrates and the doctor. "The Stoic Doctrine of the Affections of the Soul," 99, 105–7.

26. He may also prefer pleasure over pain, beauty over ugliness, strength over weakness, wealth over poverty, and so on, provided that he does not make the mistake of believing that any of these things truly make one's life any better or worse. See, e.g., Diogenes Laertius 7.102–104.

27. Dionysius of Heraclea became a renegade during an attack of ophthalmia, according to Diogenes Laertius 7.166: "So violent was his suffering that he could not bring himself to describe pain as an indifferent thing." Marcus Aurelius, who claims that a Stoic can be happy even while being torn apart by wild animals (*Meditations* 7.68), was never actually torn apart by wild animals.

28. Stobaeus 4.671–73 (*LS* 57–G).

29. As Annas points out, what Hierocles depicts is "a situation where I cease to be indifferent to people and regard them more in the way in which I regard people to whom I have particular commitments." *Morality of Happiness,* 268.

30. *De Ira* 3.37.3.

31. See, e.g., Marcus Aurelius, *Meditations* 5.36; Epictetus, *Discourses* 1.29.31, 2.5.20.

32. Francis Hutcheson, "Reflections Upon Laughter," 37.

33. Cf. Stanley Cavell, "Knowing and Acknowledging," 68–71. See also Arne Johan Vetlesen, *Perception, Empathy, and Judgment,* 159.

34. Cf. William O. Stephens, "Epictetus on How the Stoic Sage Loves," 195.

35. *Discourses* 3.24.4–5.

36. *Nicomachean Ethics* 1115a.

37. Epictetus admits that shame and grief over one's moral shortcomings are better than indifference toward them, but these emotions, like joy at one's own moral improvement (itself a indifferent matter), are not ultimately classified as rational. They may be useful on the way to attaining virtue, but would not be present in a fully virtuous person. *Discourses* 3.7.27, 4.10.3. Cf. Sorabji, *Emotion and Peace of Mind,* 51–52.

38. Epictetus, *Discourses* 4.10.8; see also *Encheiridion* 8. Cf. Camus, *The Stranger,* 121.

39. *The Myth of Sisyphus,* 21.

40. Marcus Aurelius, who likes to redescribe significant happenings in insipid mechanistic language, does appear to view life as a sequence of meaningless events in, for instance, *Meditations* 8.3. As for Epictetus, his uncompromising denial of value to everything other than volition is noted by Sorabji (*Emotion and Peace of Mind,* 169–70) as well as Long (*Epictetus,* 131–32, 202). "I think it is clear that what we must absolutely avoid doing, if we are faithful to the spirit of the Stoic conception, is to attach to the indifferents, to external goods, the sort of value that most ordinary people are seen to attach to them," Nussbaum writes. This is because the Stoics are "committed to denying the intrinsic worth of external worldly action and even, as they explicitly assert, the instrinsic worth of life itself." *Therapy of Desire,* 362.

41. Kierkegaard, *Purity of Heart Is to Will One Thing,* KW 15.107; SV 11.100. Steere translation.

42. Augustine, for example, believes that so-called autonomy enslaves a person under the dominion of his own will, whereas when we are moved by love we are in a sense liberated by submitting to a power greater than ourselves. See *De Libero Arbitrio* 3.6. Cf. Kant, *The Metaphysics of Morals,* 161.

43. Seneca describes love as "a state of affairs which is disturbed, powerless, subservient to another and worthless to oneself." Letter 116 (*LS* 66–C). Long and Sedley translation.

44. *Discourses* 2.16.31. The idea that participation is the precondition of tragedy is defended by Peter Kramer: *Listening to Prozac,* 258. Jason Xenakis writes that

Stoicism, like Cynicism, is ultimately concerned with "avoiding or cushioning hurt, tragedy, despair, disappointment, anxiety," and so on: "No ties, no loss, no tragedy." "Hippies and Cynics," 4–5.

45. Camus, *Myth of Sisyphus,* 30. "This divorce between man and his life, the actor and his setting, is properly the feeling of absurdity." *Myth of Sisyphus,* 6.

46. Epictetus, *Discourses* 1.6.19–20. The sympathy of Adam Smith's "spectator" is unbiased, not impassive. *The Theory of Moral Sentiments,* 10. Compare Byron on the Stoic: "And there he stood with such *sang froid,* that greater / Could scarce be shown even by a mere spectator." *Don Juan* 5.11.

47. *Walden,* 85 (my italics).

48. Chrysippus, SVF III 4. For Zeno's original position on the fiery vitality of the cosmos, see Stobaeus 1.213. The analogy between human and universal nature is central to Stoic philosophy. With the dawn of Stoicism, writes Alasdair MacIntyre, "morals become unintelligible apart from cosmology." *A Short History of Ethics,* 104.

49. Chrysippus, SVF III 698. Cf. Bryan Magee, *The Philosophy of Schopenhauer,* 301–5.

50. Nicholas P. White, "Stoic Values," 42–43.

51. On preferred indifferents, see Stobaeus 2.84 and Diogenes Laertius 7.102.

52. Frede, "Stoic Doctrine," 93. He cites Diogenes Laertius 5.31; one might add Sextus Empiricus, *Outlines of Pyrrhonism* 3.236 and Aristotle, *Nicomachean Ethics* 1109a. It is clear that most things really are viewed as indifferent by the Stoics. See, e.g., Stobaeus 2.83 and Epictetus, *Discourses* 1.4.27, 4.1.136–38.

53. Sorabji thinks that some of the "good passions" [*eupatheiai*] are what we would call emotions. *Emotion and Peace of Mind,* 49. Sherman doubts whether this is the case. *Making a Necessity of Virtue,* 117. Cf. Inwood, *Ethics and Human Action,* 173. Lawrence Becker concedes that the Stoics "certainly appear to have assumed (as opposed to have argued) that the sages's *eupatheia* would be tranquil." *A New Stoicism,* 131.

54. See Cicero, *De Finibus* 3.42.

55. "The rational emotions are those of a perfectly rational reason whose sentiments are not colored and intensified or weakened by any false assumptions . . . concerning the value of the things we are attracted or repelled by. Only the emotions of the wise man will be rational, because only the reason of a wise man is perfectly rational, undistorted by any false beliefs. Since none of us is wise, all the emotions we have, and all the emotions we are familiar with, are irrational and thus affections of the mind. Thus, if by 'emotion' we mean the kinds of emotions we are familiar with, the Stoic sage will, indeed, be free from emotion." Frede, "Stoic Doctrine," 94.

56. Marcus Aurelius writes that externals should not disturb a person because they "do not impose themselves upon you but in a sense you yourself go out to them." *Meditations* 11.11. Epictetus goes further toward denying the reality of the external world, saying that a violent storm is "nothing other than" an impression, and therefore, nothing to be troubled about. *Discourses* 2.18.30.

57. Aristo's position is described in Diogenes Laertius 7.160 and Sextus Empiricus, *Against the Professors* 11.64–67. His extremism was to give "the Stoic teaching [on the worthlessness of externals] a rigorously literal and unambiguous construction," as James Porter puts it, arguing that we should actually be indifferent about the "indifferents." "The Philosophy of Aristo of Chios," 157. Augustine's objection to Stoic hypocrisy is stated in *City of God* 9.4; see also *City of God* 14.9.

58. "The kiss must be the expression of a particular passion," writes one of Kierkegaard's pseudonymous authors. "A kiss is a symbolic act that is meaningless if devoid of the feeling it is supposed to signify." *Either/Or, KW* 3.416–17; *SV* 2.384.

59. *Discourses* 2.14.8.

60. *Metaphysics of Morals*, 204–5.

61. Wilde, *De Profundis*, 196.

62. Robert Frost, "Desert Places," lines 1, 10–12.

63. *Discourses* 1.23.5–6.

FOUR. Integrity without Apathy?

1. *Twilight of the Idols*, 25.

2. James Hillman, *Emotion*, 281.

3. A. A. Long, "The Logical Basis of Stoic Ethics," 87–88.

4. Frankfurt, *What We Care About*, 91. Socrates felt that caring for the wrong things was a vice worth mentioning. *Apology* 41e.

5. E. M. Cioran, *Drawn and Quartered*, 85.

6. Stoic ethics is strenuous, no doubt: it is no surprise to find (Diogenes Laertius 7.179) that Chrysippus was a long-distance runner in his pre-critical years.

7. De Sousa suggests "adequate emotional response" as a "mystical" alternative to the Stoic ideal. *Rationality of Emotion*, 332–33. Cf. Aristotle, *Nicomachean Ethics* 1109a–b.

8. Cf. Freud, *Civilization and Its Discontents*, 32–33.

9. Marcus Aurelius, *Meditations* 5.21.

10. *Discourses* 4.10.25.

11. J. W. N. Sullivan, *Beethoven*, 45–47. This portrait of Beethoven's character and temperament may or may not be biographically accurate, but it does seem to fit with the spirit of the music.

12. *Spiritual Exercises*, 201–7.

13. Cf. David Michael Levin, *The Body's Recollection of Being*, 95–103.

14. See *KW* 6.321; *PAP* IV B 117: "A person must be careful about where he becomes earnest."

15. As Plotinus says in his treatise on virtue, "what is left remaining will be the good, not the purification itself." *Enneads* 1.2.4.

16. The phrase "legitimate suffering" is Jung's. See *Psychology and Religion*, 91–92.

FIVE. Interlude: The Relevance of Kierkegaard's Writings

1. Karsten Friis Johansen, "Kierkegaard on 'The Tragic'," 105.

2. Kierkegaard greatly admired Sibbern for preserving authentic motives in his work even though he held an academic position. See, e.g., *JP* 3.3309; *PAP* VII¹ A 152.

3. Undated fragment from 1844. *KW* 8.191; *PAP* V B 53:29. Modified translation.

4. In one typical journal entry, he writes that the Greeks "still remain my consolation," as opposed to "the confounded mendacity that entered into philosophy with Hegel." *JP* 3.3300; *PAP* V A 98. Niels Thulstrup notes that it is "a possibility that has not been thoroughly analyzed" that the Danish Hegelians "radically influenced Kierkegaard's understanding or, more correctly, gave him a prejudiced view which he retained when he began to read Hegel's own works." *Kierkegaard's Relation to Hegel*, 26. A more thorough analysis of Kierkegaard's relation to the Danish Hegelians and to Hegel himself can be found in Jon Stewart's *Kierkegaard's Relations to Hegel Reconsidered*, a work which also acknowledges Kierkegaard's affinity for the Greek conception of philosophy (see, e.g., 641–50).

5. Preface to *Phenomenology of Spirit*, §5–§7.

6. Kierkegaard, *JP* 3.3314; *PAP* IX A 148. Hannay translation. Cf. Thoreau, *Walden*, 16: "There are nowadays professors of philosophy, but not philosophers. Yet it is admirable to profess because it was once admirable to live."

7. *KW* 8.78–79; *SV* 6.168. W. H. Walsh comments that "the role of the philosopher, in ethics as elsewhere, was [in Hegel's view] very much a spectator's role." *Hegelian Ethics*, 7.

8. This, at least, is the claim made by "Johannes Climacus" in *Concluding Unscientific Postscript*. See *KW* 12¹.308; *SV* 10.15. Compare: "Alongside his vitriolic critique of German speculation must be set Kierkegaard's veneration for the Greeks." Louis Mackey, *Kierkegaard: A Kind of Poet*, 268.

9. The *Cumulative Index* to the Princeton edition of *Kierkegaard's Writings* lists multiple references to Zeno of Citium and Plotinus; 10–15 apiece to Chrysippus, Diogenes of Sinope, Seneca, Marcus Aurelius, and Sextus Empiricus; and over 30 each to Cicero, Diogenes Laertius, Aristophanes, and Xenophon. His references to Stoicism even mention such minor figures as Aristo of Chios and Stilpo.

10. A number of journal entries record Kierkegaard's admiration for Seneca's letters, especially *JP* 4.3906, 3908; *PAP* X⁵ A 29, 35. He cites Cicero as early as the dissertation itself: see *The Concept of Irony*, *KW* 2.181; *SV* 1.211.

11. The *DIAPSALMATA* or "Fragments" (the title is given in Greek) which open the first volume of *Either/Or* begin with the epigraph *"ad se ipsum,"* or "to himself." *KW* 3.17; *SV* 2.21. The second allusion (*KW* 15.125; *SV* 11.115) is more cryptic. As Hadot points out, "attention to oneself" is regarded as the fundamental attitude of the philosopher by a tradition that stretches back beyond Anthony of Egypt to the Hellenistic practices he inherited when, as his biographer Athanasius says, he "began to pay attention to himself." *Philosophy as a Way of Life*, 131–35.

12. See *KW* 11.645; *PAP* V B 150:26 and Epictetus, *Discourses* 2.17.34.

13. *JP* 1.1057, 1059; *PAP* X² A 328, 439.

14. *Practice in Christianity, KW* 20.81; *SV* 16.85.

15. Edward Mooney, *Selves in Discord and Resolve*, 18.

16. Sophia Scopetea, *Kierkegaard og græciteten*, 465. Cf. Plato, *Phaedo* 96a–99e. Epictetus has been praised in contrast to Plato for his concern for the problems of ordinary life (Origen, *Contra Celsus* 6.2); and the Socratic spirit of his own philosophy is noted by both Long and Adolf F. Bonhöffer. See *Epictetus*, 92, and *The Ethics of the Stoic Epictetus*, 15. Socrates is mentioned more than fifty times in the *Discourses* of Epictetus.

17. Cf. Seneca, Letters 45 and 48, and Kierkegaard, *Three Discourses on Imagined Occasions, KW* 10.82–83; *SV* 6.306.

18. See, e.g., *The Sickness Unto Death, KW* 19.22–23; *SV* 15.81–82. This medical image is found throughout Stoic writings, for instance, in Epictetus, *Discourses* 3.23.27–30.

19. Cicero, *De Finibus* 4.7.

20. "Anti-Climacus," *Sickness Unto Death, KW* 19.90; *SV* 15.143.

21. See *The Concept of Anxiety, KW* 8.138; *SV* 6.220. Compare: "An incredible want of sensibility is required to arrive at conclusions like these, and not to feel pierced to the heart." Jung, "Thoughts on the Interpretation of Christianity," 95.

22. This idea is at the heart of the remarks by "Climacus" on subjective truth that make up a notorious chapter of *Concluding Unscientific Postscript*. See *KW* 12¹.189–251; *SV* 9.157–210.

23. "Anti-Climacus," *Sickness Unto Death, KW* 19.43–44; *SV* 15.100. This may be an allusion to Part Three of Descartes' *Discourse on Method*, 13–16.

24. *JP* 3.3308; *PAP* VII¹ A 82.

25. Epictetus, *Discourses* 1.4.13–17.

26. In his notes for a preface to *Concept of Irony*, Kierkegaard aligns himself with Socrates and quotes directly from *Phaedrus* 244a. See *KW* 2.441; *PAP* III B 3.

27. *Judge for Yourself!, KW* 21.99; *SV* 17.134.

28. Nussbaum, *Therapy of Desire*, 335. See also Chrysippus, *SVF* III 177; Seneca, Letters 15 and 40; Epictetus, *Encheiridion* 1; and *SVF* II 131 (*LS* 41–D).

29. Cf. Robert C. Roberts, "Existence, Emotion, and Virtue," 179.

30. *JP* 3.3126; *PAP* IV C 57.

31. *KW* 14.66; *SV* 14.62. Passages cited in Greek in Kierkegaard's text appear in translation throughout.

32. *Concluding Unscientific Postscript, KW* 12¹.399; *SV* 10.93.

33. Undated journal entry from 1844: *KW* 7.187; *PAP* V B 3:4. For the passage by Chrysippus, see *SVF* III 102. References to Tennemann, including the quotation that follows, are to the English translation of his *Manual of the History of Philosophy*, 147–50.

34. One philosophical position that Jakob Peter Mynster shared with Kierkegaard (and Sibbern), as Thulstrup notes, is that he "was an outspoken opponent of

Hegelian logic and a decided adherent of classical logic." *Kierkegaard's Relation to Hegel*, 290. Under the heading "Copenhagen" in an 1842 notebook (*JP* 5.5572; *PAP* IV C 2), Kierkegaard gives an outline of the categories of Stoic logic; see the similar list recorded by Alexander of Aphrodisias, *SVF* II 124. Whether Kierkegaard cared much about the difference between Stoic and Aristotelian logic is unclear; what was important to him, as also to Sibbern, is that classical logic did not make existential claims or deny basic principles of reason. See also George Connell, *To Be One Thing*, 12–13; and Benson Mates, *Stoic Logic*, 2–3.

35. Kierkegaard's use of the two Danish words for love, *Elskov* and *Kjærlighed*, and its relation to the different Greek words for love, is discussed at length in chapter 9.

36. *Three Discourses on Imagined Occasions*, KW 10.47; SV 6.278. In *Either/Or* it is shown that a variety of emotions can follow from an "erotic relation": all but one of the characters in Mozart's opera stand in such a relation to Don Giovanni, and this is what grounds both Anna's hatred and Zerlina's fear. See KW 3.125; SV 2.117.

37. Robert C. Roberts, "Existence, Emotion, and Virtue: Classical Themes in Kierkegaard," 185–86.

38. As Robert C. Roberts notes in "Passion and Reflection," 88–89, the word *Lidenskab* is used in each of these two senses in Kierkegaard's authorship. For an example of the former, see *For Self-Examination*, KW 21.45; SV 17.86; of the latter, see *Concluding Unscientific Postscript*, KW 12¹.311; SV 10.18.

39. Ronald L. Hall, *The Human Embrace*, 71. It should be remembered that, for Kierkegaard as for the Stoics, the object of passionate attachment need not be a person—it could be a social cause, an artistic project, or whatever else one may care about. See Hubert L. Dreyfus and Jane Rubin, "Kierkegaard on the Nihilism of the Present Age," 16–17.

40. KW 3.163; SV 2.151. My translation.

41. Undated journal entry from 1846. KW 16.407; PAP VII¹ A 192.

42. "Johannes de Silentio" and "Anti-Climacus," respectively. See *Fear and Trembling*, KW 6.100; SV 5.91 and *Sickness Unto Death*, KW 19.39; SV 15.96.

43. See *Two Ages*, KW 14.25; SV 14.26 and *The Book on Adler*, KW 24.53; PAP VII² B 235:95.

44. KW 3.31–32; SV 2.34.

45. See, e.g., Walter Lowrie, *Kierkegaard*, 1:99; and C. Stephen Evans, *Passionate Reason*. See also Jean Wahl's discussion of Kierkegaard's attempt to discover a fusion of sensibility and thought. *Kierkegaard*, 229. David J. Gouwens writes that Kierkegaard should not be accused of a "thoughtless denigration" of rationality, since "emotion and belief are closely intertwined for him." *Kierkegaard as Religious Thinker*, 52.

46. Robert L. Perkins, "Kierkegaard, a Kind of Epistemologist," 7; and Anthony Rudd, "'Believing All Things'," 121.

47. JP 1.221; PAP II A 130 (Hannay translation); KW 25.123; Breve og Aktstykker 62 (letter to Emil Boesen, 1842).

48. *JP* 5.5187; *PAP* I A 335. Modified translation. See also *Practice in Christianity*, *KW* 20.151; *SV* 16.147.

49. *Either/Or*, *KW* 3.6; *SV* 2.11. Modified translation. Xerxes, according to Herodotus, was angry at the sea for ruining a bridge that his men had built, and ordered that it be given three hundred lashes as well as a verbal rebuke. His rage is described, with a different anecdote, by Seneca. *De Ira* 3.16.4. Also comparable is Seneca's critique of anger directed at inanimate objects. *De Ira* 2.26.2–3.

50. *Christian Discourses*, *KW* 17.7; *SV* 13.15. See also Plato, *Apology* 30a–b.

51. On the accent of passion, see "Johannes Climacus," *Concluding Unscientific Postscript*, *KW* 12^1.100; *SV* 9.86. To place the accent of pathos in the wrong place is, evidently, to go wrong in perceiving significance; it is an expression of wrong judgment, for instance, to fear what a person should not fear. See *Purity of Heart*, *KW* 15.45–46; *SV* 11.48.

52. *Works of Love*, *KW* 16.348; *SV* 12.332.

53. *Repetition*, *KW* 6.171; *SV* 5.150 and *JP* 6.6611; *PAP* X^3 A 13.

54. See *JP* 4.4514; *PAP* X^3 A 643. The passage of Epictetus to which Kierkegaard refers is *Encheiridion* 1. This is one Stoic text that he appears to have read in Danish translation: his library included *Epiktets Haandbog*, translated by E. Boye.

55. *KW* 11.40; *SV* 7.40.

56. See, on hypochondria, *Concept of Anxiety*, *KW* 8.162; *SV* 6.240; and, on depression, *Either/Or*, *KW* 4.189; *SV* 3.177.

57. See Kresten Nordentoft, *Kierkegaard's Psychology*, 4. Cf. Freud, *The Interpretation of Dreams*, 460–62, on affect in dreams.

58. *Christian Discourses*, *KW* 17.124; *SV* 13.121.

59. *Practice in Christianity*, *KW* 20.75; *SV* 16.81.

60. *KW* 7.82–83; *SV* 6.75–76. The phrase "spurious emotionality and sentimentality" occurs in an 1846 journal entry. *JP* 1.566; *PAP* VII^1 A 161.

61. Cf. Alastair Hannay, *Kierkegaard*, 239.

62. Young's words (4.629–30) are: "Are *Passions*, then, the Pagans of the Soul? / *Reason* alone baptiz'd?" Kierkegaard puts a loose Danish translation at the opening of *Either/Or*, and ends up closer to the English lines quoted in the text. *KW* 3.1; *SV* 2.5.

63. *JP* 3.3125; *PAP* I A 117. See also two letters to Emil Boesen, 1842: *KW* 25.123, 135; *Breve og Aktstykker* 62, 68.

64. See, e.g., *JP* 4.4863; *PAP* X^1 A 448.

65. *Purity of Heart*, *KW* 15.45–46; *SV* 11.48. Cf. Aristotle, *Rhetoric* 1382a–1383a.

66. This is the view of the "Married Man" in *Stages on Life's Way*, *KW* 11.135; *SV* 7.122.

67. *JP* 3.3070; *PAP* II A 755. Hannay translation.

68. *JP* 4.4512; *PAP* IV A 44.

69. On the wretched contentment of those who are past feeling, see *Concept of Anxiety*, *KW* 8.94; *SV* 6.181–82. Regarding the escspe from suffering, see *Purity of Heart*, *KW* 15.13; *SV* 11.20.

70. *Ethics and the Limits of Philosophy*, 24. Williams introduces the ethical skeptic as a skeptic in the more general philosophical sense, and names him Callicles (22–23); see Plato, *Gorgias* 481e–527e.

71. *Three Discourses on Imagined Occasions*, KW 10.99–100; SV 6.320–21.

72. *KW* 12¹.194–95; SV 9.162–63. Modified translation.

73. See *Three Discourses on Imagined Occasions*, KW 10.78; SV 6.302 and *Eighteen Upbuilding Discourses*, KW 5.322; SV 4.286. *Betydning* is the Danish word for "significance," and is rendered this way in the Hongs' translation.

74. On "providence versus atoms" see, e.g., Marcus Aurelius, *Meditations* 6.10. For Kierkegaard's view of providence, see *The Point of View for My Work as an Author*, *KW* 22.87; SV 18.134 and *Practice in Christianity*, KW 20.189–90; SV 16.180–81.

75. *Fear and Trembling*, KW 6.15; SV 5.17. Modified translation. "Johannes de Silentio" opens his "Eulogy on Abraham" with this question.

76. See, e.g., *JP* 1.888; *PAP* III A 185 and *KW* 8.209; *PAP* V B 68.

77. *JP* 3.3127; *PAP* V A 44. Cf. *Works of Love*, KW 16.361; SV 12.344.

78. See *Concluding Unscientific Postscript*, KW 12¹.584–85; SV 10.250 and *Two Ages*, KW 14.69; SV 14.64.

79. See, e.g., Marcus Aurelius, *Meditations* 4.3 and Hadot, *Inner Citadel*, 105. On this point it is worth noting that J. L. Heiberg, the leading advocate of Hegelian philosophy in Kierkegaard's Denmark, spoke of the human good as the satisfaction of our "striving for detachment from restraint" by external objects. See Thulstrup, *Kierkegaard's Relation to Hegel*, 20.

80. See *From the Papers of One Still Living*, KW 1.76; SV 1.34–35.

81. This organizing principle is introduced in *Either/Or*: See, e.g., KW 4.147; SV 3.139. See also *Stages on Life's Way*, KW 11.476; SV 8.266 and *Concluding Unscientific Postscript*, KW 12¹.294; SV 9.247. Although I have used the spheres of existence as an organizing principle, my interpretation is guided by the idea that Kierkegaard's writings are meant to get us thinking about certain issues, not to show us what Kierkegaard himself believes.

82. On the idea of an ascent of love, see *Either/Or*, KW 4.18; SV 3.32–33 and Nussbaum, *Upheavals of Thought*, 457–714. On passion and religiousness, see *Book on Adler*, KW 24.104; *PAP* VII² B 235:190 and *The Instant* (#6), KW 23.209; SV 19.200. I will be following Lowrie and translating *Øieblikket* as *The Instant* instead of *The Moment*.

SIX. **Aesthetics and Sentimentality**

1. *Either/Or*, KW 3.42; SV 2.43. Modified translation.

2. *Either/Or*, KW 3.24; SV 2.27. We are told by the "editor" that the young man's fragments do not appear in any particular order.

3. *Either/Or*, KW 3.22; SV 2.25.

4. *Either/Or*, KW 3.21; SV 2.25 and *KW* 3.20; SV 2.24.

5. *Either/Or*, KW 4.6; SV 3.12 and *KW* 4.102; SV 3.98.

6. Here, "sentimental" will be used neither as a loose synonym for "emotional" nor in the technical sense introduced by Schiller in his essay on naïve and sentimental poetry. Instead, the term will be used to indicate a range of emotional phenomena which share a few structural flaws. I explain this critical use of the term at greater length in "Poetics of Sentimentality."

7. *JP* 3.3125; *PAP* I A 117. Hannay translation.

8. *Either/Or*, KW 3.24; SV 2.27. Milan Kundera defines *homo sentimentalis* as the person who values feelings themselves rather than letting them be responsive to value; as with a person who, in being "in love," is really infatuated by the beauty of her own emotion. *Immortality*, 194–211.

9. *Either/Or*, KW 4.318; SV 3.293.

10. *Either/Or*, KW 4.196; SV 3.183.

11. *JP* 2.2120; *PAP* IX A 402.

12. Rudolph Allers, "The Cognitive Aspect of Emotions," 637; Wilde, *De Profundis*, 200.

13. *Concluding Unscientific Postscript*, KW 12^1.432; SV 10.120. For the Hongs' "esthetic" (for *æsthetisk/œsthetiske*) I substitute "aesthetic" here and throughout.

14. Robert C. Roberts, "Existence, Emotion, and Virtue," 197.

15. Mackey, *Kierkegaard: A Kind of Poet*, 3.

16. *Either/Or*, KW 3.23; SV 2.26.

17. *Either/Or*, KW 3.19; SV 2.23. The author of the "Seducer's Diary" also has an aesthetic relation to emotions with unhappy significance, as when he admires Cordelia in her sadness and pain. This is not the same as admiring a negative emotion because it is sincere and appropriate, as when Rilke praises Kappus's "beautiful anxiety about life" (*Letters to a Young Poet*, 32). The seducer attends not to the meaning of his victim's emotion but to the attractiveness it lends her. *Either/Or*, KW 3.314; SV 2.291.

18. Freud discusses people who distort reality out of a need to keep experiencing unpleasantness. *Beyond the Pleasure Principle*, 22. Michael Tanner adds that sentimental people actually enjoy cultivating what, if sincere, would be unpleasant emotions. Tanner has in mind those who, when "grieving," are not thinking "this person whom I loved is gone" but something like "how admirable it is to experience grief." "Sentimentality," 140. Both are guilty, like Dewey's "fuzzy sentimentalist," of allowing their own wishes to color what they take to be the object of their emotion. See John Dewey, *Art as Experience*, 248. Cf. Nietzsche, *On the Genealogy of Morals*, first essay, §1.

19. *Either/Or*, KW 3.306; SV 2.284 (on stimulation) and *KW* 3.42; SV 2.43 (on salmon).

20. *JP* 3.3802; *PAP* I A 142 and *Three Discourses on Imagined Occasions*, KW 10.16; SV 6.253. Kierkegaard elsewhere condemns "the indefinable frauds of indefinite feelings." *JP* 3.3301; *PAP* V B 14.

21. One could also say: his Romantic soul, with a capital R. George Stack points out that an "underlying trait of all romanticism is a disillusionment generated by the juxtaposition of quixotic possibility and prosaic actuality." "Kierkegaard and Romantic Aestheticism," 60. Examples of this attitude in English Romantic poetry include, for example, "Childe Harold's Pilgrimage" by Byron and "Constancy to an Ideal Object" by Coleridge. James Collins argues that one of Kierkegaard's central questions is: "What can be salvaged from Romanticism?" *The Mind of Kierkegaard*, 75.

22. Cf. Wilde, *De Profundis*, 123.

23. *Either/Or*, KW 3.26–27; SV 2.29–30.

24. Mark Jefferson argues in "What is Wrong With Sentimentality?" that it is a morally relevant variety of cognitive falsification to impose qualities onto objects for the sake of feeling a certain predetermined way about them.

25. KW 12^2.17; *PAP* VI B 29. Cf. Kant, *Dreams of a Spirit-Seer*. On Grundtvig, see also Bruce H. Kirmmse, *Kierkegaard in Golden Age Denmark*, 483–85.

26. "Vigilius Haufniensis," *Concept of Anxiety*, KW 8.121–22; SV 6.205–6. Michael Slote writes that self-deception "may have its uses, and an incurable cancer victim may . . . benefit from his ability to misread or deceive himself about the evidence that he has terminal cancer," but that "we commonly regard such a person as less to be admired than someone who faces similar facts squarely." *From Morality to Virtue*, 130. See also Bernard Williams, *Truth and Truthfulness*, 118: "Even if it is for good reasons of concern for her, I do not give her a chance, in this particular respect, to form her own reactions to the facts . . . but give her instead a picture of the world which is a product of my will."

27. *Either/Or*, KW 4.191–92; SV 3.179.

28. *Concept of Irony*, KW 2.255–56; SV 1.271.

29. *Either/Or*, KW 3.23 and 3.39–42; SV 2.27 and 2.40–44. "A" uses Spinoza's phrase *aeterno modo*. See *Ethics*, 219 (Part V, Proposition 36). He continually tries to adopt the view from nowhere, which prohibits the kind of acknowledgement that can be made only within ordinary moral life. Cf. Stanley Cavell, "Knowing and Acknowledging," 68–69, and *The Claim of Reason*, 382–83.

30. For Marcel, Albertine comes to be seen as "the generating center of an immense construction that rose above the plane of my heart"; and he speaks of how the art of living is to detach our emotions from individuals and convert them, as it were, into a beautiful tapestry. See *Remembrance of Things Past*, 3:445, 3:932–45. See also Martha Nussbaum's discussions of this aesthetic tendency in Proust. *Love's Knowledge*, 271–74, and *Upheavals of Thought*, 511–19. Charles Larmore has pointed out to me that Proust favors the aesthetic attitude because he believes that it is preferable to be liberated from human suffering. From this point of view, it is not a failure but an achievement to "rise above" the realm of the passions. Cf. Schopenhauer, *World as Will and Representation*, 1:196–99.

31. KW 3.324–34; SV 2.301–9.

32. *An Actor Prepares*, 129.

33. See, e.g., Roger Scruton, *Art and Imagination*, 128. Noël Carroll develops the point: "The author presenting a fiction in effect says to the audience: 'hold these propositions before your mind unasserted'—that is, 'suppose p' or 'imagine p' or 'entertain p unasserted.'" "Art, Narrative, and Emotion," 210. This is Coleridge's "willing suspension of disbelief," as described in chapter 14 of *Biographia Literaria*, and it may involve what Wollheim calls "forms of conviction that fall short of . . . that form of assent which is belief." *On the Emotions*, 67. This fits with the Stoic idea that presentation of an object is prior to assent, see, e.g., *SVF* II 974, 991. Some primal versions of fear may similarly involve less than fully conscious belief. See Jon Elster, *Alchemies of the Mind*, 268–69, and Jonathan Lear, *Open Minded*, 94–95, for physiological and psychoanalytic illustrations.

34. "Shakespeare and the Stoicism of Seneca," 111.

35. *Two Ages*, KW 14.73; SV 14.68. Italics removed.

36. See *JP* 1.149; *PAP* V A 97. Sartre, likewise, distinguishes the emotions of an actor, which are *fictitious,* from *false* emotions that invest real objects with false qualities. *The Emotions*, 72–73.

37. Roger Poole, "The Unknown Kierkegaard," 53.

38. In *Either/Or*, "A" says that Byron errs in making Don Juan into a character, since that is precisely what he isn't—he loves an ideal woman in many faces and resists the particularities of care which define a person's character. KW 3.106; SV 2.100. In a journal entry, Kierkegaard claims that all of Faust's knowledge was good for nothing, since it did not answer any of his existential questions. JP 2.1182; PAP II A 29.

39. *Either/Or*, KW 4.5; SV 3.11.

40. Cf. Scruton, *Sexual Desire*, 333: "To take responsibility for one's past is also to project that responsibility forward into the future." The person who honestly feels remorse, therefore, should want to refrain from similar actions in the future.

41. *For Self-Examination*, KW 21.75; SV 17.112.

42. Compare the judge's warning about "the disintegration [*opløste*] of your essence into a multiplicity," which sets up an allusion to Luke 8:30 on the demoniac whose name was legion. *Either/Or*, KW 4.160; SV 3.152.

43. For example: "sadness—yearning for the absent good—hope that it will be ours—the desire to bring it about—the courage to make the attempt—the decision to act." Brentano, *Psychology from an Empirical Standpoint*, 236–37.

44. Cf. Daniel Berthold-Bond, "A Kierkegaardian Critique of Heidegger's Concept of Authenticity," 132–35.

45. *Notes from Underground*, 121. Although he oscillates between regretting his "sentimentality" and admitting that it was not sentimentality but "true feeling" (106–9), Dostoevsky's narrator ends up spitefully refusing to acknowledge either Liza's emotion or his own. Compare the discussion of this text by Merold Westphal in *God, Guilt, and Death*, 83–84.

46. John Barth, *The End of the Road,* 360, 390, 430.

47. *Upbuilding Discourses in Various Spirits, KW* 15.290; *SV* 11.268. Modified translation. See also Luke 11:29–37.

48. Camus, *The Stranger,* 32, 99.

49. See *Either/Or, KW* 3.292–95; *SV* 2.269–72. The passage of Marcus Aurelius appropriated by the aesthete is from *Meditations* 7.2.

50. *Either/Or, KW* 3.306; *SV* 2.284. Hannay translation.

51. George Pattison, *Kierkegaard: The Aesthetic and the Religious,* 58.

52. *Either/Or, KW* 3.411; *SV* 2.379.

53. *Either/Or, KW* 3.445; *SV* 2.410. The last sentence is Hannay's translation.

54. These are the terms she uses in her first letter in response to "Johannes". *Either/Or, KW* 3.312; *SV* 2.289. I have been using masculine pronouns more often than not when referring to the aesthetic sentimentalist, for the sake of being consistent with the gender of Kierkegaard's characters. Of course, the story could be told with the roles reversed. Whatever else may be said of Kierkegaard's treatment of his own fiancée, it was not light-minded. As Lowrie writes, Regine was "not an episode" in his life. *Kierkegaard,* 1:229.

55. Kierkegaard inveighs against the "merely phenomenological personality" in *Papers of One Still Living, KW* 1.82; *SV* 1.40. Whether or not his use of *phœnomenologiske* is consistent with its technical use in phenomenology, we can see what he means. A misguided reduction would be made if an experience of awe in which the subject is aware of some awesome object were reduced to a merely phenomenal sensation, in which the experience itself would be studied and the object forgotten. Still, even when Husserl says that the emotion of wonder should lead one into the purely theoretical attitude, the study of the world that he recommends is at least *of the world*—in other words, it is not objectless. *The Crisis of European Sciences and Transcendental Phenomenology,* 276–85.

56. Aristotle discusses drama and possibility in *Poetics* 1451a. See also Nussbaum, *Upheavals of Thought,* 238–48.

57. *KW* 11.460; *SV* 8.252–53. Modified translation.

58. See *JP* 1.1051; *PAP* IX A 154. Although this entry from 1848 applies to those who treat the church like a theater, its diagnosis of spectatorship as "enjoyment" without "earnestness" is also applicable to the aesthete who exhibits this same tendency, treating all the world like a stage and wanting sensuous enjoyment, or stimulation, without earnest engagement.

59. *Either/Or, KW* 4.122; *SV* 3.117 and *KW* 3.120; *SV* 2.113. Cf. Thoreau, *Walden,* 85: "I *may* be affected by a theatrical exhibition; on the other hand, I *may not* be affected by an actual event which appears to concern me much more."

60. This is one Hegelian phrase that Kierkegaard ought to have admired. See Hegel, *Aesthetics: Lectures on Fine Art,* 1:46–47.

61. See *A Portrait of the Artist as a Young Man,* 164, 98.

62. *Selves in Discord*, 67.

63. As a shellfish also cannot. See Plato, *Philebus* 21c.

64. John Vignaux Smyth, *A Question of Eros*, 230.

65. As the aesthete says in an address composed for a symposium of those who are effectively dead. *Either/Or, KW* 3.224–25; *SV* 2.205–6. On not wanting to discover at the end of life that one has not lived, see also Thoreau, *Walden*, 60.

66. See *Either/Or, KW* 4.321; *SV* 3.295.

67. This image is also used by the judge. *Either/Or, KW* 4.219; *SV* 3.203. Compare the words of another of Dostoevsky's narrators: "You hear and see people living— living in reality, you see that for them life is not something forbidden, their life does not fly asunder like dreams . . . I often drift like a shadow, morose and sad, without need or purpose, through the streets and alleyways of Petersburg." "White Nights," 26.

68. Henry James, "The Beast in the Jungle," 311. My interpretation of this text is heavily indebted to Robert Pippin's discussion in *Henry James and Modern Moral Life*, 92–105.

69. *Either/Or, KW* 4.199, 4.204; *SV* 3.186, 3.190. Lowrie translation.

SEVEN. Virtues of Ethical Resolution

1. On the relation between aesthetic perception and moral awareness, see also Kant, *Critique of Judgment*, §42, §59. Cf. Epictetus, *Discourses* 4.11.25–29. In a journal entry, Kierkegaard notes that the "identity of virtue and beauty is also seen by Aristotle." See *JP* 5.5591; *PAP* IV C 22, with reference to *Nicomachean Ethics* 1115b.

2. "The Accounting," in *On My Work as an Author* (within *Point of View*), *KW* 22.7; *SV* 18.65.

3. Kierkegaard writes that the first part of *Either/Or* "continually gets stranded on time," while the second part affirms temporal commitment, showing "that the meaning of finitude and temporality is to be able . . . to gain a history." *JP* 1.907; *PAP* IV A 213. It is the editor, "Victor Eremita," who states that Judge William's papers "contain an ethical view of life." *Either/Or, KW* 3.13; *SV* 2.19. Because "ethical" [*ethisk*] is used by Kierkegaard as a technical term to designate a particular form of moral existence, I try to refrain from using it in a more generic sense.

4. *Either/Or, KW* 4.11; *SV* 3.16.

5. *KW* 16.441; *PAP* VIII^2 B 35:8. Modified translation.

6. See, e.g., *Book on Adler, KW* 24.18–20; *PAP* VII^2 B 235:16–19. Cf. Scheler, *Formalism in Ethics and Non-Formal Ethics of Values*, 165–66: "'Morality' does not lie in the realm of ideal meanings *alone*. It is not in the light of such ideal meanings alone that 'premoral facts' *become* moral ones. There are *originaliter* moral facts that are distinct from the sphere of the meanings of moral concepts. . . . [For instance,] a child feels the kindness of his mother without having even vaguely comprehended an idea of the good."

7. *JP* 4.4826; *PAP* IV C 110. Kierkegaard begins by quoting from Aristotle, *Poetics* 1449b, acknowledges the controversy over this passage, then offers his own reading.

8. Cf. Iris Murdoch, *The Sovereignty of Good*, 19–23.

9. As Nietzsche would seem to agree: see his discussion of how an aesthetic response can lead to life-enhancing transformation as well as empathetic understanding. *The Will to Power*, §804, §809.

10. *Either/Or, KW* 4.8; *SV* 3.14.

11. As Kierkegaard suggests. *JP* 1.954; *PAP* VIII¹ A 410. See also the judge's remarks on "the summit of the aesthetic." *Either/Or, KW* 4.137; *SV* 3.130.

12. Kierkegaard discusses the implied progress from (aesthetic) admiration to (ethical) imitation in a journal entry: *JP* 4.4454; *PAP* X¹ A 134. In another entry, he laments that what we admire in the theater finds no expression in our moral life. *JP* 1.953; *PAP* VIII¹ A 398.

13. Cf. Scruton, *Art and Imagination*, 131. See also Holden Caulfield's account of the lady sitting next to him at the movie theater, who is moved by what she sees on the screen but is insensitive to the child at her side: "You take somebody that cries their goddam eyes out over phony stuff in the movies, and nine times out of ten they're mean bastards at heart." J. D. Salinger, *The Catcher in the Rye*, 140.

14. As the judge suggests in his treatise on marriage. See *Stages on Life's Way, KW* 11.154; *SV* 7.139. "Some Reflections on Marriage in Answer to Objections," although it is signed by a "Married Man," is discovered at Judge William's country house by the snooping revelers who are out for a morning walk after holding a symposium on love the night before.

15. *Stages on Life's Way, KW* 11.163; *SV* 7.146.

16. See *Works of Love, KW* 16.90; *SV* 12.92. Epictetus discusses the faculty of assent in *Discourses* 1.28.1–5.

17. I may "fall in love" willingly (that is, I may decide not to resist it) but I cannot make myself love someone by force of will. Love is not love that can be turned on or off as easily as a light switch or a water faucet. But someone who takes a firm stand against the nascent inspiration of romantic love may, says the "Married Man," be able to thwart it: *Stages on Life's Way, KW* 11.176; *SV* 7.158. An account of "learning to fall," that is, the process of deciding *not* to resist, can be found in Nussbaum, *Love's Knowledge*, 274–80.

18. *Either/Or, KW* 4.250; *SV* 3.231.

19. The phrase "willing receptivity" is used by Mooney to describe the non-assertive mode of volition, the power of assent, that the judge is talking about. *Selves in Discord*, 16–22. James J. Valone writes that "the ethical type of personality" seeks beauty and love just as the aesthete does; however, he does so "in a form which demands commitment." *The Ethics and Existentialism of Kierkegaard*, 130–31.

20. *Three Discourses on Imagined Occasions, KW* 10.55; *SV* 6.284. Although when the judge calls "A" sentimental he uses the word *sentimental* (*Either/Or, KW* 4.179; *SV* 3.168), here the word translated as "sentimentality" is *Kjelenskabet*. Only a sentimental

kind of emotionalism, not all emotion, would be excluded by the "resolution" that Kierkegaard is talking about.

21. See *Either/Or*, KW 4.206; SV 3.192. This decision is, as Mark C. Taylor says, the initial step into ethical existence. *Kierkegaard's Pseudonymous Authorship*, 185. On the idea that a voluntary action need not be spontaneous, since it can arise out of a characteristic reaction, see Aristotle, *Nicomachean Ethics* 1105b–1106b, 1114a–b.

22. See *Two Ages*, KW 14.77–78; SV 14.72. On the earnestness of suffering in person and being present in one's own experience, see *JP* 2.2108; *PAP* XI¹ A 322.

23. See *PAP* X⁴ A 175, a fragment in which Kierkegaard credits Augustine with the discovery that the idea of *liberum arbitrium* is fantastic, because the will has "a history, a continuous history." Hannay translation.

24. "Johannes Climacus," *Concluding Unscientific Postscript*, KW 12¹.253; SV 9.211.

25. See *Concluding Unscientific Postscript*, KW 12¹.288; SV 9.241.

26. Ted Cohen, "Sports and Art," 272–73. He invites us to see the sports fan's purity of heart as not only admirable in itself but also as an expression of the same capacity that makes morality possible.

27. The Stoic categories of emotion associated with good and evil in the present tense are described in *SVF* III 391. See also Aristotle, *Nicomachean Ethics* 1156b.

28. "Concern constitutes the relation to life, [and] to the actuality of the personality." *Sickness Unto Death*, KW 19.5; SV 15.67.

29. *Concept of Irony*, KW 2.282; SV 1.294. Cf. *Concept of Anxiety*, KW 8.9; SV 6.109.

30. See, Dostoevsky, *Notes from Underground*, 6–8. See also David L. Hall, *Richard Rorty: Prophet and Poet of the New Pragmatism*, 138: "If one takes the ironist's comments seriously, he is able to say: 'But I was only joshing!' . . . Rorty, as a master of irony, is aware of this characteristic of irony and uses it, as all ironists do for purposes of attack and defense. He chooses to take seriously philosophic theories when such a response is crucial to the construction of his narratives and he takes up a lightminded stance toward them when that serves his purpose."

31. *Either/Or*, KW 4.87; SV 3.85.

32. *Either/Or*, KW 4.141; SV 3.133 and *KW* 4.179; SV 3.168.

33. Cf. *Either/Or*, KW 3.295; SV 2.272.

34. *Either/Or*, KW 4.256; SV 3.237.

35. *Either/Or*, KW 3.34; SV 2.36.

36. *Either/Or*, KW 3.36; SV 2.38.

37. See *Either/Or*, KW 4.37–38; SV 3.40–41.

38. On this point, many readers of *Either/Or* are in agreement with its "editor" (see KW 3.13; SV 2.19). Connell refers to the aesthete's "apotheosis of temporal atomism" and Taylor shows that the aesthete "moves from one momentary experience to another without establishing any continuity among them." See *To Be One Thing*, 134, and *Kierkegaard's Pseudonymous Authorship*, 151.

39. *Rosencrantz and Guildenstern Are Dead,* 61.

40. Letter to Emil Boesen, 1842. *KW* 25.123–24; *Breve og Aktstykker* 62.

41. Milan Kundera, *The Book of Laughter and Forgetting,* 25, 30, 119. For Kierkegaard's criticism, of Andersen in particular, see *From the Papers of One Still Living, KW* 1.76–77; *SV* 1.34–35.

42. Cf. *Concept of Anxiety, KW* 8.91–92; *SV* 6.179.

43. *JP* 3.3705; *PAP* IX A 365.

44. *Stages on Life's Way, KW* 11.113–15; *SV* 7.102–4.

45. *Stages on Life's Way, KW* 11.91–92; *SV* 7.85.

46. Kundera, less optimistic than Kierkegaard's ethicist, also acknowledges that the heaviest of burdens can crush us. "The heaviest of burdens crushes us, we sink beneath it, it pins us to the ground. . . . Conversely, the absolute absence of a burden causes man to be lighter than air, to soar into the heights, take leave of the earth and his earthly being, and become only half real, his movements as free as they are insignificant." *The Unbearable Lightness of Being,* 5.

47. *Either/Or, KW* 4.309–10; *SV* 3.284–85.

48. Alasdair MacIntyre says that practical wisdom involves being able to identify what circumstances are morally relevant and to respond appropriately, including with appropriate emotion. See *Whose Justice? Which Rationality?,* 132, and *After Virtue,* 149. Cf. Aristotle, *Nicomachean Ethics* 1104b.

49. Cf. Patricia S. Greenspan, *Emotions and Reasons,* 10. See also Aristotle, *Nicomachean Ethics* 1111b, 1114b.

50. On Kierkegaard's view of the self as a "network of relationships" with a "relational, intersubjective nature" see Mooney, *Selves in Discord,* 94, and Merold Westphal, *Becoming a Self,* 143.

51. As does Ronald M. Green, in *Kierkegaard and Kant,* 42.

52. This is Aristotle's example: *Nicomachean Ethics* 1170a.

53. *Either/Or, KW* 4.109; *SV* 3.104. Heidegger's discussion of mood and attunement can be found in *Being and Time,* §29.

54. See Aristotle, e.g., *Nicomachean Ethics* 1106b.

55. *Either/Or, KW* 3.497; *PAP* III B 185:1.

56. de Sousa, *Rationality of Emotion,* 262.

57. On this topic, see Alexander of Aphrodisias, *Ethical Problems* 29 and Augustine, *De Libero Arbitrio* 3.1.

58. C. Stephen Evans, *Passionate Reason,* 134.

59. See *Either/Or, KW* 4.262; *SV* 3.242.

60. See, e.g., *Either/Or, KW* 4.251; *SV* 3.232–33.

61. *Stages on Life's Way, KW* 11.117; *SV* 7.106.

62. *Either/Or, KW* 4.66; *SV* 3.67. Paul Ricoeur agrees with Scheler that there exists an emotional revelation of values in given situations—but, he says, the perception of value depends upon our loyalty, our ethical dedication. See *Freedom and Nature,* 74–75.

63. Kundera writes of the communitarian dream of a "realm of harmony where the world does not rise up as a stranger," where "everyone is a note in a sublime Bach fugue," and "anyone who refuses to be one is a mere useless and meaningless black dot." *Book of Laughter and Forgetting,* 11.

64. *Either/Or, KW* 4.167; *SV* 3.157–58.

65. See *Three Discourses on Imagined Occasions, KW* 10.52; *SV* 6.282 and Eliot, "*Hamlet,*" 49. Cf. Eliot Deutsch, *Creative Being,* 48: "Inherent in the having of emotions is the effort to appropriate them, to make them one's own, and to achieve appropriateness in their direction and intensity. It is not a matter of reason controlling the emotions, but of emotions themselves seeking a clarity that allows for their rightness."

66. Entry of 17 May in "The Florence Diary." *Diaries of a Young Poet,* 19.

67. Abandoning the unreflective aestheticism with which, two years earlier, he had celebrated "the most heart-easing things," Keats writes in an 1818 letter to John Taylor that his future "road lies through application, study and thought." He continues: "I have been hovering for some time between an exquisite sense of the luxurious and a love for Philosophy . . . I shall turn all my soul to the latter." *Letters of John Keats,* 88. The development from the "pleasant smotherings" of Keats's early verse to the unsentimental perspective of the late odes is traced by Morris Dickstein in *Keats and His Poetry.* Rilke's comparable development is discussed by Stephen Mitchell in his foreword to *Letters to a Young Poet,* v–xvi.

68. Joyce, *Portrait of the Artist,* 268–69; Proust, *Remembrance of Things Past,* 1:100. The phrase "momentary transports" is taken from Proust. Paul Ricoeur stresses the "retrospectively synthetic character of Proustian narrative," whereby the retelling of past events makes possible a moment of insight in which one perceives the whole story of one's life as the invisible history of a vocation. *Time and Narrative,* 2:84, 2:131–32.

69. See *JP* 1.990; *PAP* X³ A 248. Part of the goal of Kierkegaard's authorship, argues John Lippitt, is to articulate a version of moral perfectionism. See "Illusion and Satire in Kierkegaard's *Postscript.*" Nicholas Rescher claims that aiming at a perfectionistic goal will in all probability lead to better results than aiming at a "realistic" one. See *Ethical Idealism,* 14–18.

70. Cheshire Calhoun writes that "our patterns of knowledge and ignorance tend to reflect our personal past or present biographies. So we can ask . . . 'How do you come to know so much about that?' and expect to get a personally revealing answer ('I know the history of Panama, because I grew up in the Canal Zone.')" "Subjectivity and Emotion," 201. On the narrative characterization of good and bad ways of thinking, see Linda Trinkaus Zagzebski, *Virtues of the Mind,* 22.

71. *For Self-Examination, KW* 21.44; *SV* 17.86.

72. Kierkegaard even suggests that something like asceticism may be a condition of perceiving the truth. *JP* 3.2762; *PAP* XI¹ A 134. On the "*askēsis* of truth," see also Michel Foucault, *Ethics: Subjectivity and Truth,* 101.

73. Although the Kierkegaardian ethicist excuses himself from taking a stand on "the relation between the Aristotelian and the Kantian views of the ethical," he clearly

believes that moral agency should involve affective attention, and dispositions to have the right emotions at the right times. Kant's distrust of emotion as non-cognitive would not admit this, and the judge is operating with a moral psychology closer to Aristotle's (and that of the Stoics). See *Either/Or, KW* 4.322; *SV* 3.296. On Kant's non-cognitive view of emotion, sympathy (for example) can only be seen as an unwanted pain, an increase of the total amount of evil in the world. See *The Metaphysics of Morals,* 457. Kant does not focus upon the criterion of truth which is so crucial to Stoicism, but on the undesirability of the raw feel of emotion and, especially, the importance of maintaining control. The idea that emotions are an orientation toward the world, that they might put us in touch with reality, is not rejected so much as overlooked in his moral philosophy. When he praises the sublimity of the Stoic who has no compassion for his friend's misfortune (*Metaphysics of Morals,* 205), this is not because the Stoic's response is axiologically valid but because equanimity is desirable on hedonistic and consequentialist grounds. If his sadness, which in itself is unpleasant, also "does no good," Marcia Baron says, the Kantian wise man will *turn it off.* See *Kantian Ethics Almost without Apology,* 211–16. But if the sadness is a cognitive response to the situation, then the question of its utility has little to do with its truth, and a true belief should not be rejected because it is not useful. Ultimately, it may be most judicious to conclude that the moral perspective of Judge William is "too complicated to be capable of being traced back to any one single philosopher." Ulrich Knappe, "Kant's and Kierkegaard's Conception of Ethics," 195.

74. "The only way of expressing emotion in the form of art is by finding an 'objective correlative'; in other words, a set of objects, a situation, a chain of events which shall be the formula of that *particular* emotion; such that when the external facts . . . are given, the emotion is immediately evoked." "*Hamlet,*" 48. Iris Murdoch, writing about Eliot as a moralist, calls attention to his idea that it is more praiseworthy to be responding to the object than to be constantly searching for an object worthy of one's feelings: the latter attitude is to be blamed for a dissociation of sensibility in which "emotion parted company with thought." *Existentialists and Mystics,* 163.

75. Likewise, Aristotle's account of the formal structure of ethical life, which can be purged of the "inessential and objectionable elements" that influence his list of the particular virtues, "captures essential features not only of human practice within Greek city-states but of human practice as such." MacIntyre, *Short History of Ethics,* xviii.

76. Cf. *Concept of Anxiety, KW* 8.148; *SV* 6.228–29.

77. See MacIntyre, *After Virtue,* 216, 241–42. See also John Davenport, "Towards an Existential Virtue Ethics," 291.

78. *Kierkegaards Univers,* 65. My translation.

79. See Hegel, *The Philosophy of Right,* §209–§210. See also MacIntyre, *Whose Justice?,* 350, 391.

80. As Walsh comments, such a particularized system of values may entail "a closed rather than an open morality." *Hegelian Ethics,* 55.

81. Nicholas Rescher, *The Coherence Theory of Truth,* 44.

EIGHT. The Romantic Imagination

1. The epigraph to the aesthete's fragments is taken from Paul Pelisson-Fontanier: "Grandeur, savoir, renommée, / Amitié, plaisir et bien, / Tout n'est que vent, que fumée: / Pour mieux dire, tout n'est rien." *Either/Or, KW* 3.18; *SV* 2.22.

2. *Either/Or, KW* 3.37; *SV* 2.39. Hannay translation. Kierkegaard discusses the overestimation of youth in *Point of View for My Work as an Author, KW* 22.47; *SV* 18.99. See also Ecclesiastes 11:9. Loki is a figure in Norse mythology who, like the Greek Prometheus, suffers the fate of being chained to a rock.

3. *The Instant* (#9), *KW* 23.318; *SV* 19.299.

4. Kundera, *Unbearable Lightness of Being*, 121–22. Seneca, as we should expect, believes that what is light must therefore be bearable. See Letter 31. On the project of playfully taking everything more lightly than ever before, see Richard Rorty, *Contingency, Irony, and Solidarity*, 39–40.

5. As "Haufniensis" says, "irony is jealous of earnestness." See *Concept of Anxiety, KW* 8.150; *SV* 6.230. On how irony remains aristocratic in order to evade any reconciliation with existence, see also *JP* 2.1548; *PAP* III B 20.

6. Cf. Hannay, "Kierkegaard and What We Mean By 'Philosophy'," 7.

7. See *JP* 2.1832; *PAP* XI¹ A 288.

8. The judge compares the young man to "that Spanish knight," Don Quixote. *Either/Or, KW* 4.141; *SV* 3.133. He hopes that "A" will find a center of focus for his passionate nature, but worries that his life may "amount to nothing but tentative efforts at living". *Either/Or KW* 4.6–7; *SV* 3.12–13.

9. *Two Ages, KW* 14.20; *SV* 14.22.

10. See *Either/Or, KW* 3.295–99; *SV* 2.272–76.

11. Cf. Epictetus, *Discourses* 3.22.67–76 and Pseudo-Diogenes, *Epistle* 47.

12. *Repetition, KW* 6.201; *SV* 5.172. Modified translation.

13. *Repetition, KW* 6.138–41; *SV* 5.121–24. Lowrie translation.

14. Cf. *Sickness Unto Death, KW* 19.101; *SV* 15.152–53.

15. See Andrew Bowie, *Aesthetics and Subjectivity*, 7. See also J. G. Hamann, "Aesthetica in Nuce," 196–99. Kierkegaard's writings contain many references to Hamann, one German thinker whom he actually admired.

16. On the sense in which thought, according to Hamann, is bound up with a particular language, see Terence German, *Hamann on Language and Religion*, 7. In a journal entry entitled "Something about Hamann," Kierkegaard complains that in the present age no one can "maintain a definite impression" long enough to be able to distinguish his own voice from that of others. *JP* 2.1541; *PAP* I A 340.

17. Cf. *Christian Discourses, KW* 17.108; *SV* 13.107.

18. See *JP* 4.4885; *PAP* XI¹ A 352, where Kierkegaard scornfully alludes to Aristotle, *Politics* 1253a.

19. *Either/Or, KW* 3.25; *SV* 2.28. On passion for what is actually insignificant, see *Christian Discourses, KW* 17.124; *SV* 13.121.

20. Letter to George and Georgiana Keats, 1819. *Letters of John Keats,* 229.

21. See Jung, *Freud and Psychoanalysis,* 248–49, 287–89.

22. Cf. Ernest Becker, *The Denial of Death,* 4–7, 85.

23. *Either/Or,* KW 3.27–28; SV 2.30–31.

24. *Works of Love,* KW 16.71; SV 12.74.

25. KW 1.67–68; SV 1.27.

26. This is from the famous entry dated 1 August 1835. *JP* 5.5100; *PAP* I A 75.

27. *Kierkegaard,* 160.

28. *Either/Or,* KW 3.47; SV 2.47.

29. *JP* 3.3560; *PAP* XI¹ A 62.

30. *JP* 3.3796; *PAP* I A 130.

31. Plato, *Apology* 41e.

32. Byron, "Childe Harold's Pilgrimage," III.42.

33. Wordsworth, "Lines Composed a Few Miles above Tintern Abbey," line 131.

34. Pico della Mirandola, *On the Dignity of Man,* 7.

35. *Stages on Life's Way,* KW 11.241; SV 8.60. Here we see what Milan Kundera means when he speaks of the "miserable tranquillity of marriage." *Immortality,* 76.

36. Rudd, *Kierkegaard and the Limits of the Ethical,* 25.

37. MacIntyre, *Short History of Ethics,* 60. Cf. *Either/Or,* KW 4.327–28; SV 3.300–301 and *JP* 3.2750; *PAP* VIII¹ A 403. As Hubert L. Dreyfus points out, there is no indication in Aristotle's ethics that the virtuous person has perceived the ungroundedness of the everyday understanding of what it means to be a human being. "Could Anything Be More Intelligible than Everyday Intelligibility?," 157–66.

38. See, e.g., *Phenomenology of Spirit,* §503–§504, and *Philosophy of Right,* §150.

39. See *JP* 5.5979; *PAP* VIII¹ A 23 and *JP* 6.6706; *PAP* X³ A 650. Cf. Thoreau, *Walden,* 61: "Our life is frittered away by detail." See also, KW 16.458; *PAP* VIII² B 73.

40. KW 2.320; SV 1.325.

41. Cf. Lawrence Vogel, *The Fragile "We,"* 8–9, 71.

42. See KW 11.606; *PAP* V B 98:6 and Smyth, *A Question of Eros,* 113. On running with the herd, see *The Instant* (#10), KW 23.340–41; SV 19.318–19.

43. See KW 11.568; *PAP* V B 191 and *Two Ages,* KW 14.99; SV 14.90.

44. Vogel, *The Fragile "We,"* 16–17.

45. *Either/Or,* KW 3.34; SV 2.36. Modified translation.

46. *Either/Or,* KW 4.292; SV 3.269.

47. Klaus Mortensen, "The Demons of Self-Reflection: Kierkegaard and Danish Romanticism," 445. Thulstrup blames Heiberg, not Hegel, for literally equating the rational with the actual in the sense that is ridiculed by Kierkegaard. *Kierkegaard's Relation to Hegel,* 31. In any case, the judge's language does contain Hegelian undertones: see, e.g., the preface of *Philosophy of Right* and the *Introduction to the Philosophy of History.*

48. See *Two Ages,* KW 14.84; SV 14.77 and *JP* 1.1541; *PAP* I A 340.

49. Rudd, *Kierkegaard and the Limits of the Ethical,* 131.

50. Cf. Linda Trinkaus Zagzebski, "From Reliabilism to Virtue Epistemology," 113.

51. Emotions often involve an awareness of a difference between how things are and how we think they ought to be. "Suppose that the world either was impervious to our emotions, or instantly and utterly capitulated before them. . . . Suppose, for instance, that, whenever we loved someone, our love was never returned [or] that, whenever we were angry, the object of our anger dropped down dead. . . . Our emotions would, I suspect, die of the lack of interaction, of the lack of narrative." Wollheim, *On the Emotions,* 224.

52. Robert Musil, *The Man Without Qualities,* 1:11.

53. *Either/Or, KW* 4.167; *SV* 3.158.

54. Individuality "is the presupposition for loving," according to Kierkegaard, and love "is the source of everything and . . . the deepest ground of spiritual life." See *JP* 2.2003; *PAP* VIII¹ A 462 and *Works of Love, KW* 16.215; *SV* 12.208.

55. *Either/Or, KW* 4.216; *SV* 3.201.

56. *Either/Or, KW* 4.177; *SV* 3.166. Hannay translation. See also *Either/Or, KW* 4.215; *SV* 3.200.

57. Frithjof Bergmann argues convincingly that the concept of freedom is incoherent unless it means actively identifying with the influences by which one is guided. See *On Being Free,* 85–95.

58. He opposes romance, beauty, enjoyment, and any other form of dependence on something outside the self, even if that "something" is the will of God. See *Either/Or, KW* 4.180–84, 243; *SV* 3.169–73, 225. His language of self-positing may suggest that the judge has been influenced by a misreading of Fichte, but his notion of the not-self appears to be more closely aligned with the Stoic category of what is not up to us.

59. *Either/Or, KW* 4.343; *SV* 3.314–15.

60. *Either/Or, KW* 4.324; *SV* 3.297.

61. Cf. Nietzsche, *Daybreak,* §429.

62. *For Self-Examination, KW* 21.84; *SV* 17.120.

63. *Either/Or, KW* 4.102, 193; *SV* 3.99, 180.

64. Zeno draws a comparison between giving assent to an impression and clenching the fist upon an object, according to Cicero. See *SVF* I 66 (*LS* 41–A).

65. *Point of View for My Work as an Author, KW* 22.30; *SV* 18.86.

66. This phrase is from the Gilleleje journal. *JP* 5.5100; *PAP* I A 75.

NINE. Love as Necessary Premise

1. See, e.g., *SVF* III 462, 475; Seneca, *De Ira* 1.7.4; Epictetus, *Discourses* 2.1.1; and Cicero, *Tusculan Disputations* 3.61.

2. See, e.g., Diogenes Laertius 7.88, 110 and Marcus Aurelius, *Meditations* 4.23, 29.

3. My intention in emphasizing these terms is only to point out that we are moving from *something like* coherence to *something like* correspondence as we move from the "structural" to the "fundamental" aspect of the inquiry.

4. Irving Singer, *Meaning in Life*, 24–25.

5. *Two Ages*, KW 14.96; SV 14.88. Cf. Gouwens, *Kierkegaard as Religious Thinker*, 86. Kierkegaard's remarks on the direct path from the aesthetic to the religious appear in *On My Work as an Author*, KW 22.7–8; SV 18.65.

6. *Either/Or*, KW 4.341–54; SV 3.313–24. Cf. Robert L. Perkins, "Either/Or/Or: Giving the Parson his Due," 222–28.

7. Robert C. Roberts argues that the judge "is a very religious man by any but the most stringent standards"—that is, by standards other than Kierkegaard's. "The Socratic Knowledge of God," 133.

8. *Either/Or*, KW 4.351–53; SV 3.321–23.

9. "Johannes de Silentio" also suggests that these questions should not be answered in terms that "level all existence to the idea of the state or the idea of a society." See *Fear and Trembling*, KW 6.62; SV 5.58.

10. JP 2.2126; PAP X³ A 356. See also Plato, *Apology* 41e and Seneca, Letter 31.

11. JP 3.3131; PAP X³ A 583.

12. The aesthete's case-specific critique of what is valued in his society is different from that of the Stoic, who wants to make sure that nothing at all is hallowed. In Zeno's ideal city there are supposed to be no temples and nothing sacred. See Plutarch, *On Stoic Self-Contradictions* 1034b.

13. See the aesthete's sarcastic remarks in *Either/Or*, KW 3.34; SV 2.36. In a journal entry, Kierkegaard writes: "Most people lead far too sheltered lives, and for that reason they get to know God so little. They have permanent appointments . . . they have the solace of wife and children. I shall never talk disparagingly of that happiness, but I believe it my task to do without all this." JP 5.5962; PAP VII¹ A 222. Hannay translation. People who live with too much objective security "have no idea at all of what it means to be a Christian," since their worldly assurance prohibits them from knowing God as "the infinitely compelling subjectivity." JP 4.4555; PAP X² A 401. Hannay translation.

14. Thoreau, citing an unnnamed contemporary in "A Plea for Captain John Brown," 39. Further proof of Brown's madness, according to popular opinion, was that he was inspired to work against slavery with a feeling of religious vocation (46). "The next thing is that such sentiments assume even the guise of piety," Hegel says, as if conscientious nonconformists had "the highest of justifications for despising the ethical order and the objectivity of law." But, he continues, "if it is piety of the right sort, it sheds the form of this emotional region so soon as it leaves the inner life" and develops reverence for "the universal" moral order as revealed in the laws of the state. Preface to *Philosophy of Right*, 6.

15. Richard Rorty, "Cultural Politics and the Question of the Existence of God," 61. Cf. Hegel, *Phenomenology of Spirit*, §351. See also *Fear and Trembling*, KW 6.60;

SV 5.56: "As soon as I speak, I express the universal, and if I do not do so, no one can understand me."

16. In the midst of a discussion of Skepticism, Jason Xenakis asks: "Can't the System, as well as the individual, be sick (or make for sickness)?" "Noncommittal Philosophy," 200. Cf. Sextus Empiricus, *Outlines of Pyrrhonism* 1.160–61, 164–66. See also Norman O. Brown, *Life Against Death,* 143–44: "While cultural activities may be distinguished from individual neurosis by their social character, it does not follow that all socially integrated behavior is non-neurotic."

17. *Love and Its Place,* 153.

18. *Either/Or, KW* 4.200; *SV* 3.186.

19. Camus, *The Rebel,* 101. Hegel, of course, would share the judge's distrust of anyone who interprets feelings of estrangement as the source of a potentially genuine ethical or religious commitment: he scorns as capricious fancies all emotional responses that are at odds with the Establishment, calling it "the quintessence of shallow thinking" to give any credence to our feelings about the possibility of a better world. Preface to *Philosophy of Right,* 4–5. In other words, Hegel opposes any moral revolt arising from a "merely emotional response to the modern world." Mark Shelton, "The Morality of Peace," 382. Camus himself agrees that revolt ought to lead to a qualified "consent to the relative"; this is hardly the longing of the Unhappy Consciousness which cannot come to terms with *any* actual circumstances. See *The Rebel,* 290; see also *The Phenomenology of Spirit,* §230.

20. *JP* 1.219; *PAP* II A 127.

21. *Repetition, KW* 6.227; *SV* 5.191.

22. *JP* 5.5100; *PAP* I A 75.

23. Henri Bergson, *The Two Sources of Morality and Religion,* 100. "Life" is what Bergson has in mind, although in another place he refers to this "creative energy" as Love itself, which is the prime mover of "a universe which is the mere visible and tangible aspect of love and the need for loving" (256).

24. "Devoid of imagination, as the Philistine always is, he lives in a certain trivial province of experiences as to how things go, what is possible, what usually occurs. . . . Philistinism tranquilizes itself in the trivial." *Sickness Unto Death, KW* 19.41; *SV* 15.97–98. Lowrie translation. The philistine always seems to be busy; and yet "to be busy in a world where nothing is of true significance is, naturally, comical." Sløk, *Kierkegaards Univers,* 32–33. See also David Michael Levin, *The Opening of Vision,* 173: "The self always exists within social practices. But social practices do not totally determine the being of the self."

25. *JP* 4.4112; *PAP* VII¹ A 63. Hannay translation. The passage quoted is from Schelling's preface to the posthumously published papers of Steffens. On Kierkegaard's connection, via Sibbern, to Steffens's lectures on Schelling, see Connell, *To Be One Thing,* 11–12.

26. One of Hegel's central tasks, according to Michael Forster, is to show "that truth is constituted by community consensus"; he ascribes to Hegel an "enduring

community consensus theory of truth," according to which it is "sufficient for a claim's truth that it be agreed upon and continue to be agreed upon by a community." *Hegel's Idea of a Phenomenology of Spirit,* 14–15, 226–27. Even Franz Grégoire, who insists that the Hegelian state is not *totalitarian,* admits that the state, not the individual, is "the superior term," and that there is "a predominance on the side of the state." "Is the Hegelian State Totalitarian?", 105–7. This is arguably why Kierkegaard is "opposed to just that sense of community ultimately deified by Hegel. Kierkegaard refers to Hegel's Spirit as 'the Crowd,' 'the Public,' the 'collective Idea,' 'the Christian hordes,' and variously compares them to geese, sheep, and factory products." Robert C. Solomon, *In the Spirit of Hegel,* 621.

27. The state has "the highest right over the individual," Hegel says, and therefore it ought to be honored as "the divine on earth." *Philosophy of Right,* §258, §272. Grégoire can give only a weak apology for Hegel's apparent divinization of the state: he points out that by calling something divine Hegel does not mean that it is the *exclusive* site of divinity, but then concedes that even a partial deification of the state could reasonably be classified as idolatry. "A Semi-Legend: The 'Divinity' of the State in Hegel," 291–300.

28. In other words, Aristotle can show us how to be virtuous, but he does not radically question what are regarded as virtues in his society. Vigen Guroian says that we could describe Orthodox Christian morality as a kind of virtue ethics, as long as we add the qualification that, on this view, it is impossible to become virtuous without the transfiguring power of love to animate and guide one's life. *Incarnate Love: Essays in Orthodox Ethics,* 13.

29. Berthold-Bond, "Kierkegaardian Critique," 133. In Heidegger's language, it is the mood of anxiety that points Dasein toward its possible authenticity. See *Being and Time,* §40.

30. *Eighteen Upbuilding Discourses,* KW 5.86; SV 4.83. Modified translation. On how the imagination lures us out into existence, see also *JP* 2.1832; *PAP* XI^1 A 288.

31. *Either/Or,* KW 3.291; SV 3.268. Swenson translation.

32. Kierkegaard points out that it is difficult for a person to fulfill his or her need for heroic significance at a time when "the age of heroes is past." *Two Ages,* KW 14.87; SV 14.85. Alluding to *Rameau's Nephew* by Diderot, Hegel locates the "nihilistic game" in which moral life is stripped of its significance in the historical era in which the truth of the Enlightenment is still struggling to prevail by force over the ancien régime. *Phenomenology of Spirit,* §521. And yet even a confirmed Hegelian can admit of *Rameau's Nephew* that "there is something universal in the text," since it exposes the insincerity upon which the rituals of social life are predicated in any historical period, thereby calling into question the idea of established values. See Heyde, *The Weight of Finitude,* 14. Cf. Lionel Trilling, *Sincerity and Authenticity,* 31.

33. *Either/Or,* KW 3.291; SV 3.268. By "primitive" [*primitiv*] Kierkegaard has in mind a human being's native capacity to receive significant impressions without being

influenced by "the others." See, e.g., *JP* 3.3560; *PAP* XI¹ A 62. The crowd can have a pernicious influence on the emotional dispositions of a moral agent, since it buzzes like a swarm of insects with confused yet infectious passions, which are supposedly shared by "everyone" and yet are not grounded in anyone's individual, or primitive, sense of value. See *JP* 2.2061; *PAP* XI¹ A 319. See also *Purity of Heart*, *KW* 15.28; *SV* 11.33: "Like the world's contempt, the world's honor is a maelstrom, a play of disordered forces, a false instant . . . as when a swarm of insects in the distance appears to the eye to be one body, an illusion, as when the noise of a crowd in the distance seems to the ear like one voice. Even if this honor be unanimous, it is still meaningless." Modified translation.

34. Cf. Connell, "The Importance of Being Earnest," 138–39. As Jankélévitch points out, there is this essential difference: love is not a contract, but marriage is. See *Les Vertus et L'Amour*, 2:246.

35. *Selves in Discord*, 58–59. Judge William's claim about the "real constituting element" in marriage occurs early in his first letter. *Either/Or*, *KW* 4.32; *SV* 3.35.

36. *Three Discourses on Imagined Occasions*, *KW* 10.59, 10.78; *SV* 6.288, 302. See also *JP* 2.1108, 2.1365; *PAP* IV A 117, VIII¹ A 670.

37. With regard to Hegel's position, see, e.g., *Lectures on the Philosophy of Religion*, 473; *Encyclopedia Logic*, §1. For Kierkegaard's view, see *JP* 2.2165; *PAP* X³ A 231: "Christianity rests on the idea that the truth *is* the single individual." Hannay translation. Truth, Kierkegaard asserts, is "anything but the result of a unified effort. . . . To become an individual, to continue as an individual, is the way to the truth." *JP* 4.4887; *PAP* XI¹ A 438. Modified translation.

38. *Eighteen Upbuilding Discourses*, *KW* 5.87; *SV* 4.84. See also *Three Discourses on Imagined Occasions*, *KW* 10.98–99; *SV* 6.320–21.

39. *Three Discourses on Imagined Occasions*, *KW* 10.96, 73–74; *SV* 6.317, 298–99. See also *KW* 10.79; *SV* 6.303: "Have any notion you wish, fanciful or true, about your life, about its importance for everybody, about its importance for yourself"; the "thought of death" explains "that this security is false."

40. *Three Discourses on Imagined Occasions*, *KW* 10.83; *SV* 6.306.

41. Cf. *Eighteen Upbuilding Discourses*, *KW* 5.127; *SV* 4.118: "What is the good, where is the perfect to be found? If it exists, where is its source?" In *Book on Adler*, Kierkegaard points out that if I receive a letter, what I want to know is: who is it from? *KW* 24.32; *PAP* VII² B 13:63.

42. See, e.g., *JP* 2.2266; *PAP* II A 523. By now we are familiar with the distinction made by Epictetus between what is "up to us" and what is not; this is described as his "main thesis" by Kierkegaard in a journal entry that alludes to *Discourses* 1.1.17–27. In his essay on love, Hegel writes: "Nothing is unconditioned; nothing carries the root of its own being in itself." *Early Theological Writings*, 304.

43. See F. W. J. Schelling, *Bruno; or, On the Natural and the Divine Principle of Things*, 157–59.

44. *Book on Adler*, KW 24.62; PAP VII² B 235:107. Later in this text, Kierkegaard says that religiousness should not be seen as something that a person *has* (in the sense of ownership or egoistic seizure); instead, one should be *"had* by it" in more of a passionate sense. KW 24.107; PAP VII² B 235:194.

45. Nagel, *The View from Nowhere*, 119. The claim that "what a person most fundamentally is" is not entirely within his or her control is made by Saul Smilansky. See *Free Will and Illusion*, 128. He has in mind Epictetus' distinction between "what is up to us" and what is not, which he cites (14). "What gives?" is a question whose relevance to phenomenology is noted by Marion, *Reduction and Givenness*, 38–39.

46. *Works of Love*, KW 16.215; SV 12.209. Modified translation.

47. *Works of Love*, KW 16.8–10; SV 12.13–15 (Kierkegaard quotes Proverbs 4:23).

48. *Eighteen Upbuilding Discourses*, KW 5.87; SV 4.84. "God is infinite wisdom," Kierkegaard writes in another discourse, and then (one sentence later): "God is love." *Without Authority*, KW 18.11; SV 14.135.

49. "How could one speak properly about love if you were forgotten, you God of love, source of all love in heaven and on earth . . . you who are love, so that one who loves is what he is only by being in you!" *Works of Love*, KW 16.3; SV 12.10. On existing *in* that upon which one depends, see also O'Meara, *Plotinus*, 26–27.

50. *Eighteen Upbuilding Discourses*, KW 5.55; SV 4.57.

51. Protagoras, Fragment 1; Heraclitus, Fragment 45 (Diels).

52. *Works of Love*, KW 16.62–63; SV 12.66.

53. See, e.g., *Works of Love*, KW 16.182; SV 12.176. See also, by way of contrast, Hegel's discussion of "the subjectively knowing spirit for which God is object." *Lectures on the Philosophy of Religion* (1984 edition), 1:381.

54. Ephesians 3:13. Kierkegaard cites this phrase in *Eighteen Upbuilding Discourses*, KW 5.80; SV 4.78. See also 1 John 4:8, in which it is written that "anyone who does not love does not know God, for God is Love." The authorized contemporary Danish translation of this passage is: "Den, der ikke elsker, kender ikke Gud, for Gud er kærlighed." Canonical Edition, authorized by Queen Margrethe II, February 1992. For Kierkegaard, an emotional person is not self-creating. But it *is* possible to reject love, and hence to become closed to the possibility of emotion.

55. On the differentiation of self and world out of a primary "oceanic" condition, see Kresten Nordentoft's discussion of *Eighteen Upbuilding Discourses*, KW 5.165; SV 4.150. *Kierkegaard's Psychology*, 104–5. See also Nordentoft's remarks on the differentiation of subject from object as a "subject-constituting separation," in which certain objects are charged with significance: "Erotic Love," 90–91. Kierkegaard writes of a time in which "the child has not yet separated himself from his surroundings," in which his identity is "gestalted in vague and fleeting outlines," just like ocean waves; this is the time when the child "is still at as good as one with the mother." See JP 4.4398; PAP I C 126 and *Christian Discourses*, KW 17.62; SV 13.64. Here we begin to see why Kierkegaard has been described as a "post-Freudian." See Ernest Becker, *Denial of Death*, 68.

56. Kierkegaard's understanding of love as a kind of *care* prompts Ferreira to read *kjerlighed* as "caring". *Love's Grateful Striving*, 43–44. Neighborly love, then, involves caring for each human being "according to (i.e., not in spite of or regardless of) his particularity." Hannay, *Kierkegaard: A Biography*, 362.

57. Nordentoft, *Kierkegaard's Psychology*, 385. Even though it is a spontaneous "event over which we have no control," Elsebet Jegstrup points out that love can be refined into a deliberate way of being: "To let the other be is how Kierkegaard understands love as obligation," and truthful subjective comportment requires that one be "attuned to being as love." "Text and the Performative Act," 125.

58. Thomas Langan, *Being and Truth*, 311.

59. Arnold B. Come, "Kierkegaard's Ontology of Love," 91–92.

60. *Works of Love, KW* 16.12; *SV* 12.18. See also *Either/Or, KW* 4.125; *SV* 3.119. The "truly loving" person, writes Kierkegaard, "loves every human being according to his distinctiveness; but 'his distinctiveness' is what for him is *his own*; that is, the loving one does not seek his own; quite the opposite, he loves what is the other's own." *Works of Love, KW* 16.269; *SV* 12.258.

61. *Works of Love, KW* 16.112; *SV* 12.112. Cappelørn suggests "love is an emotional passion" as a translation of "Kjerlighed er en Følelses Lidenskab." (Personal communication.) See also *Works of Love, KW* 16.107; *SV* 12.107.

62. *Works of Love, KW* 16.121; *SV* 12.120. Kierkegard elsewhere suggests that the Third Person of the Holy Trinity sustains mental life more generally. *JP* 1.296; *PAP* II A 419. Cf. Nicholas of Cusa, "On the Vision of God," 267–68.

63. *Love's Grateful Striving*, 72. Cf. Bowen, "Kierkegaard on the Theological Ethics of Love," 25: "In any relationship of love, Love (i.e., *God himself*) is the aforementioned 'third term' and eternal Reality." See also Wahl, *Kierkegaard*, 172–73.

64. Alastair Hannay writes that "love has the form of an interest in the interests of the other." "The Dialectic of Proximity and Apartness," 178. Harry G. Frankfurt claims that the requirements of love have "not simply power but authority," since our individuality is defined by "what we cannot help caring about." *Necessity, Volition, and Love*, 138.

65. Kierkegaard associates love with providence, and uses both terms to designate the source of individual human distinctiveness. See, e.g., *JP* 1.909, 2.1372; *PAP* IV B 170, IX A 182. See also *Works of Love, KW* 16.84–85; *SV* 12.86; and *JP* 3.3225, 2.2083; *PAP* XI² A 177, and XI² A 259. On God as "the source and origin of all distinctiveness" who gives being to each of us, see *Works of Love, KW* 16.271; *SV* 12.260. On the sense in which we human beings are capable of nothing apart from God, see *Eighteen Upbuilding Discourses, KW* 5.319; *SV* 4.283–84.

66. Kierkegaard describes one who "has pondered upon the nature of God, upon the fact that God is love," and who has reflected "upon what follows from this as a consequence," that "all things must work together for good." Even this person, he says, could sometimes doubt "whether after all God is love." *Christian Discourses, KW* 17.197–98; *SV* 13.188–89. Lowrie translation. It is all-important, however, to make this

affirmation in spite of any doubts (see *JP* 3.2809; *PAP* VII¹ A 186)—in Kierkegaard's view, it is only when "you believe that God is love" that "all things serve you for good." *Christian Discourses*, KW 17.193; SV 13.185.

67. See Lingis, *The Imperative*, 119–20.

68. "The Dream of a Ridiculous Man," in *A Gentle Creature and Other Stories*, 108.

69. *Christian Discourses*, KW 17.237; SV 13.223. Iris Murdoch writes, "We differ not only because we select different objects out of the same world but because we see different worlds." *Existentialists and Mystics*, 82–83.

70. Jonathan Lear, *Happiness, Death, and the Remainder of Life*, 32–33.

71. *Phenomenological Interpretations of Aristotle*, 69.

72. See *Works of Love*, KW 16.225–28; SV 12.218–20.

73. *Works of Love*, KW 16.180; SV 12.175. See also *Christian Discourses*, KW 17.109; SV 13.108 and *Repetition*, KW 6.140; SV 5.123. The sense of infinity that is "inherent in all true love" (according to Schlegel) need not send the romantic imagination on a flight from actuality; it could also open up the experience of sacred meaning *within* contingent existence. See Hannay, *Kierkegaard: A Biography*, 145, 198. See also *JP* 2.1108, 2.1832; *PAP* IV A 117, XI¹ A 288.

74. 1 Peter 4:7–12 is cited in *Eighteen Upbuilding Discourses*, KW 5.55, 69; SV 4.57, 69.

75. *Judge for Yourself!*, KW 21.104–6; SV 17.138–40.

76. *Eighteen Upbuilding Discourses*, KW 5.55–56; SV 4.57–58. Kierkegaard might be alluding to Aristotle, for whom anger at being wronged involves the pleasant expectation of revenge: see *Rhetoric* 1378b.

77. Anders Nygren, *Agape and Eros*, 6. Pseudo-Dionysius speaks of love as what "holds all things together". *Divine Names* 4.10–11 [708b–709d]. The "cause of the universe," he adds, is manifested in "the loving care it has for everything." *Divine Names* 4.13 [712a]. Plotinus appears at times to identify the One with Love (e.g., *Enneads* 6.8.15, 6.9.9), but it is Pseudo-Dionysius who develops a thorough account of love as an ontological force, as the creative basis of all things in their distinct individual qualities. Other Christian thinkers who do not view *erōs* and *agapē* [or *amore* and *caritas*] as contradictory terms include Augustine (*City of God* 14.7; *Homily on the First Epistle of Saint John*), Origen ("Commentary on the Song of Songs"), and Catherine of Siena (*The Dialogue*, 25–26). Unlike Nygren, who considers Saint Augustine to be the archenemy of "Christian" love, Kierkegaard believes in the religious significance of love, in both its metaphysical origin and its human *works*. In this respect, he is directly opposed to the Lutheran tendency of reducing love to "a purely human, carnal, sensuous force"; at its worst, this reduction threatens to replace love of others with a self-interested eschatological faith. Cf. Scheler, *Ressentiment*, 105–6.

78. A variant spelling is *Kjerlighed*; the modern Danish word is *Kærlighed*. In notes to *Three Discourses on Imagined Occasions* and to *Christian Discourses*, Hong

and Hong also draw this parallel between *Elskov/erōs* and *Kjærlighed/agapē*. See *KW* 10.161, 17.444. Unfortunately, their translations often misrepresent the distinction, impertinently rendering *Elskov* as "erotic love" (as if it always meant something lewd or profane) although in many cases the single inclusive term "love" would be a more accurate translation—e.g., "If you yourself have never been in love, you do not know whether anyone has ever been loved in the world, although you do know how many have affirmed that they have loved, have affirmed that they have sacrificed their lives for erotic love [*Elskov*]." In this passage (from *Christian Discourses, KW* 17.237; *SV* 13.223), the Hongs give the misleading impression that Kierkegaard changes the subject all of a sudden, when in fact he has been using the verb *elske* all along. He does not mean to single out the erotic as *opposed* to other kinds of love at any point in this sentence, just as he does not intend to instigate an orgy by declaring "Du *skal* elske" (you *shall* love) throughout *Works of Love*. E.g., *KW* 16.17–43; *SV* 12.23–48.

79. See *Three Discourses on Imagined Occasions* (*KW* 10.47; *SV* 6.277), referring to the speech of "Phaedrus" at *Symposium* 178b. In *Concept of Irony*, Kierkegaard uses the word *Kjærlighed* repeatedly in reference to Plato's *Symposium*. See *KW* 2.41–52; *SV* 1.96–107. See also *Either/Or, KW* 4.32; *SV* 3.35 and *Works of Love, KW* 16.22–25, 112–14; *SV* 12.28–30, 112–14.

80. Kierkegaard argues in *Works of Love* that our aim should be to distinguish the most unselfish love (*Kjærlighed*) from deviant forms. *KW* 16.7; *SV* 12.13. Erotic love (*Elskov*) and friendship (*Venskab*) are not "the truest form of love," and it is crucial to identify the ways in which they fall short of the ideal. *Works of Love, KW* 16.267; *SV* 12.256 and *JP* 3.2410, 3.2428; *PAP* VIII¹ A 196, X² A 63.

81. *Works of Love, KW* 16.139–43; *SV* 12.137–41. In the opening chapter of this work, Kierkegaard declares that love "flows" from a single hidden source "along many paths"; the varieties of "love in its manifestations" are announced as the theme of his treatise. *KW* 16.9; *SV* 12.14–15. Nordentoft remarks that Kierkegaard's reason for paying attention to "the pre-Christian, Greek form of erotic love" is to emphasize that "love may take a variety of forms." "Erotic Love," 92. Cf. Guroian, *Incarnate Love*, 17–18: Christian love "does not negate but sublimates and transforms all so-called natural or human loves. This is why such Greek writers as John Chrysostom and Nicholas Cabasilas used [*philia, agapē*, and *erōs*] interchangeably."

82. *Letters and Documents, KW* 25.66–67; *Breve og Aktstykker* 21. Kierkegaard alludes to *Phaedrus* 229d–230a and *Symposium* 220c–d, respectively, in *Book on Adler* (*KW* 24.139; *PAP* VII² B 235:226) and *For Self-Examination* (*KW* 21.9; *SV* 17.55). On the lover as *entheos*, see *Phaedrus* 255b and *Symposium* 179a.

83. Jegstrup, "Text and the Performative Act," 124.

84. *Stages on Life's Way, KW* 11.121–22; *SV* 7.109–11. See also *Either/Or, KW* 4.148; *SV* 3.140: "Duty is only one thing: it is to love in truth, in one's inmost heart; and duty is just as protean as love itself."

85. *JP* 3.2387; *PAP* III A 61. Hannay translation.

86. *JP* 3.3323; *PAP* III B 26.

87. This claim is made by Patricia J. Huntington. "Heidegger's Reading of Kierkegaard Revisited," 52. Kierkegaard's most explicit comparison between the Socratic *daimon* and his own sense of religious vocation is made in *JP* 2.1373; *PAP* IX A 242. Cf. Sophia Scopetea, *Kierkegaard og græciteten,* 395.

88. *Concept of Irony, KW* 2.158; *SV* 1.193. Kierkegaard cites *Theages* 128d; see also *Theages* 128b. On love as a source of moral improvement and religious insight see, e.g., *Symposium* 178c–d and *Phaedrus* 254e. See also *Works of Love, KW* 16.212, 228; *SV* 12.205–6, 220–21.

89. *Concept of Irony, KW* 2.45–46, 41; *SV* 1.100–101, 97. The portrait of the lover's soul in the speech of Socrates "is a totally empty abstraction," Kierkegaard writes; in the *Phaedo,* the soul is "understood just as abstractly as the pure essence of the things that are the object of its activity." *Concept of Irony, KW* 2.68; *SV* 1.120.

90. *Eighteen Upbuilding Discourses, KW* 5.75; *SV* 4.74. Here, my interpretation is deeply indebted to Niels Nymann Eriksen, "Love and Sacrifice in *Repetition,*" 29–34. See also *Repetition, KW* 6.185; *SV* 5.160: "From a religious point of view, one could say it is as if God used this girl to capture him, and yet the girl herself is not an actuality but is like the lace-winged fly with which a hook is baited." Cf. Plato, *Symposium* 210a–211c.

91. Plato, *Symposium* 219d; see also Perkins, "Woman-Bashing in Kierkegaard's 'In Vino Veritas': A Reinscription of Plato's *Symposium,*" 87–89. Gregory Vlastos finds in both the *Phaedrus* and the *Symposium* a neglect of the individual, not only "in the uniqueness and integrity of his or her individuality," but also as "a valuing subject" with his or her own emotions. "The Individual as Object of Love in Plato," 31–32. See, e.g., *Phaedrus* 250e, 255a.

92. See *Stages on Life's Way, KW* 11.34–40; *SV* 7.35–40. See also *JP* 2.1411; *PAP* X³ A 374. Even as much of a value objectivist as Scheler recognizes this difference between Platonic and Christian love. For the Christian, "it is the activity and movement of love which embues life with *its highest meaning and value.*" *Ressentiment,* 83.

93. *Works of Love, KW* 16.159; *SV* 12.154.

94. On knowing what is worthy of love, see Epictetus, *Discourses* 2.22.2–3; Diogenes Laertius 6.11 and 7.129–30 (on Antisthenes, Zeno, and Chrysippus); and Stobaeus 2.66, 115. Epictetus opposes *erōs* and recommends a more reasonable affection, which he usually refers to as *philia. Discourses* 1.11.16–19, 2.21.7–8, 2.22.34–37, 3.13.10–12, 3.24.7–30. The early Stoics did speak well of *erōs,* although their use of this term was unconventional: in their writings, "love" could mean a source of friendship and civic harmony (Athenaeus 561c); a chase after well-endowed youngsters (Plutarch, *On Common Conceptions* 1073b); or, the desire to have intercourse with beautiful young people and to educate them in virtue (Andronicus, *SVF* III 397). "It is to be presumed," Malcolm Schofield writes, "that Zeno did not think of erotic love as what the Stoics called a passion," since if he did, "he could hardly have allowed that

the sage will love." *The Stoic Idea of the City,* 29–30. A. W. Price suggests that, if they counted as passions, then "the sage's loves must have counted as *eupatheiai,*" or "good" emotions. "Plato, Zeno, and the Object of Love," 190.

95. Cicero, *Tusculan Disputations* 4.75–76.

96. Epictetus, *Discourses* 3.8.1–4; Marcus Aurelius, *Meditations* 6.52. On the Stoic idea of the cataleptic impression, in which the perceiving subject has a "true and full apprehension of the value and significance of the object perceived," see A. C. Bouquet, "Stoics and Buddhists," 213; see also *SVF* I 73.

97. Mooney, *Selves in Discord,* 71.

98. *JP* 4.3898; *PAP* IX A 383. Kierkegaard cites Marcus Aurelius, *Meditations* 11.3. See also Seneca, Letter 23. Nussbaum worries about this self-isolating tendency in Stoicism *Upheavals of Thought,* 207, while Hadot applauds it (*The Inner Citadel,* 83–84).

99. *JP* 3.2447; *PAP* XI¹ A 411. For Kierkegaard, love "must open the self in the direction of the world," creating "a passage through which things can enter." Pia Søltoft, "Love and Continuity," 222–24. For Epictetus, however, the divine principle of the world, which is instantiated in one's own mind, is "nothing other than reason itself." Bonhöffer, *Ethics of the Stoic Epictetus,* 14.

100. Chrysippus argues in *On Love* that "love has friendship for its object." Diogenes Laertius 7.130. Cf. Xenophon, *Symposium* 8.18. Schofield writes that, according to early Stoicism, "Friendship consummates love—and replaces it." *Stoic Idea of the City,* 34.

101. On the nonspecific uniformity of affection in the Stoic city, see Diogenes Laertius 7.131; for Aristotle's critique of this idea in Plato's *Republic,* see *Politics* 1262a, 1264b. In *Either/Or,* it is said that Aristotle "bases the concept of justice on the idea of friendship." The allusion is presumably to *Nicomachean Ethics* 1159b–1161a. See *KW* 4.322; *SV* 3.296.

102. *Works of Love, KW* 16.83–84; *SV* 12.85–86. Cf. Guroian, *Incarnate Love,* 18: "*Eros* [in Greek Orthodox thought] no longer is simply a human yearning for the divine. It is a divine-human love, the ascending mode of charity itself, whereby the mind 'ravished by divine knowledge' seeks God, but in so doing discovers from a divine point of view the infinite value and perfect equality of all human persons."

103. Aristotle, *Nicomachean Ethics* 1159a. Cf. *Nicomachean Ethics* 1155b, 1166a; *Rhetoric* 1380b–1381a.

104. Vlastos, "The Individual as Object of Love in Plato," 4–6.

105. Nussbaum, *The Fragility of Goodness,* 354. As Freud argues, "language has carried out an entirely justifiable piece of unification in creating the word 'love' with its numerous uses." *Group Psychology,* 30.

106. Aristotle does sometimes speak as if my highest loyalty as a loving person is to the good which may exist in someone's character, not to the value of the person as such. This is at least one aspect of what Kierkegaard means when he says that *philia,* like *erōs,* has limits. See, e.g., *Nicomachean Ethics* 1159b and compare *Works of Love,*

NOTES TO PAGES 105–106

KW 16.273; *SV* 12.262. The exclusiveness of *philia* is another limitation, as is the notion that a life of contemplation is best for human beings. See *Nicomachean Ethics* 1177a–1178a and compare *JP* 1.114; *PAP* IV C 27.

107. Only a being with *psychē* is eligible for friendship, says Aristotle. *Nicomachean Ethics* 1155b. See also 1159a: "If we have been right to say that a friend wishes good things to the other for the sake of the other himself, then the other must continue to be whatever he is."

108. *Works of Love, KW* 16.223; *SV* 12.216. Augustine says that each person *is* what he *loves*. *Homily on the First Epistle of Saint John* §2.

109. *JP* 2.2274, 6.6211; *PAP* III A 5, IX A 178.

110. M. Jamie Ferreira, *Love's Grateful Striving*, 287. Loewald observes that both the loving subject "and that which is loved are distinguished in the act of loving . . . in such a relatedness, both oneself as subject and the other as object are established." "Transference and Love," 552–57. See also Merleau-Ponty, *Phenomenology of Perception*, 154: "Let us try to see how a thing or a being begins to exist for us through love and we shall thereby come to understand better how things and beings can exist in general."

111. See *Works of Love, KW* 16.264–79; *SV* 12.254–68. On the love that asks for nothing in return, see *Works of Love, KW* 16.345–58; *SV* 12.329–41.

112. Even the seducer in *Either/Or* recognizes that "for one who loves everything ceases to have intrinsic meaning and has meaning only through the interpretation that love gives to it." *KW* 3.407; *SV* 2.375. And yet, not only does he appropriate Cordelia into his own scheme of ends, but he also resists this gift of significance, refusing to allow his love to develop into a lasting disposition. Apparently, he is ignorant of the fact that the passion of love "is not simply a momentary feeling, but a deep caring commitment, which can be cultivated and developed. Without passion the individual's life lacks unity and continuity; only through passion can a person truly 'become a self.'" C. Stephen Evans, *Existentialism*, 22.

113. *Eighteen Upbuilding Discourses, KW* 5.59–60; *SV* 4.60–61. See also *Works of Love, KW* 16.226–28; *SV* 12.219–21, where love is called the opposite of mistrust. "Fundamentally all understanding depends upon how one is disposed toward something," Kierkegaard writes. If a misfortune should occur at a time when we are trusting in love, then we can explain why this might providentially have happened just now, because we have the strengh to bear it, because we can learn from it, etc. "From this we see that a person's whole view of life actually is a confession of the state of his inner being." *JP* 4.4554; *PAP* X² A 355.

114. *Eighteen Upbuilding Discourses, KW* 5.72–75; *SV* 4.71–74. Love which is "tortured by preoccupation with itself" is liable to become a selfish jealousy in which one loves only insofar as one is loved. "True love," on the other hand, is a fundamental spiritual disposition in which one does not ask for anything in return. See *Works of Love, KW* 16.34–35; *SV* 12.39–40.

115. Ferreira, *Love's Grateful Striving*, 160. "Love is certainly an emotion," as Kierkegaard reminds us: *KW* 16.436; *PAP* VIII² B 32:6. He characterizes "faith in God's

love" as a necessary condition of "a life that is truly worth living." *Christian Discourses, KW* 17.200; *SV* 13.190–91.

116. *Works of Love, KW* 16.254–55; *SV* 12.245. This kind of decision, as M. Jamie Ferreira notes, "embodies a tension between passive and active," since it is "both our action and dependent on the power or attraction of something outside of us" (much like falling in love). *Transforming Vision*, 116–17.

117. *KW* 11.590–91; *PAP* V B 103:5. See also *Works of Love, KW* 16.140–41; *SV* 12.137–38. Kierkegaard discusses a literary character who "is in love, and yet at the same time he is constantly wishing to be so," wishing "every moment to be what he already is at that very moment." *Letters and Documents, KW* 25.67; *Breve og Aktstykker* 21.

118. *Eighteen Upbuilding Discourses, KW* 5.157; *SV* 4.144. On the proper attitude toward this grounding power, see *KW* 19.142; *PAP* VIII² B 170:2 and *Works of Love, KW* 16.3; *SV* 12.10.

119. *Eighteen Upbuilding Discourses, KW* 5.312–13; *SV* 4.278–79. See also *Works of Love, KW* 16.209–24; *SV* 12.203–17. The belief that "love builds up" implies a very different kind of fundamentalism than that of the "narrow-minded" Christianity which Kierkegaard accuses of worshipping the tail end of the donkey that Christ rode upon. *JP* 3.3048; *PAP* VIII¹ A 118. On the contrary, "according to Kierkegaard's Christian anthropology . . . love *is* in the fundament." Nordentoft, *Kierkegaard's Psychology*, 380. Cf. *Catechism of the Catholic Church*, §27: "If man exists, it is because he has been created through Love, and by Love is continuously held in existence. He cannot live fully according to truth unless he freely acknowledges that love and entrusts himself to his creator."

120. Rolf Johnson, *Three Faces of Love*, 103.

121. Richard L. Rorty, *Contingency, Irony, and Solidarity*, 29; Nordentoft, *Kierkegaard's Psychology*, 91.

122. Augustine, *Homily on the First Epistle of Saint John* §4–§8. Catherine Osborne argues that the phrase "God is love," in the Greek New Testament, "does not so obviously imply that God is loving; it is usual for the Patristic commentators . . . to take it in a different sense, namely to refer to God as the source or origin from which all other lovers derive their love." She refers to Origen and Gregory of Nyssa, along with Augustine: *Eros Unveiled*, 41. On the Augustinian "understanding of all reality as sheer intelligibility and the whole cosmos as erotic," see David Tracy, *On Naming the Present*, 38–39.

TEN. **Suffering as Logical Consequence**

1. Cf. *Works of Love, KW* 16.215; *SV* 12.208. The beliefs that "God is love" and "all is good" are explicitly and repeatedly linked by Kierkegaard. See, e.g., *PAP* VII¹ A 186.

2. Love's "deep sustaining power" and the "vulnerability" to which it gives rise are noted by Edward Mooney in *Knights of Faith and Resignation*, 59–60.

3. José Ortega y Gasset, *On Love,* 37. Kierkegaard's own use of ocean waves as a metaphor for emotion has been noted above. See also *PAP* I A 64 and I C 126 and *Eighteen Upbuilding Discourses, KW* 5.165; *SV* 4.150.

4. See *Three Discourses on Imagined Occasions, KW* 10.47; *SV* 6.278 and *JP* 4.4692; *PAP* X⁴ A 630. On love as the sacred origin of pain and suffering, see also *KW* 10.35; *SV* 6.269 and *JP* 2.1123; *PAP* VIII¹ A 649. Kierkegaard's late writings make increasing reference to the idea of "suffering" for the truth. I am not focusing on the meaning that he introduces into this phrase toward the end of his life, but it is worth noting that even at the height of this phase, he writes that "to be a Christian is to suffer, *including* having to suffer for the doctrine," indicating that being persecuted is merely one sense in which a Christian must suffer, in addition to the main one: namely, that love renders a person liable to "suffering" in the sense that Schopenhauer, whom Kierkegaard is discussing in this same 1854 passage, has in mind when "in his gloomy Indian view" he says that "to live is to suffer": *JP* 4.3881; *PAP* XI¹ A 181 (my italics). Cf. Schopenhauer, *Parerga and Paralipomena,* 2:157. See also, e.g., Radhakrishnan, *An Idealist View of Life,* 59: "To love is to suffer. The more we love, the more we suffer."

5. Bergson, *Two Sources of Morality,* 99.

6. Lines 1–2 and 5 of an untitled 1946 poem: Larkin, *Collected Poems,* 6–7. This poem alludes to Schopenhauer's tale of the porcupines who crowd together to avoid being frozen to death, only to move apart due to the pain of one another's quills: *Parerga and Paralipomena,* 2:396.

7. Cioran, *Drawn and Quartered,* 147.

8. *JP* 3.2447; *PAP* XI¹ A 411. See also *The Sickness Unto Death, KW* 19.126; *SV* 15.175.

9. *Discourses* 4.1.147. Cf. Marion, *Prolegomena to Charity,* 167: the beloved other is "the uncontrollable, the unforeseeable, and the foreign stranger who will affect me, provoke me, and—possibly—love me. Love of the other . . . empties its world of itself in order to make place there for what is not like it, what does not thank it, what— possibly—does not love it."

10. *Stages on Life's Way, KW* 11.176; *SV* 8.158. The "free" heart has no concerns and (therefore) no history; however, for a loving person, "the heart must be bound." *Works of Love, KW* 16.148–49; *SV* 12.145–46.

11. *Christian Discourses, KW* 17.200–201; *SV* 13.191. See also *Works of Love, KW* 16.130–32; *SV* 12.129–30. Again, see Kundera, *Unbearable Lightness of Being,* 5: "The heavier the burden, the closer our lives come to the earth, the more real and truthful they become."

12. Kierkegaard's word for "suffering" [*liden*] is a direct cognate of "passion" [*lidenskab*], and carries the Greek sense that a passion is something suffered rather than something done. Antigone, for instance, is not merely active but in a crucial sense acted upon: "Her pain is now increased by her love, by her sympathetic suffering with the one whom she loves." *Either/Or, KW* 3.164; *SV* 2.151.

13. In *Sickness Unto Death,* "Anti-Climacus" writes that "the formula for all despair" is "to will to be rid of oneself," that is, "to tear [the] self away from the power that established it." *KW* 19.20; *SV* 15.79. Elsewhere, Kierkegaard asks the "suffering" person: "Have you reflected upon what it means to despair? It means to deny that God is love!" *Purity of Heart Is to Will One Thing, KW* 15.101; *SV* 11.95.

14. See *Eighteen Upbuilding Discourses, KW* 5.301–7; *SV* 4.174–79. See also *Works of Love, KW* 16.175–78, 16.267–69; *SV* 12.170–73, 256–58. Cf. Fichte, "On the Foundation of Our Belief in a Divine Government of the Universe," 20–21.

15. *Eighteen Upbuilding Discourses, KW* 5.312–13; *SV* 4.278–79. In *Gospel of Sufferings,* this self-knowledge is more explicitly associated with the weighty and passionate task of taking up one's cross. *KW* 15.221–22, 252–57; *SV* 11.206–7, 234–39. Kierkegaard's belief that sacred love and meaningful suffering have shaped his own life is expressed in an 1848 journal entry: *JP* 5.6135; *PAP* VIII[1] A 650.

16. On the belief among rich "Christians" that material wealth is evidence of their favored status, see Nordentoft, *Kierkegaard's Psychology,* 254. Regarding what Weber calls the "theodicy of good fortune," see Hans Joas, *The Genesis of Values,* 29. In a journal entry from 1853, Kierkegaard discusses his former belief "that God expressed his love by sending earthly gifts, happiness, prosperity," and his later realization that "to love is to suffer." *JP* 6.6837; *PAP* X[5] A 72.

17. *Eighteen Upbuilding Discourses, KW* 5.314–17; *SV* 4.279–82. "Although I have the most inspired conception that God is love, I also have the conception that in time and temporality one must be prepared to suffer everything . . . [T]he point is to be receptive to the terrors." *KW* 11.613–14; *PAP* V B 119:3. Unpublished passage from 1844.

18. *Eighteen Upbuilding Discourses, KW* 5.321; *SV* 4.285–86. Kierkegaard is quoting Philippians 4:4.

19. *Eighteen Upbuilding Discourses, KW* 5.322–26; *SV* 4.286–89.

20. *Works of Love, KW* 16.41; *SV* 12.45 and *Christian Discourses,* 17.95–96; *SV* 13.95–96. Cf. *JP* 6.6895; *PAP* XI[1] A 382. On how someone who is "moved by God's love" consequently "takes care" in such a way that "his life will become suffering," see *JP* 1.538; *PAP* X[4] A 624.

21. Kierkegaard affirms that (a) God is love, (b) love is not itself an object, and (c) we can be God-like only as loving subjects. With regard to (a) and (c) see *Works of Love, KW* 16.62–63; *SV* 12.66. Regarding (b) see *Works of Love, KW* 16.182; *SV* 12.176. The equation between "to love God" and "to be loving," can be found in *Christian Discourses, KW* 17.130; *SV* 13.126. Unselfish love is not dependent upon its object, but it is not "proudly independent" of all objects either. As Kierkegaard says, it looks "down to earth" in order to love "the person one sees" in his or her contingency. See *Works of Love, KW* 16.66–67, 174; *SV* 12.70, 169.

22. On the question of whether the self should be affirmed or annihilated, and how this is answered in different religions, see the remarks about "Christianity and Selfhood" in Walter J. Ong, *Hopkins, the Self, and God,* 41–45. Because, for Kierkegaard, the "absolute significance" of the distinct individual is the "very principle" of

Christianity (*JP* 2.1997; *PAP* VIII[1] A 9), despair must be "a failure to face the challenge of realizing the inherent value of one's life." Alastair Hannay, "Kierkegaard and the Variety of Despair," 337.

23. For Kierkegaard it is not possible that a reverent person could avoid being involved in relationships, as it is for Epictetus: *Discourses* 3.22.69.

24. *Works of Love, KW* 16.383; *SV* 12.364. Cf. Levinas, *Ethics and Infinity,* 98; see also Epictetus, *Discourses* 1.15.5.

25. Schopenhauer, *World as Will and Representation,* 1:390. Of course, Schopenhauer's conclusion is that we should be relieved to be liberated from individuality. This is not simply because of the "sum total of misery, pain, and suffering" in life, but because individuality (according to Schopenhauer) is not the locus of significant truth but is fundamentally illusory. *Parerga and Paralipomena,* 2:156.

26. While Luther "turns Christianity upside down" by making it into a soothing reassurance, Schopenhauer (according to Kierkegaard) has the right notion of Christianity: *JP* 3.2550; *PAP* XI[1] A 193. Schopenhauer argues that Christianity is similar to Buddhism in denying life rather than affirming it. See, e.g., *Parerga and Paralipomena,* 2:156 and *The World as Will and Representation,* 2:584. This is why Kierkegaard makes reference to Schopenhauer in some of his late rants about how the human race ought to bring itself to extinction: see *JP* 4.3970, 4.4998; *PAP* XI[2] A 202, XI[1] A 141. Cf. *The Instant* (#7), *KW* 23.238–39; *SV* 19.228–29. In these life-hating writings from 1854–55, Kierkegaard frequently contradicts the religiousness he affirms in *Works of Love.* The ideal of realizing God's love by loving one's neighbor as oneself is suddenly replaced by such extreme claims as (a) God is hateful and must be loved as an object withdrawn from the world, and (b) one must hate oneself and everything in the world because God hates all things human. All of this may be of some biographical interest, but it is obviously at odds with the religiousness of Kierkegaard's earlier writings. On (a) see, e.g., *The Instant* (#5), *KW* 23.177; *SV* 19.171 and *JP* 3.2454; *PAP* XI[2] A 426. On (b) see, e.g., *JP* 6.6902; *PAP* XI[1] A 445 and *The Instant* (#9), *KW* 23.316; *SV* 19.298. Here, we are far from the vision of the cross as the symbol of total emotional involvement; instead, we find (what cannot be found in the bulk of Kierkegaard's work) an otherworldly religious vision in which "war is declared on life, nature, and the will to life; nonentity is deified, and the will to nonbeing declared holy." Nietzsche, *The Antichrist,* 22.

27. In *Works of Love,* Kierkegaard writes that a person "in whom the spirit has awakened does not as a consequence abandon the visible world," and adds that "the most dangerous of all escapes is wanting to love only the unseen." *KW* 16.209, 161; *SV* 12.203, 156. But the late Kierkegaard sometimes falls prey to the notion that a love which "flies over actuality completely" is loftier than a love which finds its expression in this world. Prior to the onset of his Manichaean period, Kierkegaard notes appreciatively that Augustine "crushes everything in order to rebuild it again" (*JP* 1.29; *PAP* I A 101). Toward the end, however, his own work shows little interest in rebuilding. In Kierkegaard's last writings, the Augustinian openness of *Works of Love* gives way to

an Augustinian fear of "being given to and for others" (Nussbaum, *Upheavals of Thought,* 610), along with the disdain toward flesh-and-blood persons that accompanies such a fear.

28. See *JP* 2.1399; *PAP* X² A 241, a journal entry which goes on to suggest that things of this world should be regarded as harmless but ultimately distracting playthings from which a child is weaned. See also *JP* 3.2888; *PAP* X⁴ A 260. Cf. Marcus Aurelius, *Meditations* 5.36. It is noteworthy that some of Kierkegaard's late apocalyptic writings explicitly conflate Stoicism and Christianity. See *JP* 2.1266; *PAP* X⁴ A 13 and *JP* 4.4518; *PAP* X⁵ A 63. Kierkegaard recognizes, most of the time, that the two schools are antithetical, however, he sometimes advises a *contemptus mundi* attitude. Similarly, Augustine denies the value of human life in favor of an unearthly future, demonstrating "a callous lack of love for neighbors . . . and an otherworldly hatred of all things temporal" (Gerald W. Schlabach, *For the Joy Set Before Us,* 101–2) which Hannah Arendt describes as "pseudo-Christian" since its "denial of human existence" makes neighborly love impossible (*Love and Saint Augustine,* 27–30). See *City of God* 12.1 and 22.22, *De Libero Arbitrio* 1.27, and *On the Good of Marriage* 10. The strain of unloving self-interested eschatology in some of Kierkegaard's own later works can be found, e.g., in *The Instant* (#2) and (#8), *KW* 23.121 and 21.304; *SV* 19.121 and 19.285. See also *JP* 3.2551, 4.3642, 4.4670, and 4.4940; *PAP* XI¹ A 297, X⁴ A 174, X⁴ A 158, and X⁵ A 41.

29. Mooney, *Knights of Faith,* 49. On the risk of being torn apart or "care-buried" as a consequence of loving, see also de Sousa, *Rationality of Emotion,* 231–32.

30. Nietzsche, *Genealogy of Morals,* first essay, §10.

31. Gouwens, *Kierkegaard as Religious Thinker,* 170. See also *JP* 1.307–8; *PAP* VIII¹ A 343–44.

32. Cf. Nietzsche, *Will to Power,* §2.

33. *Eighteen Upbuilding Discourses, KW* 5.43; *SV* 4.44–45.

34. "Highly emotional people perceive the events of their daily lives as . . . more significant than do those with less emotional sensitivity." Ben-Ze'ev, *Subtlety of Emotions,* 151. Compare: "At first sight, I perceived that he was a poet—if for no other reason I saw it in the fact that a situation that would have been taken easily in stride by a lesser mortal expanded into a world event for him." *Repetition, KW* 6.230; *SV* 5.194. See also Nietzsche, *Daybreak,* §142–§143.

35. As is suggested by Thorvaldsen's statues of the apostles in Vor Frue Kirke, some of whom hold the instruments of their martyrdom while making questioning gestures in the direction of Christ. Roger Poole gives a powerful commentary on these sculptures in *Kierkegaard: The Indirect Communication,* 236–41. Gouwens claims that "the problem that plagues [Kierkegaard] is how a person can survive the debilitating and numbing effects of suffering" without ceasing to believe. *Kierkegaard as Religious Thinker,* 164–66.

36. *Eighteen Upbuilding Discourses, KW* 5.94–95; *SV* 4.90–91.

37. See *JP* 1.741; *PAP* III A 195.

38. *Tess of the D'Urbervilles,* 98. Hardy wrote this novel immediately after studying Schopenhauer.

39. "Tess's Lament," in *Tess of the D'Urbervilles,* 487–88.

40. *Works of Love, KW* 16.300–301; *SV* 12.288–89.

41. Kierkegaard writes in an 1849 journal entry that "my life's significance corresponds precisely to my suffering." In other words, it has been so constitutive of who he is that it cannot be dismissed as something unfortunate that "he" might have avoided. See *PAP* X⁴ A 92. On the link between particular sufferings and the tragic sense of life in general, see also Hannay, "Kierkegaard and the Variety of Despair," 332, and Nordentoft, *Kierkegaard's Psychology,* 314.

42. John Kekes, *Moral Tradition and Individuality,* 224.

43. See, e.g., Job 1:1, 1:13–22, 2:1–8, 29:4. Kierkegaard's remarkable discourse on Job is located in *Eighteen Upbuilding Discourses, KW* 5.109–24; *SV* 4.103–16.

44. *Eighteen Upbuilding Discourses, KW* 5.118; *SV* 4.110. On the grounds for his resentment, see Job 6:1–2. At 3:1–3, he curses the day of his birth. He does not, however, "curse God and die," as his wife recommends (2:9–13), even after he is so disfigured by his affliction that even his "friends" do not recognize him.

45. *Gospel of Sufferings, KW* 15.264–68; *SV* 11.245–48.

46. The dangers of acting out a desperate refusal to acknowledge that we human beings are not omnipotent is one of the main themes of Ernest Becker's (largely Kierkegaardian) work in social anthropology. See, e.g., "Everyman as Pervert" and *Escape from Evil.*

47. *Repetition, KW* 6.197; *SV* 5.169. Modified translation. Cf. Job 1:22, 19:25–27.

48. See *Repetition, KW* 6.204–205, 208; *SV* 5.174–76, 177.

49. Job 1:20–21. See *Eighteen Upbuilding Discourses, KW* 5.109; *SV* 4.103.

50. *Eighteen Upbuilding Discourses, KW* 5.122; *SV* 4.114. Kierkegaard refers to 1 Corinthians 13:1. See also *Gospel of Sufferings, KW* 15.273–74; *SV* 11.253–54.

51. See *Eighteen Upbuilding Discourses, KW* 5.110–12; *SV* 4.104–6.

52. *Eighteen Upbuilding Discourses, KW* 5.119; *SV* 4.111–12.

53. *Eighteen Upbuilding Discourses, KW* 5.120; *SV* 4.112.

54. Job 1:20–21; see *Eighteen Upbuilding Discourses, KW* 5.121; *SV* 5.113.

55. *Eighteen Upbuilding Discourses, KW* 5.123–24; *SV* 4.115–16.

56. *Selves in Discord,* 32. See also Job 38:1–41:26.

57. Cf. Hall, *The Human Embrace,* 79. Kiekegaard says that the lover who doesn't realize that it is an honor to be in love, even if he must suffer because of his beloved, is not really loving at all. *KW* 12².136; *PAP* VII¹ B 88. The "individual passion of two lovers is just as inexplicable as is the quite special individuality of any person," Schopenhauer argues; "indeed, at bottom the two are one and the same." *World as Will and Representation,* 2:536.

58. See *Repetition, KW* 6.197; *SV* 5.169 and *Eighteen Upbuilding Discourses, KW* 5.119; *SV* 4.111. On the understandable fear that "it might just all be wrong," see *JP* 4.3999; *PAP* II A 584.

59. *Works of Love*, KW 16.5; *SV* 12.11.

60. *JP* 2.1401; *PAP* X² A 493. We are invited to place faith in love, Gary Starr Bowen points out, "even though there is no *objective* assurance either of the eternal love of God, or of the temporal love of the beloved." "Kierkegaard on the Theological Ethics of Love," 26.

61. Journal entry from 1848, *JP* 3.3746; *PAP* IX A 486. Mark C. Taylor discusses the sense in which the "humanistic atheist" does not realize that the death of God would mean "the death of the self" in *Erring: A Post-Modern A/Theology*, 20.

62. See, e.g., Schopenhauer, *The Fourfold Root of the Principle of Sufficient Reason*, 23, and Schelling, *Ages of the World*, 132–34.

63. Letters to Regine Olsen and P. M. Stilling. *Letters and Documents*, KW 25.64 and 25.338; *Breve og Aktstykker* 18 and 241. For Kierkegaard as for Marcus Aurelius, what is at issue is whether or not the individual is *cared for* (see, e.g., *JP* 3.3628; *PAP* VII¹ A 130). He suggests that to believe in providence is a matter of existential commitment rather than an empirical conclusion. See *JP* 2.1117; *PAP* VII¹ A 61. Cf. *Meditations* 9.28, 12.14.

64. *JP* 2.1449; *PAP* XI² 133. Hannay translation. See also *JP* 4.4901; *PAP* X⁴ A 613: "In the unconditioned all teleology vanishes." Cf. Arnold B. Come, "Kierkegaard's Ontology of Love," 96–98.

65. As Ortega points out. *On Love*, 189.

66. *Fear and Trembling*, KW 6.15; *SV* 5.17. Modified translation.

67. Camus, *Myth of Sisyphus*, 41.

68. See, e.g., *JP* 2.1254, 4.4554; *PAP* VIII¹ A 522, X² A 355.

69. Simone Weil, *Waiting for God*, 121. Cf. *Christian Discourses*, KW 17.196; *SV* 13.187. Christ was "led to the border, as it were, of justifiably mistrusting that God is indeed love, when he cried out: My God, my God, why have you abandoned me." But, Kierkegaard adds, none of us could genuinely endure this thought for long. *Gospel of Sufferings*, KW 15.270; *SV* 11.250.

70. See *JP* 3.2442; *PAP* X⁵ A 50. See also *Eighteen Upbuilding Discourses*, KW 5.71; *SV* 4.71: "Indeed, even if love has led a person astray, even if it cannot acquit him later, it will nevertheless say: Would I abandon you in the hour of need?"

71. *JP* 6.6884; *PAP* XI¹ A 215. Kierkegaard is making reference to Schopenhauer's remark that we are disappointed either by hope itself or by the attainment of the object that was hoped for. See *World as Will and Representation*, 2:573.

72. See, e.g., *Stages on Life's Way*, KW 11.374; *SV* 8.178: "The person who wills religiously must have receptivity precisely for the terrible." The more a person is moved by the eternal force of love, the more difficult her life in time is apt to become. See *JP* 2.1434; *PAP* X⁵ A 55. Cf. Nietzsche, *Will to Power*, §686. Schopenhauer points out that suffering "does not flow in upon us from outside, but everyone carries around within himself its perennial source." *World as Will and Representation*, 1:318.

73. *World as Will and Representation*, 2:579–80.

74. Cf. Malantschuk, *Kierkegaard's Thought*, 130.

75. See *Two Ages*, 14.74–75; *SV* 14.68–69. See also Scheler, *On the Eternal in Man*, 267–69. Cf. Ernest Becker, *Denial of Death*, 70–92.

76. See, e.g., *JP* 5.6135; *PAP* VIII¹ A 650. Lear argues that the fundamental restlessness of the human psyche "is not itself good or bad; indeed, it is not a principle of any teleological system. It exists *before good and evil*." *Happiness*, 89.

ELEVEN. Value on the Other Side of Nihilism

1. de Sousa, *Rationality of Emotion*, 329.

2. Cf. Seneca, *De Ira* 1.8, 2.13.

3. Cf. Augustine, *City of God* 14.7.

4. Sløk, *Kierkegaards Univers*, 46–47. Gouwens points out that Judge William "holds out to the aesthete a richer *emotional* life," and that the "religious" sphere of existence is also marked by a concern "with the emotional life." *Kierkegaard as Religious Thinker*, 86–87.

5. Gouwens, *Kierkegaard as Religious Thinker*, 202. Cf. Rudd, "'Believing All Things'," 123. On the Romantic mood of "axiomatic disillusionment," see Laura Quinney, *The Poetics of Disappointment*, 81.

6. *Either/Or*, *KW* 3.32–33; *SV* 2.35.

7. This latter passage, from an 1849 journal entry, refers to the one preceding (see note 6). *JP* 3.3608; *PAP* X¹ A 481. Modified translation. Cf. William James, *The Varieties of Religious Experience*, 73–74.

8. As Kierkegaard suggests. See *The Gospel of Sufferings*, *KW* 15.306; *SV* 11.282. Cf. Thoreau, *Walden*, 194: "I love to weigh, to settle, to gravitate toward that which most strongly and rightfully attracts me."

9. On the relation between love and wonder, see *JP* 2.1254; *PAP* VIII¹ A 522. See also Vacek, *Love, Human and Divine*, 6–7, 12. In spiritual matters, Kierkegaard writes, all *receptivity* also involves *productivity*. See *JP* 1.878; *PAP* II A 536. This is why a love potion is a conceptual impossibility (see Plotinus, *Enneads* 4.4.43): the mind must be receptive and assent to the emotion.

10. Kierkegaard writes in an 1843 journal entry that a religious disposition "is precisely a matter of being able to believe in God in small things . . . it is a matter of drawing God into the actualities of the world, where he certainly is, after all." *JP* 2.1108; *PAP* IV A 117.

11. *Works of Love*, *KW* 16.84; *SV* 12.86. See also *Works of Love*, *KW* 16.222–23; *SV* 12.215–16. In *JP* 1.432; *PAP* II A 250, Kierkegaard contrasts the symbolic meaning of the Greek cross, which signifies perfection in earthly development, with that of Roman cross, which symbolizes infinite, heavenly striving. My focus is on the "Greek" aspect of this disjunction. On the need to cultivate a heartfelt love of one another, see *JP* 3.2400; *PAP* IV B 148. Robert C. Solomon argues that justice requires that we "care about the well-being of *particular* other people." *A Passion for Justice*, 96.

12. *Works of Love, KW* 16.301; *SV* 12.289. Cf. *Works of Love, KW* 16.141; *SV* 12.138.

13. *Book on Adler, KW* 24.112–14; *PAP* VII² B 235:199–201. See also *JP* 1.896; *PAP* IV C 96, where Kierkegaard claims that "everything religious is passion." To live with a belief that love is sacred is, of course, to be religious in a different sense than "by virtue of living in geographical Christendom": Kierkegaard does not speak with the authority of one who says "follow me and you will be saved," but asks us to place our trust in a source of guidance that is manifest in every human psyche. Cf. Fromm, *The Art of Loving,* 64–65.

14. *Works of Love, KW* 16.32; *SV* 12.36. See also *Works of Love, KW* 16.384; *SV* 12.365.

15. *Purgatorio* 17.104–105. See also *Works of Love, KW* 16.166–67; *SV* 12.161.

16. See, e.g., *Book on Adler, KW* 24.108; *PAP* VII² B 235:195.

17. Michael Strawser, *Both/And,* 210. Cf. Augustine, *Confessions* 10.29; Dante, *Paradiso* 3.85. Bergson argues that the morality of the New Testament is that of the "open" soul, and is not consistent with "closed" morality. *Two Sources of Morality,* 59.

18. See, e.g., *JP* 2.1997; *PAP* VIII¹ A 9. On the "cares that make integrity possible and life worth living," see also Mooney, *Selves in Discord,* 73–74.

19. Hannay, *Kierkegaard,* 335. Cf. Lear, *Love and Its Place,* 12.

20. See Marcus Aurelius, *Meditations* 2.9 and 3.6, and Epictetus, *Discourses* 1.1.4–7, 2.8.12–13. On the relation between metaphysics and moral awareness in Stoic philosophy, see Long, *Epictetus,* 118–19. See also Diogenes Laertius 7.88, 138–49. John Rist suggests that, in Augustinian Christianity, love takes the place of "right reason" in Stoicism. *Augustine,* 168.

21. Epictetus, *Discourses* 4.1.41.

22. See *JP* 3.3579; *PAP* X⁴ A 663. See also Lear, *Love and Its Place,* 181–82.

23. Marcus Aurelius, *Meditations* 10.31, 12.24. Cf. Thomas Nagel, *The View from Nowhere,* 209–10.

24. The strategy of reducing things to absurdity is practiced with particular vigor by Marcus Aurelius. His way of denying the subjective "illusion" of significance involves mentally chopping things up into fragments, which no longer appear to be meaningful. So a purple robe can be depicted as a mere piece of wool dyed with blood, human life as nothing but sperm and ashes. See *Meditations* 6.13, 4.48. This scientific method is explicitly affirmed in, e.g., *Meditations* 7.29, 11.16. For a sympathetic reading of the "almost medical" scientism that can be found in Stoicism see Hadot, *Philosophy as a Way of Life,* 185–87.

25. Kallistos Ware, *The Orthodox Way,* 119; Schlabach, *For the Joy Set Before Us,* 53.

26. *JP* 2.2299; *PAP* IX A 438. Modified translation.

27. *Prolegomena to Charity,* 160. Cf. Simone Weil, *The Need for Roots,* 242: "Truth is the radiant manifestation of reality. . . . To desire truth is to desire direct contact with a piece of reality. To desire contact with a piece of reality is to love." On apathetic reason and "the consciousness that is aware of nothing," see *KW* 11.558; *PAP* V B 183:12.

28. Cf. Edward Collins Vacek, *Love, Human and Divine,* 44–47, and Bergson, *Two Sources of Morality,* 35–39.

29. This is from an 1849 journal entry which compares Socrates, who himself embodied his philosophical teachings, to the inhumanity of modern systematic philosophy. *JP* 6.6360; *PAP* X¹ A 146. See also David R. Law, *Kierkegaard as Negative Theologian,* 104.

30. See Plato, *Phaedrus* 244a, 256e, and *Apology* 31c–d. See also Xenophon, *Memorabilia* 1.1.5. The ancient debate between the Stoics, who admire Socrates for his anti-passionate ratiocination, and others who view him as a man of religious conviction, is recorded by Sextus Empiricus and Origen, among others. See *Against the Professors* 9.101 and *Contra Celsum* 3.66–67. I am with those who argue that "belief in a special, direct relation between himself and divine forces must be accepted in any account of [Socrates'] mentality which lays claim to completeness." W. K. C. Guthrie, *Socrates,* 84. Cf. Mark L. McPherran, *The Religion of Socrates,* 2–7. Dispassionate reason is not the basis of Socrates' firmest certainties; this is one reason for Kierkegaard's feeling of affinity with him. See, e.g., *PAP* X³ B 4 and compare Niels Jørgen Cappelørn, "The Retrospective Understanding of Søren Kierkegaard's Total Production," 19. See also *JP* 3.2341, 4.4847, 4.4886, 5.5100; *PAP* V A 74, IV A 42, XI¹ A 355, I A 75. On the dangerous fiction of a pure knowing subject, see Nietzsche, *Genealogy of Morals,* third essay, §12; compare Hegel, *Phenomenology of Spirit,* §217. The "musical thinking" that Hegel ridicules as less than rational would be decomposed into its notes by Marcus Aurelius (*Meditations* 11.2); however, it is this kind of emotional consciousness that constitutes and situates the self.

31. See J. L. Mackie, "The Subjectivity of Values," 111.

32. Cf. Anthony O'Hear, *The Element of Fire,* 16–19. Kathleen Raine, the Neoplatonist poet, writes that "the primary experience of perception is itself, in its kind and quality, determined by what [one] believes to be the qualitative nature of the things perceived." *Defending Ancient Springs,* 114.

33. See *JP* 3.3705; *PAP* IX A 365 and *KW* 3.497; *PAP* III B 185:2. Here, we are close to the idea that "our sense of reality, and the claims it makes on us, is inseparable from the creative imagination," such that apart from passionate embodiment there is no place on earth where we could feel at home. Charles Larmore, *The Romantic Legacy,* 8. The only other method of reconciliation would consist in denying the human need for meaning, as Lev Shestov ultimately does, criticizing Kierkegaard for embracing a notion of belief grounded in love instead of Luther's non-rational "faith alone." See, e.g., *Kierkegaard and the Existential Philosophy,* 127–38.

34. See *Book on Adler, KW* 24.19; *PAP* VII² B 235:18. See also *JP* 2.1177; *PAP* I A 88 and *Letters and Documents, KW* 25.62–63; *Breve og Aktstykker* 17. On the basis of moral awareness in the perception of value, see Vetlesen, *Perception, Empathy, and Judgment,* 137. The notion that "truth pertains to the individual person" is defended by Nishida Kitarō. *An Inquiry Into the Good,* 26.

35. See *Works of Love, KW* 16.234–35; *SV* 12.227 and *Philosophical Fragments, KW* 7.82; *SV* 6.75. On "rational" and passionate impressions, see Diogenes Laertius 7.51 and Sextus Empiricus, *Against the Professors* 7.247; see also Michael Frede, "Stoics and Skeptics on Clear and Distinct Impressions," 152–55. José Neto writes that "Kierkegaard's concept of belief is . . . similar to Sextus's concept of *dogma*," although he does not draw the same conclusions. *The Christianization of Pyrrhonism,* 74.

36. *Works of Love, KW* 16.5; *SV* 12.11. Cf. Mooney, *Knights of Faith,* 49. The suggestion that we ought to remain spectators and not participants is made by Epictetus in *Discourses* 1.6.19–20; he names *ataraxia* as a goal in 2.17.31. See also Anthony Rudd, "Kierkegaard and the Sceptics," 75–77, and Nordentoft, *Kierkegaard's Psychology,* 333–34.

37. *Works of Love, KW* 16.5–6; *SV* 12.11–12. The conviction that apathy is a way of deceiving oneself out of life sets Kierkegaard in opposition to appropriations of *apatheia* as a normative goal by such early Christian authors as Clement and Evagrius. See *Stromateis* 7.14 and *Praktikos* 34–36. Cf. Sorabji, *Emotion and Peace of Mind,* 385–99. Arendt and Scheler criticize this self-isolating (and anti–Christian) tendency. See *Love and Saint Augustine,* 41–42, and *Ressentiment,* 103.

38. Rhees adds that "if such a change does come, it is not because [one] sees any *reason* for it," for it "is a matter of being able to thank God for the world,—no matter what the world is like." See "Gratitude and Ingratitude for Existence," 162–64. See also Kundera, *Unbearable Lightness of Being,* 247: "The dispute between those who believe that the world was created by God and those who think it came into being of its own accord deals with phenomena that go beyond our reason and experience. Much more real is the line separating those who doubt being as it is granted to man (no matter how or by whom) from those who accept it without reservation."

39. *JP* 4.4555; *PAP* X² A 401. Hannay translation. On the sense in which love is an inexplicable fact which cannot be explained by any number of reasons, see Jerome Neu, "*Odi et Amo,*" 64–66, and Nussbaum, *Upheavals of Thought,* 123. Pierre Hadot writes that this "something more" in love corresponds to life in its deepest mystery. *Plotinus,* 50. The idea of perceiving objects in a way that is not governed by the principle of sufficient reason is discussed by both Schopenhauer and Heidegger. See, e.g., *World as Will and Representation,* 1:179, 1:483, and "The Principle of Reason," 126–27.

40. Since love is a kind of understanding, it is tragic to to be misunderstood in one's love, or by the beloved. See *JP* 1.118; *PAP* I A 33.

41. Diogenes Laertius 7.123. Advocates of "thick," unscientific description include a range of moral philosophers, from Paul Grice to Alphonso Lingis. See, e.g., *The Conception of Value,* 63 and *Dangerous Emotions,* 193. Cf. Mooney, *Selves in Discord,* 18.

42. Calhoun, "Subjectivity and Emotion," 207–8. See also Alison Jaggar, "Love and Knowledge," 157–60.

43. See, e.g., Plato, *Meno* 81a–84b, *Phaedo* 72e–77d; Epictetus, *Discourses* 2.18.19–22, 3.22.33. The following discussion is indebted to both John D. Caputo,

Radical Hermeneutics, 16–20, and Mooney, "*Repetition*," 295–96. Pseudo-Dionysius distinguishes eternity as "the home of being" from time as "the home of things that come to be" in *Divine Names* 10.3 [940a].

44. *Three Discourses on Imagined Occasions*, KW 10.52; SV 6.282. On the link between emotional discernment and ethical resolution see *Two Ages*, KW 14.22–24; SV 14.24–25 and *Either/Or*, KW 4.202; SV 3.290. See also Marino, *Kierkegaard in the Present Age*, 20–23.

45. *Johannes Climacus*, KW 7.118–19; PAP IV B 1:105–106.

46. *Repetition*, KW 6.131; SV 5.115. Modified translation. On the soul which attempts to sneak out of the body into the "wild blue yonder" of abstraction, see Kierkegaard's discussion of *Phaedo* 79a–80b and 114c in *Concept of Irony*, KW 2.73–74; SV 1.124–25.

47. Niels Nymann Eriksen, "Kierkegaard's Concept of Motion," 296; see also Eriksen, *Kierkegaard's Category of Repetition*, 12–14.

48. On the love that persists throughout the duration of time, see *Works of Love*, KW 16.132–33; SV 12.130–31. This is contrasted with the "love that flares up and is forgotten." *Purity of Heart Is to Will One Thing*, KW 15.101; SV 11.95. See also *Works of Love*, KW 16.37; SV 12.41.

49. JP 2.1587; PAP III A 1. Hannay translation. This passage echoes back to the Gilleleje journal of 1835, in which existentially relevant truth is described as that by virtue of which a person is "grafted into the divine": "What is truth but to live for an idea? When all is said and done, everything is based on a postulate; but not until it no longer stands outside [a person], not until he lives in it, does it cease to be a postulate for him." See JP 5.5100; PAP I A 75. In *Johannes Climacus*, Kierkegaard speaks again of consciousness as the medium in which the metaphysical and the contingent, or the ideal and the actual, come together in the instant of repetition: KW 7.171; PAP IV B 1:149–50.

50. On the ideal of a "sound and healthy love" which is opposed to a sentimental escape from the world see *Concept of Irony*, KW 2.329; SV 1.330–31. On a kind of truthfulness which is also a mode of being, see *Practice in Christianity*, KW 20.205–206; SV 16.192–93.

51. See, e.g., *Repetition*, KW 6.142–46; SV 5.125–29 (his plan to deceive "the girl"), KW 6.165–67; SV 5.145–47 (his voyeurism in the theater, mixed with a nostalgic remembrance of his nursemaid), KW 6.173–76; SV 5.151–54 (his disillusioned return from Berlin, and a moment of cosmic bliss), and KW 6.179–84; SV 5.155–59 (the chronicle of his complacency back home, where his observation is unruffled by the "inconveniences and disasters" of passion). See also Isak Holm, "Kierkegaard's Repetitions," 19–23, and Amy Laura Hall, *Kierkegaard and the Treachery of Love*, 91–100.

52. See, e.g., *Repetition*, KW 6.134–41; SV 5.117–24 (the young man's melancholy longing which leaps over reality altogether), KW 6.200–201; SV 5.171–72 (his desola-

tion and inability to realize the significance of his love), and *KW* 6.220–21; *SV* 5.185–86 (his self-contained rejuvenation in an eternal poetic idealism, upon learning of the girl's engagement to another). In an 1844 fragment, Kierkegaard suggests that the young man "advances further" toward the "religious category" of repetition. *PAP* IV A 169. See also Mackey, *Points of View*, 95, and Eriksen, *Kierkegaard's Category of Repetition*, 32–33.

53. The young man in *Repetition* bears a conspicuous resemblance to "A" in *Either/Or*. See, e.g., *KW* 3.32, 225; *SV* 2.35, 206. His attitude toward love is also similar to that of the "Young Man" in *Stages on Life's Way*, *KW* 11.32–38; *SV* 7.34–39.

54. Constantin's promise to continue believing in repetition is recorded in an unpublished letter written in his name in reply to Heiberg's review of *Repetition*. See *KW* 6.319; *PAP* IV B 117:300. Whether we ought to describe as non-metaphysical this new category, without which "all life dissolves into an empty, meaningless noise," is unclear: "Repetition is the *interest* of metaphysics," Constantin writes, playing upon *inter-esse*, "and also the interest upon which metaphysics comes to grief." *Repetition*, *KW* 6.149; *SV* 5.131. This could mean either that metaphysics would need to be changed in order to make room for a non-disinterested being-in-the-midst-of-things, or else that such a perspective is precisely what metaphysical thinking cannot accommodate.

55. *Works of Love*, *KW* 16.161; *SV* 12.156. Modified translation.

56. Robert Frost, "Birches," lines 53–54.

57. On the girl's "lovableness" see *Repetition*, *KW* 6.184; *SV* 5.160. This quotation is from a late draft of a nearby passage. See *KW* 6.277; *PAP* IV B 97:8. On the "romantic stage" of existence, in which "a question arises about a satisfaction lying beyond the world and which therefore cannot be found in the world," see *JP* 4.4398; *PAP* I C 126. At this stage, Kierkegaard adds, the life of the individual has not yet developed "a center of gravity within itself."

58. He is still attuned to the music of the sheres, as evidenced by his yearning for purity and for absolute satisfaction. But this is limited to the "dream world" that "glimmers in the background of the soul," not the real world in which being moved requires embracing vulnerability and change. See *Repetition*, *KW* 6.152; *SV* 5.133. When he claims that a religious individual "is composed within himself and rejects all the childish pranks of actuality" (*KW* 6.230; *SV* 5.193), Constantin exposes himself as a kind of Stoic who is indifferent to external contingency.

59. Harry G. Frankfurt, "Some Mysteries of Love," 8–10. Italics removed. Repetition is linked with a "higher" version of ethical disposition, an "acquired originality" which is different from habit. See, e.g., *Repetition* (*KW* 6.133; *SV* 5.116), *Concept of Anxiety* (*KW* 8.148–49; *SV* 6.228–29), and *JP* 3.3795; *PAP* V B 69. The "insight into objective values can be experienced as a personal invitation to act in the name of these values," Joas points out. *Genesis of Values*, 96. Note the discrepancy between a repetition in which things are renewed in their significance due to a shift in the perceiver and that which is said to alter "nothing in the object," only "something in the

mind which contemplates it." Gilles Deleuze, *Difference and Repetition*, 70–71. Cf. Alexander Nehemas, *Nietzsche*, 150: "Eternal recurrence is not a theory of the world, but a view of the self." In Kierkegaardian "repetition," things are renewed in their own significance when a person attains a "point of view from which the finite world *as a whole* is grasped as having a transcendental origin from which all value stems." Hannay, *Kierkegaard*, 69.

60. On repetition as the "passion of the absurd" see *Concept of Anxiety*, KW 8.17; SV 6.116. Cf. *JP* 1.10; *PAP* X⁶ B 79. See also Sebastian Gardner, *Irrationality and the Philosophy of Psychoanalysis*, 122, on the exemplary psychological state in which "past experience informs rational action."

61. *Repetition*, KW 6.146; SV 5.128.

62. *Repetition*, KW 6.229–30; SV 5.193. Lowrie translation.

63. *Repetition*, KW 6.200; SV 5.171.

64. See, e.g., KW 6.315; *PAP* IV B 117:296. On the difference between a passionate inspiration which is brought into a consistent view of life and that which simply runs amok, see *Book on Adler*, KW 24.19; *PAP* VII² B 235:18. Cf. Victor Kestenbaum, *The Phenomenological Sense of John Dewey*, 14: "Complete experience is an intensification of the field of time; the present is a dramatic overture to the future and fulfillment of the past."

65. See *Repetition*, KW 6.150–71; SV 5.132–50. After returning from his failed attempt to achieve repetition by going through the motions of an earlier experience, Constantin is taken to task by the first letter from the young man, who asks whether it is not "a kind of mental disorder" to subjugate every emotion to such dispassionate mastery. *Repetition*, KW 6.189; SV 5.163. On the "compulsion to repeat" in the pejorative sense, see Freud, *Civilization and its Discontents*, 46.

66. See *Stages on Life's Way*, KW 11.10–11; SV 7.15–16. On the ideal condition in which the self has its ground in the power that established it, see *Sickness Unto Death*, KW 19.14; SV 15.74. The "religious person" is described as being "continually in passion" in KW 11.646; *PAP* VI B 8.

67. Eriksen, "Kierkegaard's Concept of Motion," 32.

68. Gouwens, *Kierkegaard as Religious Thinker*, 76.

69. On the eternal power of love and the sense of possibility, see *Works of Love*, KW 16.252–53; SV 12.242–44. The awareness that one has certain "things to do" is predicated upon "the certainty that God is love". See *The Gospel of Sufferings*, KW 15.276–79; SV 11.256–59. On the role of imagination in "the development of the self with respect to knowing," see *Sickness Unto Death*, KW 19.31; SV 15.89. "Anti-Climacus" claims, in this passage, that "the intensity of this medium is the possibility of the intensity of the self."

70. See *Either/Or*, KW 4.216; SV 3.200–201. On whether there is something in the circumstances of life that, in a moral sense, *binds* us in the time being, see also *Stages on Life's Way*, KW 11.197–98; SV 8.21. Discussing *Antigone*, "A" writes that "one does not want to be so isolated" that one does not view "inherited characteristics as a

component of his truth." *Either/Or, KW* 3.160; *SV* 2.148. Heidegger speaks of a fate which one has inherited and yet chosen in *Being and Time*, §74.

71. See Epictetus, *Discourses* 1.12.15–17, and Marcus Aurelius, *Meditations* 10.21. See also Nietzsche, *Ecce Homo*, 16, 37–38. On the error of associating repetition in the human spirit with patterns of automatic recurrence in nature, see Kierkegaard's reply to Heiberg's review of *Repetition. KW* 6.306–11; *PAP* IV B 117. The notion of life as a meaningless sequence of events is also foreign to Kierkegaard's idea of repetition; but see, e.g., Nietzsche, *Will to Power*, §55, and Marcus Aurelius, *Meditations* 4.33–35. It is beyond the range of my concern to get into Nietzsche's doctrine of "eternal recurrence," the canonical description of which can be found in *The Gay Science*, §341. Suffice it to say that, if the Nietzschean affirmation is made with full awareness that suffering is not "a problem to be overcome," since it "results inevitably from the engagement with life" (Tyler T. Roberts, *Contesting Spirit*, 165–70), it is consistent with the Kierkegaardian conception of repetition. However, there seems to be a cosmological argument at the background of Nietzsche's discussion which is similar to naturalistic repetition as described in Stoic physics. See, e.g., Alexander of Aphrodisias, *On Aristotle's Prior Analytics* 180.33 (*LS* 52–F): the Stoics "hold that after the conflagration all of the same things recur in the world numerically, so that the same distinctively qualified individual as before exists and comes to be again in that world, as Chrysippus says in *On the Cosmos*."

72. On the oscillation between "awakening" and "composure" in the constitution of the person, see *JP* 2.2013; *PAP* IX B 63:8. See also *Concluding Unscientific Postscript, KW* 12¹.259–60; *SV* 9.217: "Inwardness in love does not consist in consummating seven marriages with Danish maidens, and then cutting loose on the French, the Italian, and so forth . . . [but] in loving one and the same woman, and yet being constantly renewed in the same love, making it always new in the luxuriant flowering of the mood." Swenson translation. Cf. *Repetition, KW* 6.132; *SV* 5.115–16: "One never grows weary of the old, and when one has that, one is happy." See also Sløk, "Kierkegaard as Existentialist," 461–63.

73. *Repetition, KW* 6.140; *SV* 5.123. See also *Book on Adler, KW* 24.287–88; *PAP* VII² B 235:161–62.

74. Malantschuk, *Kierkegaard's Thought*, 136. Regarding what follows, see also Proust, *Remembrance of Things Past*, 3:568, where Marcel incoherently concludes that his love for Albertine has been "less a love for her than a love in myself."

75. *Repetition, KW* 6.155; *SV* 5.136–37. Modified translation. Cf. José Ortega y Gasset, *The Revolt of the Masses*, 156–57: he uses the image of shipwreck for the situation of crisis in which the self clings to the convictions that will define its life. Hannay writes that the "idea" stands for whatever conception "motivates and guides theoretical and practical activity," enabling a person to see life itself, and his or her own participation in it, as meaningful. *Kierkegaard: A Biography*, 13–14.

76. See *KW* 6.302; *PAP* IV B 117 and *JP* 3.2348; *PAP* V C 6. For the image of "running aimlessly," see *Gospel of Sufferings, KW* 15.313; *SV* 11.288. The metaphor of being

carried away by passion like a runner in his or her forward momentum is used, for instance, in Seneca, *De Ira* 2.4 and *SVF* III 462.

77. *Sickness Unto Death, KW* 19.30; *SV* 15.87–88. See also *KW* 19.21; *SV* 15.80.

78. Sylviane Agacinski, "We Are Not Sublime," 145. She adds that love "does not treat the finite individuality to which it attends as if it were an absolute; it sustains and affirms its finitude through a tenderness which is as singular—as random and unfair—as existence itself."(146) Nonetheless, since the lover does in a sense give the beloved a space in which to be, "any threat to the possibility of existing in the space of empathy" becomes "a threat to the lover's being in an existential sense. Extended separation, or inability to establish empathy (as in arguments), or fear of loss of the other (as in jealousy), or worst of all an actual end to the relationship, will therefore precipitate existential anxiety in its most classic form." Ralph D. Ellis, *Eros in a Narcissistic Culture,* 70, 82.

79. See Nietzsche, *Human, All Too Human,* §51–§52. The idea that truthfulness is not achieved by volitional effort but by "learning to accept the realities of a sometimes tragic existence" is defended by M. Guy Thompson, who adds: "Pretending that a slight or disappointment isn't genuinely painful, or denying that we love someone whom we do, may culminate in a *complex* of denials strung together, each supporting the other, until we no longer know how we feel or what we believe." *The Truth about Freud's Technique,* 130–31.

80. "Anti-Climacus," *Practice in Christianity, KW* 20.189; *SV* 16.180. Unsettling are both the expansive factor and the concretion of moral involvement, that is, both the "anxious possibilty of *being able*" and the passionate realization that one "cannot do otherwise." *Concept of Anxiety, KW* 8.44; *SV* 6.138 and *Sickness Unto Death, KW* 19.126; *SV* 15.175. Kierkegaard talks about the uncertainties involved in venturing in reliance upon God, and explains why this is not to be confused with wishful thinking or rational planning, in *Judge for Yourself!, KW* 21.98–101; *SV* 17.133–35. Cf. Merleau-Ponty, *Phenomenology of Perception,* 453: "The world is already constituted, but also never completely constituted: in the first case we are acted upon, in the second we are open to an infinite number of possibilities."

81. Mackey, *Kierkegaard: A Kind of Poet,* 125.

82. *Works of Love, KW* 16.90; *SV* 12.91–92. Cf. Gouwens, *Kierkegaard as Religious Thinker,* 109–14.

83. Cf. Tyler T. Roberts, *Contesting Spirit,* 200: Religion can be defined "as a certain openness or responsiveness in which divinity is not so much encountered as realized."

84. See Schopenhauer, *Parerga and Paralipomena,* 2:172a. See also Clément Rosset, *Joyful Cruelty,* 15–19. Rosset writes: "Either joy consists of an ephemeral illusion of having gotten rid of the tragic nature of existence, in which case joy is not paradoxical but illusory, or it consists of an approbation of existence which is held to be irremediably tragic, in which case joy is paradoxical, but it is not illusory."(17) The

image of the dance is used to illustrate what it means to say that love abides in *Works of Love*, KW 16.307; SV 12.294.

85. From a journal entry dated April 1838. *JP* 1.1024; *PAP* II A 711. Hannay translation. In his final letter to Constantin, the "young man" uses a musical analogy for his feeling of emotional wholeness: "The discord in my nature is resolved, I am again unified." *Repetition*, KW 6.220; SV 5.185. Lowrie translation.

86. Mooney, *Selves in Discord*, 102.

87. Sullivan, *Beethoven*, 45, 78. Scott Burnham shows how the heroic notion of the self as realized in time is enacted by some of the music itself. *Beethoven Hero*, 118–22.

88. *Stages on Life's Way*, KW 11.236; SV 8.55. Religious trust is not the same as "knowing" what God intends. Compare Epictetus when he says to a sick person: "If I really knew that it was ordained for me to be ill right now, I would wish to be; just as the foot, if it had a mind, would aspire to be muddied." *Discourses* 2.6.10. This inhumanity in response to suffering is accompanied in Stoicism by a tendency to protest too much on the side of a divinity whose ends are always comprehensible to us. Of course, sickness and death are good for us; of course, bedbugs and rodents serve a purpose in the scheme of things; and so on. See, e.g., Epictetus, *Discourses*, 3.20.12. On the hypocrisy of knowing "how blessed it is to have a personal God," see *JP* 2.1437; *PAP* XI[1] A 35. Cf. *JP* 3.3020; *PAP* X[4] A 338.

89. Clifford Holt Ruprecht, *Language, Subjectivity and Absolute Possibility in Kierkegaard and Lacan*, 272.

90. Kierkegaard defines resignation as "the consciousness of the limitation that every effort must have." *JP* 2.1676; *PAP* I A 239. Cf. Lear, *Love and Its Place*, 160. On mourning and melancholia, see also Nordentoft, *Kierkegaard's Psychology*, 259–60.

91. This phrase is from an 1839 journal entry. *JP* 5.5368; *PAP* II A 347.

92. See, e.g., *Fear and Trembling* (KW 6.34; SV 5.32–33), *Stages on Life's Way* (KW 11.312–46; SV 8.122–53), and *Christian Discourses* (KW 17.129; SV 13.125). When Kierkegaard speaks in his own voice, the worry is less that love could misguide us (cf. Plato, *Symposium* 210a) than that *we* may fail to recognize and follow its directive (cf. Plotinus, *Enneads* 3.5.1). Amy Laura Hall writes of the "illusive, fragile overestimation of [the lovers'] ability each to make the other happy" and why it needs to be exposed: "It would be to invite yet another form of self-delusion" were we to think that accepting the command to love unselfishly would bring the unhappy lover "back to William's beautiful, enclosed garden." "Stages on the Wrong Way," 30–31, 45–46.

93. Even a person who is weary of sighing and on the verge of suicide (see Tobit 3:10) could still, perhaps, have the courage to love without expecting anything in return. *Works of Love*, KW 16.123; SV 12.122. Cf. Nietzsche's account of the soul that responds to the most painful losses with an increase in the blissfulness of its love (with reference to Dante, *Inferno* 3.4–6: "I, too, was created by eternal love"). *Will to Power*, §1030. With regard to the difficulties of living at the mercy of an eternal power, see also Hegel, *Phenomenology of Spirit*, §748–§753.

94. See *KW* 6.276–77, 320; *PAP* IV B 97, 118. Alluding to the biographical fact that Kierkegaard revised the work at the last minute after hearing of his ex-fiancée's new engagement, Poole comments: "*Repetition* becomes a Golden Bowl. . . . It is invisibly cracked, defeated by the decisive action of a young Danish girl who decided not to languish forever." *Kierkegaard: The Indirect Communication*, 79.

95. *Works of Love, KW* 16.132–33; *SV* 12.130–31.

96. *Concept of Irony, KW* 2.327; *SV* 1.329. Cf. *Works of Love, KW* 16.157; *SV* 12.152–53.

97. Mooney, *Knights of Faith*, 46. Gouwens agrees that the blighted ideal of "resignation" stands for a mode of existence in which the formative influence of emotion is not renounced entirely, and that it therefore should not be confused with "apathy." *Kierkegaard as Religious Thinker*, 111.

98. *JP* 2.1152; *PAP* XI² A 115. Kierkegaard's ethic of love does, I believe, recommend care for other living creatures, although this is a topic worthy of further discussion. The God who gives being to all things in their distinctiveness is the ground of existence for the lily of the field and the bird of the air, not merely for human beings. See *Works of Love, KW* 16.271; *SV* 12.260. See also *Without Authority, KW* 18.17–18; *SV* 14.141. In favor of the possibility of nonhuman "neighbors," Alastair Hannay writes: "*Works of Love* presents the Christian ideal of love of one's neighbour in the form of a generalized selflessness. Part of what emerges is that it is only by removing personal preferences that values inherent in other persons, but also in nature, can be truly acknowledged and allowed their fulfillment." "Søren Kierkegaard," 444.

99. See *Works of Love, KW* 16.90; *SV* 12.92–93 and *JP* 6.6824; *PAP* X⁴ A 673. The "romantic" is defined as "a continual grasping after something which eludes one" in *JP* 3.3816; *PAP* I A 306. The "profound woe and misery of the individual," on Schopenhauer's view, has to do with the fact that "the individual will" is "eternally insatiable." *Parerga and Paralipomena*, 2:145. Cf. Marcus Aurelius, *Meditations* 7.73–74; Epictetus, *Discourses* 1.22.18–19, 4.4.35.

100. *Selves in Discord*, 8. Kierkegaard writes that there exists "an eternal purpose" for each human being. *Purity of Heart Is to Will One Thing, KW* 15.93; *SV* 11.88. He also claims that everything Christian is a concretion of concern, and that what Christianity means is to follow one's primitivity. *JP* 1.773, 84; *PAP* III A 4, XI¹ A 385. Eriksen points out the connection between "authentic historicality" and "a 'happy' relation to the other" in *Kierkegaard's Category of Repetition*, 11.

101. Realizing "the distinctiveness of individuality" in one's own case is described as "the presupposition for loving" other human beings: *JP* 2.2003; *PAP* VIII¹ A 462. Since "to love people is the only thing worth living for," Kierkegaard says, we really should not need to be commanded to love; however, we must learn to love "unselfishly, freely, faithfully" by practicing a way of loving in which we seek nothing in return. *Works of Love, KW* 16.375, 358; *SV* 12.357, 341. Since the quest to secure one's own personal immortality turns love of neighbor into a means of attaining a selfish

end, the "absurd" Christian who lacks hope in a future life (Camus, *Myth of Sisyphus*, 112) may be in the best position to cultivate an other-regarding love without ulterior motives. The "religious" category of repetition is something other than hope: See *Repetition*, KW 6.131–32; SV 5.115 and JP 3.3794; *PAP* IV A 169. For a minimalistic conception of hope as a mode of patient responsiveness, see Gabriel Marcel, *Homo Viator*, 52–60.

102. Mass consensus assumes that "most people, the majority of people, are of the truth," but this is false: "if you have anything you call your conviction" then you should not expect help from the world. *Gospel of Sufferings*, KW 15.338–40; SV 11.293–94. It is dangerous to deify the crowd, when its significance is actually less than that of "the most insignificant individual human being." See *Sickness Unto Death*, KW 19.118; SV 15.168. In contrast with "Hegel's notion of the embodiment of spirit in the institutions of a civilized state," Kierkegaard traces social justice to the individual sense of value which is not derived from "the prescriptions of civic duty." Hannay, *Kierkegaard*, 51. Love of neighbor is intended to have political consequences, such as might be expected if we could replace the violence of mass passions with the loving perception of individual human beings. Cf. Lear, *Love and Its Place*, 200–202.

103. "Being an author is . . . not voluntary; on the contrary, it is in line with everything in my personality and its deepest urge." JP 5.5962; *PAP* VII[1] A 222. Hannay translation. "I also know with God that precisely my work as an author was the prompting of an irresistible inner need." *Point of View for My Work as an Author*, KW 22.24; SV 18.82. Sadly enough, *the world* is likely to view love's inspiring enthusiasm as madness, and the establishment "will not put up with" each person's relating himself or herself to a sacred power. See *Works of Love*, KW 16.185; SV 12.179–80 and *Practice in Christianity*, KW 20.91; SV 16.93. To live in accordance with the love that builds each person up from the ground is not merely to submit to the force of social conditioning: this is why spiritual compromise frequently leads to worldly success. See JP 1.613; *PAP* X[2] A 397 and *Sickness Unto Death*, KW 19.34; SV 15.91.

104. Here we are quite far from the idea that a person is merely a placeholder in the space of reasons, which itself confers meaning on the individual, just as the state might provide him or her with a license to drive. See Terry Pinkard, *Hegel's Phenomenology*, 7–8. Kierkegaard gives authority to the inward source of moral imperatives which are meant to be realized in the actual world. See JP 3.3628; *PAP* VII[1] A 130 and KW 19.159; *PAP* X[5] B 18. The love that flows from the heart and forms the heart can therefore be seen as what impels each human being toward an authentic appropriation of the inauthentic. Cf. Franz Rosenzweig, who interprets the commandment to love in Deuteronomy 6:5 as "the voice of love itself." *The Star of Redemption*, 176–77. On being attentive "not simply to the thoughts, values, hopes, and memories of the Other, but also to the Other's touch of madness," that is, to "the metaethical insistence at the heart of the personality," see Eric Santner, *The Psychotheology of Everyday Life*, 82–83.

TWELVE. Conclusion: The Tragicomedy of Passionate Existence

1. *JP* 2.2003; *PAP* VIII[1] A 462. In this 1847 journal entry, Kierkegaard goes on to say that "In this far deeper sense one sees the significance of the Hebraic expression—to know one's wife." See, e.g., Genesis 4:1.

2. Cf. Donna M. Orange, *Emotional Understanding*, 21. Stanley Cavell's remarks on skepticism are relevant to this discussion of a mode of knowing that requires love: "I cannot be more certain than I am of some beliefs, so that when I say I know, what I am expressing is . . . a different stance I take toward that certainty. . . . And if I refuse ever to take such steps, I am not being *cautious* but irresponsible or obsessional." *Themes Out of School*, 214.

3. See *Eighteen Upbuilding Discourses*, KW 5.59–60; SV 4.60–61 and *Works of Love*, KW 16.158–59; SV 12.153–54. See also Jean-Luc Marion, *Reduction and Givenness*, 190–92.

4. We must, as Helm says, "appeal to a kind of holism that rejects both the assumption that the world is ontologically prior to our cognitions and the assumption that our conations are ontologically prior to the world." *Emotional Reason*, 58.

5. Ferreira, *Love's Grateful Striving*, 104–107.

6. Schopenhauer, *World as Will and Representation*, 2:433–34.

7. Lines 9–12 of an untitled poem by Philip Larkin, "Sinking like sediment through the day." *Collected Poems*, 27.

8. Cf. Kundera, *Book of Laughter and Forgetting*, 86: "If there were too much incontestable meaning in the world (the angels' power), man would succumb under its weight. If the world were to lose all its meaning (the devils' reign), we could not live either."

9. See, e.g., Kafka, diary entry for 15 October 1913: "Perhaps I have caught hold of myself again . . . and now I, who already despair in loneliness, have pulled myself up again. But the headaches, the sleeplessness! Well, it is worth the struggle, *or rather, I have no choice.*" *Diaries: 1910–1923*, 231. My italics. David Wiggins suggests that "happiness" is less important in moral philosophy than the question of life's meaning. *Needs, Values, Truth*, 88.

10. See, e.g., *JP* 6.6166; *PAP* IX A 70 (on his melancholy and upbringing), *JP* 6.6385; *PAP* X[1] A 260 (on having felt obligated "to demolish an authentic love"), *JP* 5.5664; *PAP* IV A 107 (on realizing after the fact that there had been no religious grounds for rejecting this love and breaking his engagement), and *JP* 5.5962; *PAP* VII[1] A 222 (on the overwhelming and persistent creative imperative which must, "one would think," be a divine calling). Not only does Kierkegaard never question his love for Regine, but he even says that nothing is more certain than his love for her. See *PAP* III A 166, VIII[1] A 641.

11. In *JP* 5.5913; *PAP* VII[1] A 126, Kierkegaard presents himself as a tragic figure whose task in his work has been to offer guidance to those who, unlike himself, are still capable of attaining happiness. He laments his inability to let anyone become

"deeply and intimately attached" to him, and says that his melancholy would have made Regine unhappy in spite of his love for her. See *JP* 5.5517; *PAP* III A 161 and *JP* 6.6163; *PAP* IX A 67. Also worth noting in this regard is his ill-fated attempt to reconcile himself with his ex-fiancée in a way that would allow her to "realize her significance" to him. *JP* 6.6162, 6.6471–73; *PAP* IX A 66, X⁵ A 148–50. See also *PAP* X² A 83 and *Letters and Documents*, *KW* 25.322–37; *Breve og Aktstykker* 235–39.

12. On the proximity of tragedy and comedy, see *JP* 4.4823; *PAP* I A 34 and *Stages on Life's Way*, *KW* 11.420; *SV* 8.218–19.

13. See *Book on Adler*, *KW* 24.164; *PAP* VIII² B 12:55.

14. Kierkegaard envisions "a novel in which the main character would be a man who had obtained a pair of glasses, one lens of which reduced images as powerfully as an oxyhydrogen microscope and the other magnified on the same scale, so that he perceived everything relatively." *JP* 5.5281; *PAP* II A 203. This kind of relativism is not what emotional perception should be, as is shown by the fragment in which "A" says: "My observation of life makes no sense at all. I suppose that an evil spirit has put a pair of glasses on my nose, one lens of which magnifies on an immense scale and the other reduces on the same scale." *Either/Or*, *KW* 3.24; *SV* 2.28.

15. *Letters and Documents*, *KW* 25.62–63; *Breve og Aktstykker* 17 (to Regine Olsen). Under a line drawing of a figure who appears to be suspended in a volleyball net, Kierkegaard explains that it is in fact a picture of himself standing on a bridge and looking through a telescope: "This is Knipplesbro. I am that person with the spyglass. As you know, figures appearing in a landscape are apt to look somewhat curious. You may take comfort, therefore, in the fact that I do not look quite that ugly and that every artistic conception always retains something of the ideal, even in caricature. Several art experts have disagreed as to why the painter has not provided any background whatsoever. Some have thought this an allusion to a folk tale about a man who so completely lost himself in the enjoyment of the view from Knippelsbro that at last he saw nothing but the picture produced by his own soul, which he could just as well have been looking at in a dark room. Others have thought that it was because he lacked the perspective necessary for drawing—houses. But the spyglass itself has a unique characteristic about which tradition tells us the following: the outermost lens is of mirror glass so that when one trains it on *Trekroner* and stands on the left side of the bridge at an angle of 50° off Copenhagen, one sees something quite different from what is seen by all the other people about one; thus, in the midst of a friendly chat about the view of the ships, one sees or thinks one sees, or hopes to see, or wishes to see, or despairs of seeing that which the secret *genie* of the spyglass reveals to him who understands how to use it correctly. Only in the proper hands and for the proper eye is it a divine telegraph; for everybody else it is a useless contrivance."

BIBLIOGRAPHY

Works of Søren Kierkegaard in Danish

Søren Kierkegaards Skrifter, edited by N. J. Cappelørn et al. 4th ed. Copenhagen: Gads Forlag, 1997–. This edition has been consulted whenever possible; however, for the sake of uniformity, all citations have been made to one of the complete editions listed below.

Samlede Værker, edited by A. B. Drachmann et al. 3rd ed. Copenhagen: Gyldendal, 1961–64. Cited as *SV*.

Søren Kierkegaards Papirer, edited by Niels Thulstrup and N. J. Cappelørn. 2nd ed. Copenhagen: Gyldendal, 1968–78. All references to Kierkegaard's papers employ its standard numbering system. Cited as *PAP*.

Breve og Aktstykker vedrørende Søren Kierkegaard, edited by Niels Thulstrup. Copenhagen: Munksgaard, 1953–54. Cited as *Breve og Aktstykker*.

Works of Søren Kierkegaard in English Translation

Kierkegaard's Writings, edited by Howard V. Hong and Edna Hong. Princeton, NJ: Princeton University Press, 1978–2000. Contain selections from published and unpublished works. Below I list the main titles and translators for the volumes I have referenced from this edition. Cited as *KW*.

Vol. 1   *Early Polemical Writings: From the Papers of One Still Living* (Julia Watkin, 1990).

Vol. 2   *The Concept of Irony; Notes of Schelling's Berlin Lectures* (Hong and Hong, 1989).

Vol. 3   *Either/Or I* (Hong and Hong, 1987).

Vol. 4   *Either/Or II* (Hong and Hong, 1987).

Vol. 5   *Eighteen Upbuilding Discourses* (Hong and Hong, 1990).

Vol. 6   *Fear and Trembling; Repetition* (Hong and Hong, 1983).

Vol. 7   *Philosophical Fragments; Johannes Climacus* (Hong and Hong, 1985).

Vol. 8   *The Concept of Anxiety* (Reidar Thomte and Albert B. Anderson, 1980).

Vol. 10   *Three Discourses on Imagined Occasions* (Hong and Hong, 1993).

Vol. 11 *Stages on Life's Way* (Hong and Hong, 1988).
Vol. 12 *Concluding Unscientific Postscript*. 2 vols., 12^1 and 12^2 (Hong and Hong, 1992).
Vol. 14 *Two Ages* (Hong and Hong, 1978).
Vol. 15 *Upbuilding Discourses in Various Spirits* (Hong and Hong, 1993).
Vol. 16 *Works of Love* (Hong and Hong, 1995).
Vol. 17 *Christian Discourses; Crisis in the Life of an Actress* (Hong and Hong, 1997).
Vol. 18 *Without Authority: The Lily in the Field and the Bird of the Air* (Hong and Hong, 1997).
Vol. 19 *The Sickness Unto Death* (Hong and Hong, 1980).
Vol. 20 *Practice in Christianity* (Hong and Hong, 1991).
Vol. 21 *For Self-Examination; Judge for Yourself!* (Hong and Hong, 1990).
Vol. 22 *The Point of View for My Work as an Author* (Hong and Hong, 1998).
Vol. 23 *The Moment and Late Writings* (Hong and Hong, 1998).
Vol. 24 *The Book on Adler* (Hong and Hong, 1998).
Vol. 25 *Letters and Documents* (Henrik Rosenmeier, 1978).
Vol. 26 *Cumulative Index* (2000).

Journals and Papers. Edited and translated by Howard V. Hong and Edna Hong. 7 vols. Bloomington: Indiana University Press, 1967–78. Cited as *JP* by volume and entry number.

Unless otherwise indicated, English translations are from the standard editions above. Other English translations I have consulted include the following:

Attack Upon "Christendom" 1854–55. Translated by Walter Lowrie. Princeton, NJ: Princeton University Press, 1968.
The Book on Adler. Also known as *On Authority and Revelation*. Translated by Walter Lowrie. In one volume with *Fear and Trembling*. New York: Knopf, 1994.
The Concept of Dread. Translated by Walter Lowrie. Princeton, NJ: Princeton University Press, 1946.
Concluding Unscientific Postscript. Translated by David F. Swenson. Princeton, NJ: Princeton University Press, 1941.
Edifying Discourses. Translated by David F. Swenson and Lillian Swenson. Minneapolis: Augsburg, 1962.
Either/Or. Volume I translated by David F. Swenson and Lillian Swenson; Volume II translated by Walter Lowrie. Princeton, NJ: Princeton University Press, 1971.
Fear and Trembling. Translated by Alastair Hannay. New York: Penguin, 1985.
Papers and Journals: A Selection. Translated by Alastair Hannay. New York: Penguin, 1996.

Purity of Heart Is to Will One Thing. Translated by Douglas V. Steere. New York: Harper and Row, 1956.

Repetition. Translated by Walter Lowrie. Princeton, NJ: Princeton University Press, 1941.

The Sickness Unto Death. Translated by Walter Lowrie. Princeton, NJ: Princeton University Press, 1941.

Training in Christianity. Translated by Walter Lowrie. Princeton, NJ: Princeton University Press, 1941.

Works by Other Authors

Agacinski, Sylviane. "We Are Not Sublime." In *Kierkegaard: A Critical Reader,* edited by Jonathan Rée and Jane Chamberlain, 129–50. Oxford: Blackwell, 1998.

Allers, Rudolf. "The Cognitive Aspect of Emotions." *Thomist* 4 (1942): 589–648.

Annas, Julia. *The Morality of Happiness.* Oxford: Oxford University Press, 1993.

Arendt, Hannah. *Love and Saint Augustine.* Edited by Joanna V. Scott and Judith C. Stark. Chicago: University of Chicago Press, 1996.

Baron, Marcia W. *Kantian Ethics Almost without Apology.* Ithaca, NY: Cornell University Press, 1995.

Barth, John. *The End of the Road.* In one volume with *The Floating Opera.* New York: Doubleday, Anchor Books, 1988.

Basore, John W., trans. *Seneca: Moral Essays, Volume I.* Loeb Classical Library. Cambridge, MA: Harvard University Press, 1978.

Becker, Ernest. "Everyman as Pervert: An Essay on the Pathology of Normalcy." In *Angel in Armor: A Post-Freudian Perspective on the Nature of Man,* 1–38. New York: Free Press, 1969.

———. *The Birth and Death of Meaning.* 2nd ed. New York: Free Press, 1971.

———. *The Denial of Death.* New York: Free Press, 1973.

———. *Escape from Evil.* New York: Free Press, 1975.

Becker, Lawrence C. *A New Stoicism.* Princeton, NJ: Princeton University Press, 1998.

Ben-Ze'ev, Aaron. *The Subtlety of Emotions.* Cambridge, MA: MIT Press, 2000.

Bergmann, Frithjof. *On Being Free.* Notre Dame, IN: University of Notre Dame Press, 1977.

Bergson, Henri. *The Two Sources of Morality and Religion.* Translated by R. Ashley Audra and Cloudesley Brereton. Notre Dame, IN: University of Notre Dame Press, 1997.

Berthold-Bond, Daniel. "A Kierkegaardian Critique of Heidegger's Concept of Authenticity." *Man and World* 24 (1991): 119–42.

Blum, Lawrence. *Moral Perception and Particularity.* Cambridge: Cambridge University Press, 1994.

Bobzien, Susanne. *Determinism and Freedom in Stoic Philosophy*. Oxford: Clarendon Press, 1998.

Bollas, Christopher. *The Shadow of the Object: Psychoanalysis of the Unthought Known*. New York: Columbia University Press, 1987.

Bonhöffer, Adolf F. *The Ethics of the Stoic Epictetus*. Translated by William O. Stephens. New York: Peter Lang, 1996.

Bouquet, A. C. "Stoics and Buddhists." *Philosophical Quarterly* 33 (1961): 205–21.

Bowen, Gary Starr. "Kierkegaard and the Theological Ethics of Love." *Duke Divinity School Review* 43 (1980): 23–32.

Bowie, Andrew. *Aesthetics and Subjectivity: From Kant to Nietzsche*. Manchester: Manchester University Press, 1990.

Bowlby, John. *The Making and Breaking of Affectional Bonds*. London: Routledge, 1979.

Brentano, Franz. *Psychology from an Empirical Standpoint*. Translated by C. Rancurello, D. B. Terrell, and Linda McAlister. London: Routledge, 1995.

Brown, Norman O. *Life Against Death: The Psychoanalytic Meaning of History*. 2nd ed. Hanover, NH: Wesleyan University Press, 1959.

Burnham, Scott. *Beethoven Hero*. Princeton, NJ: Princeton University Press, 1995.

Byron, George Gordon. *Byron's Poetry*. Edited by Frank D. McConnell. New York: W. W. Norton, 1978.

Calhoun, Cheshire. "Subjectivity and Emotion." *Philosophical Forum* 20 (1989): 195–210.

Camus, Albert. *The Stranger*. Translated by Matthew Ward. New York: Vintage, 1989.

———. *The Myth of Sisyphus*. Translated by Justin O'Brien. New York: Vintage, 1991.

———. *The Fall*. Translated by Justin O'Brien. New York: Vintage, 1991.

———. *The Rebel*. Translated by Anthony Bower. New York: Vintage, 1991.

Cappelørn, Niels Jørgen. "The Retrospective Understanding of Søren Kierkegaard's Total Production." In *Kierkegaard: Resources and Results*, edited by Alastair McKinnon, 18–38. Montreal: Wilfrid Laurier University Press, 1982.

Caputo, John D. *Radical Hermeneutics*. Bloomington: Indiana University Press, 1987.

Carroll, Noël. "Art, Narrative, and Emotion." In *Emotion and the Arts*, edited by Mette Hjort and Sue Laver, 190–211. Oxford: Oxford University Press, 1997.

Catechism of the Catholic Church. Authorized English translation by the United States Catholic Conference. New York: Doubleday, Image Books, 1995.

Cather, Willa. *My Ántonia*. Boston: Mariner Books, 1995.

Catherine of Siena. *The Dialogue*. Translated by Suzanne Noffke. New York: Paulist Press, 1980.

Cavell, Stanley. *Themes Out of School*. Chicago: University of Chicago Press, 1988.

———. "Knowing and Acknowledging." In *The Cavell Reader*, edited by Stephen Mulhall, 46–71. Oxford: Blackwell, 1996.

———. *The Claim of Reason*. 2nd ed. with new preface. Oxford: Oxford University Press, 1999.

Cioran, E. M. *Drawn and Quartered*. Translated by Richard Howard. New York: Arcade, 1998.

Cohen, Ted. "Sports and Art: Beginning Questions." In *Human Agency*, edited by Jonathan Dancy et al., 258–73. Stanford: Stanford University Press, 1988.

Coleridge, Samuel Taylor. *Biographia Literaria*. Edited by Nigel Leask. London: Everyman, 1997.

Collins, James. *The Mind of Kierkegaard*. Princeton, NJ: Princeton University Press, 1983.

Come, Arnold B. "Kierkegaard's Ontology of Love." In *International Kierkegaard Commentary: Works of Love*, edited by Robert L. Perkins, 79–119. Macon, GA: Mercer University Press, 1999.

Conant, James. "Putting Two and Two Together: Kierkegaard, Wittgenstein, and the Point of View for their Work as Authors." In *Philosophy and the Grammar of Religious Belief*, edited by Timothy Tessin and Mario von der Ruhr, 248–331. New York: St. Martin's Press, 1995.

Connell, George. *To Be One Thing: Personal Unity in Kierkegaard's Thought*. Macon, GA: Mercer University Press, 1985.

———. "The Importance of Being Earnest: Coming to Terms with Judge William's Seriousness." In *International Kierkegaard Commentary: Stages on Life's Way*, edited by Robert L. Perkins, 113–48. Macon, GA: Mercer University Press, 2000.

Davenport, John J. "Towards an Existential Virtue Ethics: Kierkegaard and MacIntyre." In *Kierkegaard After MacIntyre*, edited by John J. Davenport and Anthony Rudd, 265–323. Chicago: Open Court, 2001.

Deigh, John. "Cognitivism in the Theory of Emotions." *Ethics* 104 (1994): 824–54.

———. "Empathy and Universalizability." *Ethics* 105 (1995): 743–63.

Deleuze, Gilles. *Difference and Repetition*. Translated by Paul Patton. New York: Columbia University Press, 1994.

Descartes, René. *Discourse on Method*. Translated by Donald Cress. Indianapolis: Hackett, 1993.

de Sousa, Ronald. *The Rationality of Emotion*. Cambridge, MA: MIT Press, 1987.

Deutsch, Eliot. *Creative Being: The Crafting of Person and World*. Honolulu: University of Hawaii Press, 1992.

Dewey, John. *Art as Experience*. New York: Perigee, 1980.

Dickstein, Morris. *Keats and His Poetry: A Study in Development*. Chicago: University of Chicago Press, 1971.

Diderot, Denis. *Rameau's Nephew*. Translated by Jacques Barzun and Ralph H. Bowen. Indianapolis: Hackett, 2001.

Dostoevsky, Fyodor. *Crime and Punishment*. Translated by Constance Garnett. New York: Bantam, 1987.

———. *Notes from Underground*. Translated by Richard Pevear and Larissa Volokhonsky. New York: Vintage, 1993.

———. *A Gentle Creature and Other Stories*. Translated by Alan Myers. Oxford: Oxford University Press, 1995.

Dreyfus, Hubert L. "Could Anything Be More Intelligible than Everyday Intelligibility?" In *Appropriating Heidegger*, edited by James Faulconer and Mark Wrathall, 155–74. Cambridge: Cambridge University Press, 2000.

Dreyfus, Hubert L., and Jane Rubin. "Kierkegaard on the Nihilism of the Present Age: The Case of Commitment as Addiction." *Synthese* 98 (1994): 3–19.

Dylan, Bob. *Lyrics: 1962–1985*. New York: Knopf, 1985.

Eliot, T. S. "Shakespeare and the Stoicism of Seneca." In *Selected Essays*, 107–20. New York: Harcourt, Brace and Co., 1950.

———. "Hamlet." In *Selected Prose of T. S. Eliot*, edited by Frank Kermode, 45–49. New York: Harcourt Brace Jovanovich, 1975.

Ellis, Ralph D. *Eros in a Narcissistic Culture*. Dordrecht: Kluwer, 1996.

Ellsworth, Jonathan. "Apophasis and Askēsis: Contemporary Philosophy and Mystical Theology." In *Rethinking Philosophy of Religion*, edited by Philip Goodchild, 212–27. New York: Fordham University Press, 2002.

Elrod, John W. "Passion, Reflection, and Particularity." In *International Kierkegaard Commentary: Two Ages*, edited by Robert L. Perkins, 1–18. Macon, GA: Mercer University Press, 1984.

Elster, Jon. *Alchemies of the Mind: Rationality and the Emotions*. Cambridge: Cambridge University Press, 1999.

Emerson, Ralph Waldo. "Self-Reliance." In *Essays: First and Second Series*, 23–48. New York: Gramercy, 1993.

Eriksen, Niels Nymann. "Kierkegaard's Concept of Motion." In *Kierkegaard Studies Yearbook 1998*, edited by Niels Jørgen Cappelørn and Hermann Deuser, 292–301. Berlin: Walter de Gruyter, 1998.

———. *Kierkegaard's Category of Repetition: A Reconstruction*. Berlin: Walter de Gruyter, 2000.

———. "Love and Sacrifice in *Repetition*." In *Kierkegaard Studies Yearbook 2002*, edited by Niels Jørgen Cappelørn, Hermann Deuser, and Jon Stewart, 26–35. Berlin: Walter de Gruyter, 2002.

Evans, C. Stephen. *Existentialism: The Philosophy of Despair and the Quest for Hope*. 3rd ed. Dallas: Probe Books, 1984.

———. *Passionate Reason: Making Sense of Kierkegaard's* Philosophical Fragments. Bloomington: Indiana University Press, 1992.

Evans, Dylan. *Emotion: The Science of Sentiment*. Oxford: Oxford University Press, 2001.

Ferreira, M. Jamie. *Transforming Vision: Imagination and Will in Kierkegaardian Faith*. Oxford: Clarendon Press, 1991.

———. *Love's Grateful Striving: A Commentary on Kierkegaard's* Works of Love. Oxford: Oxford University Press, 2001.

Fichte, J. G. *The Vocation of Man*. Translated by Peter Preuss. Indianapolis: Hackett, 1987.
———. "On the Foundation of Our Belief in a Divine Government of the Universe." Translated by Paul Edwards. In *Nineteenth-Century Philosophy*, edited by Forrest E. Baird and Walter Kaufmann, 17–23. Upper Saddle River, NJ: Prentice-Hall, 1997.
Findlay, J. N. *Axiological Ethics*. London: Macmillan, 1970.
Forster, Michael. *Hegel's Idea of a Phenomenology of Spirit*. Chicago: University of Chicago Press, 1998.
Fortenbaugh, W. W. *Aristotle on Emotion*. New York: Barnes and Noble, 1975.
Foucault, Michel. *Ethics: Subjectivity and Truth*. Edited by Paul Rabinow. New York: New Press, 1997.
Fox, Michael V. *A Time to Tear Down and a Time to Build Up: A Rereading of Ecclesiastes*. Grand Rapids, MI: Eerdmans, 1999.
Frankfurt, Harry G. *The Importance of What We Care About*. Cambridge: Cambridge University Press, 1988.
———. *Necessity, Volition, and Love*. Cambridge: Cambridge University Press, 1999.
———. "Some Mysteries of Love." Lindley Lecture 2000, University of Kansas.
Frede, Michael. "The Stoic Doctrine of the Affections of the Soul." In *The Norms of Nature*, edited by Malcolm Schofield and Gisela Striker, 93–110. Cambridge: Cambridge University Press, 1986.
———. "Stoics and Skeptics on Clear and Distinct Impressions." In *Essays in Ancient Philosophy*, 151–76. Minneapolis: University of Minnesota Press, 1987.
Freud, Sigmund. *The Interpretation of Dreams*. Translated by James Strachey. New York: Basic Books, 1955.
———. *Group Psychology and the Analysis of the Ego*. Translated by James Strachey. New York: W. W. Norton, 1959.
———. *Civilization and Its Discontents*. Translated by James Strachey. New York: W. W. Norton, 1961.
———. *Beyond the Pleasure Principle*. Translated by James Strachey. New York: W. W. Norton, 1961.
Fromm, Erich. *The Art of Loving*. New York: Harper and Row, 1989.
Frost, Robert. *The Poetry of Robert Frost*. Edited by Edward Connery Lathem. New York: Henry Holt, 1969.
Furtak, Rick Anthony. "Poetics of Sentimentality." *Philosophy and Literature* 26 (2002): 207–15.
Gandhi, M. K. *The Sayings of Mahātma Gandhi*. Edited by Peter Burgess. Singapore: Brash, 1984.
Gardner, Sebastian. *Irrationality and the Philosophy of Psychoanalysis*. Cambridge: Cambridge University Press, 1993.

German, Terence J. *Hamann on Language and Religion*. Oxford: Oxford University Press, 1981.

Goldman, Alvin I. *Epistemology and Cognition*. Cambridge, MA: Harvard University Press, 1986.

Gordon, Robert M. *The Structure of Emotions: Investigations in Cognitive Philosophy*. Cambridge: Cambridge University Press, 1987.

Gould, Josiah B. *The Philosophy of Chrysippus*. Albany: SUNY Press, 1970.

Gouwens, David J. *Kierkegaard as Religious Thinker*. Cambridge: Cambridge University Press, 1996.

Graham, George. "Melancholic Epistemology." *Synthese* 82 (1990): 399–422.

Graver, Margaret. "Philo of Alexandria and the Origins of the Stoic *Propatheiai*." *Phronesis* 44 (1999): 300–325.

Green, Ronald M. *Kierkegaard and Kant: The Hidden Debt*. Albany: SUNY Press, 1992.

Greenspan, Patricia S. *Emotions and Reasons: An Inquiry into Emotional Justification*. New York: Routledge, 1988.

Grégoire, Franz. "Is the Hegelian State Totalitarian?" In *The Hegel Myths and Legends*, edited by Jon Stewart, 104–108. Evanston: Northwestern University Press, 1996.

———. "A Semi-Legend: The 'Divinity' of the State in Hegel." In *The Hegel Myths and Legends*, edited by Jon Stewart, 289–300. Evanston: Northwestern University Press, 1996.

Grice, Paul. *The Conception of Value*. Oxford: Clarendon Press, 1991.

Guroian, Vigen. *Incarnate Love: Essays in Orthodox Ethics*. Notre Dame, IN: University of Notre Dame Press, 1987.

Guthrie, W. K. C. *Socrates*. Cambridge: Cambridge University Press, 1972.

Hadas, Moses. *The Stoic Philosophy of Seneca*. New York: W. W. Norton, 1958.

Hadot, Pierre. *Plotinus*. Translated by Michael Chase. Chicago: University of Chicago Press, 1993.

———. *Philosophy as a Way of Life: Spiritual Exercises from Socrates to Foucault*. Edited by Arnold I. Davidson. Translated by Michael Chase. Oxford: Blackwell, 1995.

———. *The Inner Citadel: The "Meditations" of Marcus Aurelius*. Translated by Michael Chase. Cambridge, MA: Harvard University Press, 1998.

Haines, C. R., trans. *The Correspondence of Marcus Cornelius Fronto, Volume I*. Loeb Classical Library Cambridge, MA: Harvard University Press, 1919.

Hall, Amy Laura. "Stages on the Wrong Way: Love and the Other in Kierkegaard's *Stages on Life's Way* and *Works of Love*." In *International Kierkegaard Commentary: Stages on Life's Way*, edited by Robert L. Perkins, 9–47. Macon, GA: Mercer University Press, 2000.

———. *Kierkegaard and the Treachery of Love*. Cambridge: Cambridge University Press, 2002.

Hall, David L. *Richard Rorty: Poet and Prophet of the New Pragmatism*. Albany: SUNY Press, 1994.

Hall, Ronald L. *The Human Embrace: The Love of Philosophy and the Philosophy of Love*. University Park, PA: Penn State Press, 2000.

Hamann, J. G. "Aesthetica in Nuce." In *J. G. Hamann: A Study in Christian Existence, with Selections from His Writings,* edited and translated by Ronald Gregor Smith, 195–200. London: Collins, 1960.

Hannay, Alastair. *Kierkegaard*. London: Routledge, 1982.

———. "Søren Kierkegaard" In *The Oxford Companion to Philosophy,* edited by Ted Honderich, 442–45. New York: Oxford University Press, 1995.

———. "The Dialectic of Proximity and Apartness." In *Closeness: An Ethics,* edited by Harold Jodalen and Arne Johan Vetlesen, 167–84. Oslo: Scandinavian University Press, 1997.

———. "Kierkegaard and the Variety of Despair." In *The Cambridge Companion to Kierkegaard,* edited by Alastair Hannay and Gordon D. Marino, 329–48. Cambridge: Cambridge University Press, 1998.

———. "Kierkegaard and What We Mean By 'Philosophy'." *International Journal of Philosophical Studies* 8 (2000): 1–22.

———. *Kierkegaard: A Biography*. Cambridge: Cambridge University Press, 2001.

Hardy, Thomas. *Tess of the D'Urbervilles*. New York: Penguin, 1998.

Hare, R. M. "Nothing Matters: Is 'the Annihilation of Values' Something That Could Happen?" In *The Meaning of Life,* edited by E. D. Klemke, 241–47. Oxford: Oxford University Press, 1981.

Hegel, G. W. F. *Early Theological Writings*. Translated by T. M. Knox. Philadelphia: University of Pennsylvania Press, 1971.

———. *Aesthetics: Lectures on Fine Art*. Translated by T. M. Knox. 2 vols. Oxford: Oxford University Press, 1975.

———. *Phenomenology of Spirit*. Translated by A. V. Miller. Oxford: Oxford University Press, 1977.

———. *Lectures on the Philosophy of Religion*. Translated by P. Hodgson. 3 vols. Berkeley and Los Angeles: University of California Press, 1984. Cited as "1984 edition."

———. *Lectures on the Philosophy of Religion*. Translated by P. Hodgson. One-volume edition. Berkeley and Los Angeles: University of California Press, 1988. Cited as "1988 edition."

———. *Introduction to the Philosophy of History*. Translated by Leo Rauch. Indianapolis: Hackett, 1988.

———. *The Encyclopedia Logic*. Translated by Geraets, Suchting, and Harris. Indianapolis: Hackett, 1991.

———. *Philosophy of Right*. Translated by S. W. Dyde. Amherst, NY: Prometheus, 1996.

Heidegger, Martin. "The Principle of Reason." In *The Principle of Reason,* translated by Reginald Lilly, 117–29. Bloomington: Indiana University Press, 1991.

———. *Being and Time*. Translated by Joan Stambaugh. Albany: SUNY Press, 1996.

————. *Phenomenological Interpretations of Aristotle.* Translated by Richard Roj-cewicz. Bloomington: Indiana University Press, 2001.

Helm, Bennett W. *Emotional Reason: Deliberation, Motivation, and the Nature of Value.* Cambridge: Cambridge University Press, 2001.

Heyde, Ludwig. *The Weight of Finitude: On the Philosophical Question of God.* Translated by A. Harmsen and W. Desmond. Albany: SUNY Press, 1995.

Hillman, James. *Emotion: A Comprehensive Phenomenology of Theories and Their Meanings for Therapy.* Evanston: Northwestern University Press, 1992.

Holm, Isak W. "Kierkegaard's Repetitions." *Kierkegaardiana* 15 (1991): 15–27.

Huntington, Patricia J. "Heidegger's Reading of Kierkegaard Revisited." In *Kierkegaard in Post/Modernity,* edited by Martin J. Matuštík and Merold Westphal, 43–65. Bloomington: Indiana University Press, 1995.

Husserl, Edmund. *The Crisis of European Sciences and Transcendental Phenomenology.* Translated by David Carr. Evanston: Northwestern University Press, 1970.

Hutcheson, Francis. "Reflections Upon Laughter." In *The Philosophy of Laughter and Humor,* edited by John Morreall, 26–40. Albany: SUNY Press, 1987.

Ignatius of Loyola. *Spiritual Exercises.* In *Spiritual Exercises and Selected Works,* edited by George E. Ganss, 113–214. New York: Paulist Press, 1991.

Inwood, Brad. *Ethics and Human Action in Early Stoicism.* Oxford: Clarendon Press, 1985.

Jaggar, Alison M. "Love and Knowledge: Emotion in Feminist Epistemology." In *Gender/Body/Knowledge: Feminist Reconstructions of Being and Knowing,* edited by Alison M. Jaggar and Susan R. Bordo, 145–71. New Brunswick, NJ: Rutgers University Press, 1989.

James, Henry. "The Beast in the Jungle." In *Tales of Henry James,* selected and edited by Christof Wegelin, 277–312. New York: W. W. Norton, 1984.

James, William. *The Varieties of Religious Experience.* New York: Vintage, 1990.

Jankélévitch, Vladimir. *Le Sérieux de L'Intention.* Volume 1 of *Traité des Vertus.* Paris: Flammarion, 1983.

————. *Les Vertus et L'Amour.* 2 vols. Volume 2 of *Traité des Vertus.* Paris: Flammarion, 1986.

Jefferson, Mark. "What Is Wrong with Sentimentality?" *Mind* 92 (1983): 519–29.

Jegstrup, Elsebet. "Text and the Performative Act." *Philosophy Today* 45 (2001): 121–31.

Joas, Hans. *The Genesis of Values.* Translated by Gregory Moore. Chicago: University of Chicago Press, 2000.

Johansen, Karsten Friis. "Kierkegaard on 'The Tragic'." *Danish Yearbook of Philosophy* 13 (1976): 105–46.

Johnson, Rolf M. *Three Faces of Love.* DeKalb: Northern Illinois University Press, 2001.

Joyce, James. *A Portrait of the Artist as a Young Man.* New York: Penguin, 1993.

Jung, C. G. *Psychology and Religion.* New Haven: Yale University Press, 1938.

————. "Thoughts on the Interpretation of Christianity." In *The Zofinga Lectures,* translated by Jan van Heurck, 93–111. Princeton, NJ: Princeton University Press, 1983.

———. *Freud and Psychoanalysis*. Translated by R. F. C. Hull. Princeton, NJ: Princeton University Press, 1985.

Kafka, Franz. *Diaries: 1910–1923*. Edited by Max Brod. New York: Schocken Books, 1964.

Kant, Immanuel. *Critique of Judgment*. Translated by Werner S. Pluhar. Indianapolis: Hackett, 1987.

———. *The Metaphysics of Morals*. Translated and edited by Mary Gregor. Cambridge: Cambridge University Press, 1996.

———. *Dreams of a Spirit-Seer*. Translated by Emmanuel F. Goerwitz. Bristol, UK: Thoemmes Press, 1998.

Keats, John. *Letters of John Keats*. Edited by Robert Gittings. Oxford: Oxford University Press, 1970.

Kekes, John. *Moral Tradition and Individuality*. Princeton, NJ: Princeton University Press, 1989.

Kenny, Anthony. *Action, Emotion and Will*. London: Routledge and Kegan Paul, 1963.

Kestenbaum, Victor. *The Phenomenological Sense of John Dewey: Habit and Meaning*. Atlantic Highlands, NJ: Humanities Press, 1977.

Kirmmse, Bruce H. *Kierkegaard in Golden Age Denmark*. Bloomington: Indiana University Press, 1990.

Knappe, Ulrich. "Kant's and Kierkegaard's Conception of Ethics." In *Kierkegaard Studies Yearbook 2002*, edited by Niels Jørgen Cappelørn, Hermann Deuser, and Jon Stewart, 188–202. Berlin: Walter de Gruyter, 2002.

Kramer, Peter D. *Listening to Prozac*. New York: Viking, 1993.

Kundera, Milan. *The Unbearable Lightness of Being*. Translated by Michael Henry Heim. New York: HarperPerennial, 1991.

———. *The Book of Laughter and Forgetting*. Translated by Aaron Asher. New York: Perennial Classics, 1999.

———. *Immortality*. Translated by Peter Kussi. New York: Perennial Classics, 1999.

Langan, Thomas. *Being and Truth*. Columbia: University of Missouri Press, 1996.

Larkin, Philip. *Collected Poems*. Edited by Anthony Thwaite. New York: Noonday, 1993.

Larmore, Charles. *The Romantic Legacy*. New York: Columbia University Press, 1996.

Law, David R. *Kierkegaard as Negative Theologian*. Oxford: Clarendon Press, 1993.

Lear, Jonathan. *Love and Its Place in Nature: A Philosophical Interpretation of Freudian Psychoanalysis*. 2nd ed. with new preface. New Haven: Yale University Press, 1998.

———. *Open Minded: Working Out the Logic of the Soul*. Cambridge, MA: Harvard University Press, 1998.

———. *Happiness, Death, and the Remainder of Life*. Cambridge, MA: Harvard University Press, 2000.

LeDoux, Joseph. *The Emotional Brain: The Mysterious Underpinnings of Emotional Life*. New York: Simon and Schuster, 1996.

Levin, David Michael. *The Body's Recollection of Being: Phenomenological Psychology and the Deconstruction of Nihilism*. London: Routledge and Kegan Paul, 1985.

————. *The Opening of Vision: Nihilism and the Postmodern Situation*. New York: Routledge, 1988.

Levinas, Emmanuel. *Ethics and Infinity*. Translated by Richard A. Cohen. Pittsburgh: Duquesne University Press, 1985.

Lingis, Alphonso. *The Imperative*. Bloomington: Indiana University Press, 1998.

————. *Dangerous Emotions*. Berkeley and Los Angeles: University of California Press, 2000.

Lippitt, John. "Illusion and Satire in Kierkegaard's *Postscript*." *Continental Philosophy Review* 32 (1999): 451–66.

Loewald, Hans W. *The Essential Loewald: Collected Papers and Monographs*. Introduction by Jonathan Lear. Hagerstown, MD: University Publishing Group, 2000.

Long, A. A., "The Logical Basis of Stoic Ethics." *Proceedings of the Aristotelian Society* 71 (1971): 85–104.

————. *Epictetus: A Stoic and Socratic Guide to Life*. Oxford: Clarendon Press, 2002.

Long, A. A. and D. N. Sedley. *The Hellenistic Philosophers*. 2 vols. Cambridge: Cambridge University Press, 1987. Cited as *LS*.

Lowrie, Walter. *Kierkegaard*. 2 vols. Oxford: Oxford University Press, 1938.

Luther, Martin. *The Large Catechism*. Translated by Robert H. Fischer. Philadelphia: Fortress Press, 1959.

Lyons, William. *Emotion*. Cambridge: Cambridge University Press, 1980.

MacIntyre, Alasdair. *After Virtue*. 2nd ed. Notre Dame, IN: University of Notre Dame Press, 1984.

————. *Whose Justice? Which Rationality?* Notre Dame, IN: University of Notre Dame Press, 1988.

————. *A Short History of Ethics*. 2nd ed. with new preface. Notre Dame, IN: University of Notre Dame Press, 1998.

Mackey, Louis. *Kierkegaard: A Kind of Poet*. Philadelphia: University of Pennsylvania Press, 1971.

————. *Points of View: Readings of Kierkegaard*. Tallahassee, FL: Florida State University Press, 1986.

Mackie, J. L. "The Subjectivity of Values." In *Essays in Moral Realism,* edited by Geoffrey Sayre-McCord, 95–118. Ithaca, NY: Cornell University Press, 1988.

Magee, Bryan. *The Philosophy of Schopenhauer*. Rev. ed. New York: Oxford University Press, 1997.

Malantschuk, Gregor. *Kierkegaard's Thought*. Edited and translated by Howard V. Hong and Edna Hong. Princeton, NJ: Princeton University Press, 1971.

Marcel, Gabriel. *Homo Viator*. Translated by Emma Crawford. New York: Harper, 1962.

Marino, Gordon. *Kierkegaard in the Present Age*. Milwaukee: Marquette University Press, 2001.

Marion, Jean-Luc. *God Without Being*. Translated by Thomas A. Carlson. Chicago: University of Chicago Press, 1991.

————. *Reduction and Givenness.* Translated by Thomas A. Carlson. Evanston: Northwestern University Press, 1998.

————. *Prolegomena to Charity.* Translated by Stephen E. Lewis. New York: Fordham University Press, 2002.

Mates, Benson. *Stoic Logic.* Berkeley and Los Angeles: University of California Press, 1953.

McPherran, Mark L. *The Religion of Socrates.* University Park, PA: Penn State Press, 1999.

Merleau-Ponty, Maurice. *Phenomenology of Perception.* Translated by Colin Smith. New York: Routledge and Kegan Paul, 1962.

Miyawaki, Edison. "Emotional Man." *Yale Review* 88, no. 4 (2000): 143–57.

Mooney, Edward. *Knights of Faith and Resignation.* Albany: SUNY Press, 1991.

————. *Selves in Discord and Resolve.* New York: Routledge, 1996.

————. "*Repetition:* Getting the World Back." In *The Cambridge Companion to Kierkegaard,* edited by Alastair Hannay and Gordon D. Marino, 282–307. Cambridge: Cambridge University Press, 1998.

Moore, Kathleen Dean. "The Testimony of the Marsh." In *Holdfast: At Home in the Natural World,* 19–23. New York: Lyons Press, 1999.

Mortensen, Klaus P. "The Demons of Self-Reflection: Kierkegaard and Danish Romanticism." In *Kierkegaard Revisited,* edited by Niels Jørgen Cappelørn and Jon Stewart, 442–59. Berlin: Walter de Gruyter, 1997.

Murdoch, Iris. *The Sovereignty of Good.* London: Routledge, 1970.

————. *Existentialists and Mystics: Writings on Philosophy and Literature.* New York: Penguin, 1999.

Musil, Robert. *The Man Without Qualities.* Translated by Sophie Wilkins. 2 vols. New York: Vintage, 1996.

Nagel, Thomas. *The View from Nowhere.* Oxford: Oxford University Press, 1986.

Nehemas, Alexander. *Nietzsche: Life as Literature.* Cambridge, MA: Harvard University Press, 1985.

Neto, José. *The Christianization of Pyrrhonism: Skepticism and Faith in Pascal, Kierkegaard, and Shestov.* Dordrecht: Kluwer, 1995.

Neu, Jerome. "*Odi et Amo*: On Hating the Ones We Love." In *Freud and the Passions,* edited by John O'Neill, 53–72. University Park, PA: Penn State Press, 1996.

Nicholas of Cusa. "On the Vision of God." In *Selected Spiritual Writings,* translated by H. Lawrence Bond, 233–89. New York: Paulist Press, 1997.

Nietzsche, Friedrich. *The Will to Power.* Translated by Walter Kaufmann and R. J. Hollingdale. New York: Vintage, 1968.

————. *On the Genealogy of Morals.* Translated by Walter Kaufmann and R. J. Hollingdale. In one volume together with *Ecce Homo.* New York: Vintage, 1969.

————. *The Gay Science.* Translated by Walter Kaufmann. New York: Vintage, 1974.

————. *Human, All Too Human.* Translated by R. J. Hollingdale. Cambridge: Cambridge University Press, 1986.

————. *Ecce Homo.* Translated by R. J. Hollingdale. New York: Penguin, 1992.

————. *Daybreak.* Translated by R. J. Hollingdale. Cambridge: Cambridge University Press, 1997.

————. *Twilight of the Idols.* Translated by Richard Polt. Indianapolis: Hackett, 1997.

————. *The Antichrist.* Translated by Anthony M. Ludovici. Amherst, NY: Prometheus Books, 2000.

Nishida Kitarō. *An Inquiry Into the Good.* Translated by Masao Abe and Christopher Ives. New Haven: Yale University Press, 1990.

Noddings, Nel. *Caring: A Feminine Approach to Ethics and Moral Education.* Berkeley and Los Angeles: University of California Press, 1984.

Nordentoft, Kresten. *Kierkegaard's Psychology.* Translated by Bruce H. Kirmmse. Pittsburgh: Duquesne University Press, 1978.

————. "Erotic Love." In *Kierkegaard and Human Values,* edited by Niels Thulstrup and M. M. Thulstrup, 87–99. Copenhagen: C. A. Reitzels, 1980.

Nussbaum, Martha. *The Fragility of Goodness: Luck and Ethics in Greek Tragedy and Philosophy.* Cambridge: Cambridge University Press, 1986.

————. *Love's Knowledge: Essays on Philosophy and Literature.* Oxford: Oxford University Press, 1990.

————. *The Therapy of Desire: Theory and Practice in Hellenistic Ethics.* Princeton, NJ: Princeton University Press, 1994.

————. *Upheavals of Thought: The Intelligence of Emotions.* Cambridge: Cambridge University Press, 2001.

Nygren, Anders. *Agape and Eros.* Translated by Philip S. Watson. New York: Harper and Row, 1969.

O'Hear, Anthony. *The Element of Fire: Science, Art, and the Human World.* London: Routledge, 1988.

O'Meara, Dominic J. *Plotinus.* Oxford: Clarendon Press, 1993.

Ong, Walter J., S.J. *Hopkins, the Self, and God.* Toronto: University of Toronto Press, 1986.

Orange, Donna M. *Emotional Understanding: Studies in Psychoanalytic Epistemology.* New York: Guilford Press, 1995.

Ortega y Gasset, José. *The Revolt of the Masses.* New York: W. W. Norton, 1932.

————. *On Love: Aspects of a Single Theme.* Translated by Tony Talbot. New York: Meridian, 1957.

Osborne, Catherine. *Eros Unveiled: Plato and the God of Love.* Oxford: Clarendon Press, 1994.

Pattison, George. *Kierkegaard: The Aesthetic and the Religious.* New York: St. Martin's Press, 1992.

Peperzak, Adriaan T. *Reason in Faith: On the Relevance of Christian Spirituality for Philosophy.* New York: Paulist Press, 1999.

Perkins, Robert L. "Kierkegaard, a Kind of Epistemologist." *History of European Ideas* 12 (1990): 7–18.

————. "Either/Or/Or: Giving the Parson His Due." In *International Kierkegaard Commentary: Either/Or II,* edited by Robert L. Perkins, 207–31. Macon, GA: Mercer University Press, 1995.

————. "Woman-Bashing in Kierkegaard's 'In Vino Veritas': A Reinscription of Plato's *Symposium."* In *Feminist Interpretations of Søren Kierkegaard,* edited by Céline Léon and Sylvia Walsh, 83–102. University Park, PA: Penn State Press, 1997.

Pico della Mirandola, Giovanni. *On the Dignity of Man.* Translated by Charles Glenn Wallis. Indianapolis: Hackett, 1998.

Pinkard, Terry. *Hegel's Phenomenology: The Sociality of Reason.* Cambridge: Cambridge University Press, 1996.

Pippin, Robert B. *Henry James and Modern Moral Life.* Cambridge: Cambridge University Press, 2000.

Poole, Roger. *Kierkegaard: The Indirect Communication.* Charlottesville: University Press of Virginia, 1993.

————. "The Unknown Kierkegaard: Twentieth-Century Receptions." In *The Cambridge Companion to Kierkegaard,* edited by Alastair Hannay and Gordon D. Marino, 48–75. Cambridge: Cambridge University Press, 1998.

Porter, James I. "The Philosophy of Aristo of Chios." In *The Cynics,* edited by R. Bracht Branham and Marie-Odile Goulet-Cazé, 156–89. Berkeley and Los Angeles: University of California Press, 1996.

Price, A. W. "Plato, Zeno, and the Object of Love." In *The Sleep of Reason: Erotic Experience and Sexual Ethics in Ancient Greece and Rome,* edited by Martha C. Nussbaum and Juha Sihvola, 170–99. Chicago: University of Chicago Press, 2002.

Proust, Marcel. *Remembrance of Things Past.* Translated by C. K. Scott Moncrieff, Terence Kilmartin, and Andreas Mayor. 3 vols. New York: Vintage, 1982.

Quinney, Laura. *The Poetics of Disappointment.* Charlottesville: University Press of Virginia, 1999.

Radhakrishnan, Sarvepalli. *An Idealist Way of Life.* 2nd ed. London: Unwin Paperbacks, 1980.

Raine, Kathleen. *Defending Ancient Springs.* New York: Oxford University Press, 1967.

Rescher, Nicholas. *The Coherence Theory of Truth.* Washington, DC: University Press of America, 1982.

————. *Ethical Idealism: An Inquiry into the Nature and Function of Ideals.* Berkeley and Los Angeles: University of California Press, 1987.

————. "Optimalism and Axiological Metaphysics." *Review of Metaphysics* 53 (2000): 791–805.

Rhees, Rush. "Gratitude and Ingratitude for Existence." In *Rush Rhees on Religion and Philosophy,* edited by D. Z. Phillips, 159–65. Cambridge: Cambridge University Press, 1997.

Ricoeur, Paul. *Freedom and Nature: The Voluntary and the Involuntary.* Translated by Erazim Kohák. Evanston: Northwestern University Press, 1966.

————. *Time and Narrative.* Translated by Kathleen McLaughlin and David Pellauer. 3 vols. Chicago: University of Chicago Press, 1985.

Rilke, Rainer Maria. *The Notebooks of Malte Laurids Brigge.* Translated by M. D. Herter Norton. New York: W. W. Norton, 1949.

————. *Letters to a Young Poet.* Translated by Stephen Mitchell. New York: Vintage, 1986.

————. *Diaries of a Young Poet.* Translated by Edward Snow and Michael Winkler. New York: W. W. Norton, 1997.

————. *Die Sonette an Orpheus.* Frankfurt: Insel, 1999. The two sonnets cited as epigraphs are my own translation from the German.

Rist, John M. *Augustine: Ancient Thought Baptized.* Cambridge: Cambridge University Press, 1994.

Roberts, Robert C. "Passion and Reflection." In *International Kierkegaard Commentary: Two Ages,* edited by Robert L. Perkins, 87–106. Macon, GA: Mercer University Press, 1984.

————. "The Socratic Knowledge of God." In *International Kierkegaard Commentary: The Concept of Anxiety,* edited by Robert L. Perkins, 133–52. Macon, GA: Mercer University Press, 1985.

————. "What an Emotion Is: A Sketch." *Philosophical Review* 97 (1988): 183–209.

————. "Existence, Emotion, and Virtue: Classical Themes in Kierkegaard." In *The Cambridge Companion to Kierkegaard,* edited by Alastair Hannay and Gordon D. Marino, 177–206. Cambridge: Cambridge University Press, 1998.

————. *Emotions: An Essay in Aid of Moral Psychology.* Cambridge: Cambridge University Press, 2003.

Roberts, Tyler T. *Contesting Spirit: Nietzsche, Affirmation, Religion.* Princeton, NJ: Princeton University Press, 1998.

Rorty, Richard. *Contingency, Irony, and Solidarity.* Cambridge: Cambridge University Press, 1989.

————. "Cultural Politics and the Question of the Existence of God." In *Radical Interpretation in Religion,* edited by Nancy K. Frankenberry, 53–77. Cambridge: Cambridge University Press, 2002.

Rosenmeyer, Thomas G. *Senecan Drama and Stoic Cosmology.* Berkeley and Los Angeles: University of California Press, 1989.

Rosenzweig, Franz. *The Star of Redemption.* Translated by William Hallo. Notre Dame, IN: University of Notre Dame Press, 1985.

Rosset, Clément. *Joyful Cruelty: Toward a Philosophy of the Real.* Translated by David F. Bell. Oxford: Oxford University Press, 1993.

Rudd, Anthony. *Kierkegaard and the Limits of the Ethical.* Oxford: Clarendon Press, 1993.

————. "Kierkegaard and the Sceptics." *British Journal for the History of Philosophy* 6 (1998): 71–88.

―――. "'Believing All Things': Kierkegaard on Knowledge, Doubt, and Love." In *International Kierkegaard Commentary: Works of Love,* edited by Robert L. Perkins, 121–36. Macon, GA: Mercer University Press, 1999.

Ruprecht, Clifford Holt. *Language, Subjectivity, and Absolute Possibility in Kierkegaard and Lacan.* PhD diss., University of Chicago Divinity School, 1995.

Salinger, J. D. *The Catcher in the Rye.* Boston: Little, Brown, 1951.

Sandbach, F. H. *The Stoics.* 2nd ed. Indianapolis, IN: Hackett, 1989.

Santner, Eric L. *On the Psychotheology of Everyday Life.* Chicago: University of Chicago Press, 2001.

Sartre, Jean-Paul. *The Emotions: Outline of a Theory.* Translated by Bernard Frechtman. New York: Citadel Press, 1993.

Scheler, Max. *On the Eternal in Man.* Translated by Bernard Noble. Hamden, CT: Archon Books, 1972.

―――. "*Ordo Amoris.*" In *Selected Philosophical Essays,* translated by David R. Lachterman, 98–135. Evanston: Northwestern University Press, 1973.

―――. *Formalism in Ethics and Non-Formal Ethics of Values.* Translated by Manfred S. Frings and Roger L. Funk. Evanston: Northwestern University Press, 1973.

―――. *Ressentiment.* Translated by Lewis B. Coser and William Holdheim. Milwaukee, WI: Marquette University Press, 1994.

Schelling, F. W. J. *Bruno; or, On the Natural and the Divine Principle of Things.* Translated by Michael Vater. Albany: SUNY Press, 1984.

―――. *Ages of the World.* Translated by Judith Norman. In one volume with *The Abyss of Freedom* by Slavoj Zizek. Ann Arbor: University of Michigan Press, 1997.

Schlabach, Gerald W. *For the Joy Set Before Us: Augustine and Self-Denying Love.* Notre Dame, IN: University of Notre Dame Press, 2001.

Schofield, Malcolm. *The Stoic Idea of the City.* Chicago: University of Chicago Press, 1999.

Schopenhauer, Arthur. *The World as Will and Representation.* Translated by E. F. J. Payne. 2 vols. Indian Hills, CO: Falcon's Wing Press, 1958.

―――. *Parerga and Paralipomena.* Translated by E. F. J. Payne. 2 vols. Oxford: Clarendon Press, 1974.

―――. *On the Fourfold Root of the Principle of Sufficient Reason.* Translated by E. F. J. Payne. LaSalle, IL: Open Court, 1974.

―――. *The Wisdom of Life.* In one volume with *Counsels and Maxims.* [From *Parerga and Paralipomena.*] Translated by T. Bailey Saunders. Amherst, NY: Prometheus, 1995.

Scopetea, Sophia. *Kierkegaard og græciteten.* Copenhagen: C. A. Reitzels, 1995.

Scruton, Roger. *Art and Imagination: A Study in the Philosophy of Mind.* London: Methuen, 1974.

————. *Sexual Desire: A Moral Philosophy of the Erotic*. New York: Free Press, 1986.

Shelton, Mark. "The Morality of Peace: Kant and Hegel on the Grounds for Ethical Ideals." *Review of Metaphysics* 54 (2000): 379–408.

Sherman, Nancy. *The Fabric of Character*. Oxford: Clarendon Press, 1989.

————. *Making a Necessity of Virtue: Aristotle and Kant on Virtue*. Cambridge: Cambridge University Press, 1997.

Shestov, Lev. *Kierkegaard and the Existential Philosophy*. Athens: Ohio University Press, 1971.

Singer, Irving. *Meaning in Life: The Creation of Value*. New York: Free Press, 1992.

Sløk, Johannes. "Kierkegaard as Existentialist." Translated by B. H. Mayoh. In *Contemporary Philosophy in Scandinavia*, edited by Raymond E. Olson and Anthony M. Paul, 457–63. Baltimore: Johns Hopkins University Press, 1972.

————. *Kierkegaards Univers*. 2nd ed. Viborg, DK: Centrum, 1996.

Slote, Michael. *From Morality to Virtue*. Oxford: Oxford University Press, 1992.

Smilansky, Saul. *Free Will and Illusion*. Oxford: Clarendon Press, 2001.

Smith, Adam. *The Theory of Moral Sentiments*. Edited by D. D. Raphael and A. L. Macfie. Oxford: Oxford University Press, 1976.

Smyth, John Vignaux. *A Question of Eros: Irony in Sterne, Kierkegaard, and Barthes*. Tallahassee: Florida State University Press, 1986.

Solomon, Robert C. *In the Spirit of Hegel: A Study of G. W. F. Hegel's* Phenomenology of Spirit. New York: Oxford University Press, 1983.

————. *The Passions: Emotions and the Meaning of Life*. 2nd ed. with new preface. Indianapolis: Hackett, 1993.

————. *About Love: Reinventing Romance for Our Times*. Lanham, MD: Rowman and Littlefield, 1994.

————. *A Passion for Justice*. Lanham, MD: Rowman and Littlefield, 1995.

Søltoft, Pia. "Love and Continuity: The Significance of Intersubjectivity in the Second Part of *Either/Or*." Translated by M. G. Piety. In *Kierkegaard Studies Yearbook 1997*, edited by Niels Jørgen Cappelørn and Hermann Deuser, 210–27. Berlin: Walter de Gruyter, 1997.

Sorabji, Richard. *Emotion and Peace of Mind: From Stoic Agitation to Christian Temptation*. Oxford: Oxford University Press, 2000.

Spinoza, Baruch. *Ethics*. Translated by Samuel Shirley. Indianapolis: Hackett, 1992.

Stack, George J. "Kierkegaard and Romantic Aestheticism." *Philosophy Today* 14 (1970): 57–74.

Stanislavski, Constantin. *An Actor Prepares*. Translated by E. R. Hapgood. New York: Routledge / Theatre Arts, 1936.

Stephens, William O. "Epictetus on How the Stoic Sage Loves." *Oxford Studies in Ancient Philosophy* 14 (1996): 193–210.

Stewart, Jon. *Kierkegaard's Relations to Hegel Reconsidered*. Cambridge: Cambridge University Press, 2003.

Stocker, Michael, with Elizabeth Hegeman. *Valuing Emotions*. Cambridge: Cambridge University Press, 1996.

Stoppard, Tom. *Rosencrantz and Guildenstern Are Dead*. New York: Grove Weidenfeld, 1967.

Strawser, Michael. *Both/And: Reading Kierkegaard from Irony to Edification*. New York: Fordham University Press, 1997.

Sullivan, J. W. N. *Beethoven: His Spiritual Development*. New York: Vintage, 1960.

Tanner, Michael. "Sentimentality." *Proceedings of the Aristotelian Society* 77 (1977): 127–47.

Taylor, Mark C. *Kierkegaard's Pseudonymous Authorship: A Study of Time and the Self*. Princeton, NJ: Princeton University Press, 1975.

———. "Love and Forms of Spirit: Kierkegaard vs. Hegel." *Kierkegaardiana* 10 (1977): 95–116.

———. *Erring: A Postmodern A/Theology*. Chicago: University of Chicago Press, 1984.

Tennemann, W. G. *A Manual of the History of Philosophy*. Translated by Arthur Johnson. Oxford: D. A. Talboys, 1832.

Thompson, M. Guy. *The Truth about Freud's Technique: The Encounter With the Real*. New York: New York University Press, 1994.

Thoreau, Henry David. *Walden; or, Life in the Woods*. Philadelphia: Running Press, 1987.

———. "A Plea for Captain John Brown." In *Civil Disobedience and Other Essays*, edited by Philip Smith, 31–48. New York: Dover, 1993.

Thulstrup, Niels. *Kierkegaard's Relation to Hegel*. Translated by George L. Stengren. Princeton, NJ: Princeton University Press, 1980.

Tracy, David. *On Naming the Present: God, Hermeneutics, and Church*. Maryknoll, NY: Orbis Books, 1994.

Trilling, Lionel. *Sincerity and Authenticity*. Cambridge, MA: Harvard University Press, 1971.

Unamuno, Miguel de. *The Tragic Sense of Life*. Translated by J. E. Crawford Flitch. New York: Dover, 1954.

Vacek, Edward Collins, S.J. *Love, Human and Divine: The Heart of Christian Ethics*. Washington, DC: Georgetown University Press, 1994.

Valone, James J. *The Ethics and Existentialism of Kierkegaard: Outlines for a Philosophy of Life*. Lanham, MD: University Press of America, 1983.

van Heerden, Adriaan. "Does Love Cure the Tragic?: Kierkegaardian Variations on a Platonic Theme." In *International Kierkegaard Commentary: Stages on Life's Way*, edited by Robert L. Perkins, 69–90. Macon, GA: Mercer University Press, 2000.

Vetlesen, Arne Johan. *Perception, Empathy, and Judgment: An Inquiry into the Preconditions of Moral Performance*. University Park, PA: Penn State Press, 1994.

Vlastos, Gregory. "The Individual as Object of Love in Plato." In *Platonic Studies*, 3–34. Princeton, NJ: Princeton University Press, 1981.

Vogel, Lawrence. *The Fragile "We": Ethical Implications of Heidegger's* Being and Time. Evanston: Northwestern University Press, 1994.

von Arnim, Hans, ed. *Stoicorum Veterum Fragmentas.* 3 vols. plus index. Leipzig: Teubner, 1903–05. Cited 25 *JVF.*

Wahl, Jean. *Kierkegaard: l'un devant l'autre.* Paris: Hachette Littératures, 1998.

Walsh, Sylvia. *Living Poetically: Kierkegaard's Existential Aesthetics.* University Park, PA: Penn State Press, 1994.

———. "Forming the Heart." In *The Grammar of the Heart,* edited by Richard H. Bell, 234–56. San Francisco: Harper and Row, 1988.

Walsh, W. H. *Hegelian Ethics.* Bristol, UK: Thoemmes Press, 1998.

Ware, Kallistos. *The Orthodox Way.* Rev. ed. Crestwood, NY: St. Vladimir's Seminary Press, 2001.

Weil, Simone. *Waiting for God.* Translated by Emma Craufurd. New York: G. P. Putnam's Sons, 1951.

———. "Love." Translated by Emma Craufurd. In *The Simone Weil Reader,* edited by George A. Panichas, 357–62. Wakefield, RI: Moyer Bell, 1977.

———. *The Need for Roots.* Translated by A. F. Wills. London: Routledge and Kegan Paul, 1987.

Westphal, Merold. *God, Guilt, and Death: An Existential Phenomenology of Religion.* Bloomington: Indiana University Press, 1984.

———. *Becoming a Self: A Reading of Kierkegaard's* Concluding Unscientific Postscript. West Lafayette, IN: Purdue University Press, 1996.

White, Nicholas P. "Stoic Values." *Monist* 73 (1990): 42–58.

Wiggins, David. *Needs, Values, Truth.* 3rd ed. Oxford: Clarendon Press, 1998.

Wilde, Oscar. *De Profundis.* New York: Penguin, 1986.

Williams, Bernard. *Ethics and the Limits of Philosophy.* Cambridge, MA: Harvard University Press, 1985.

———. *Truth and Truthfulness.* Princeton, NJ: Princeton University Press, 2002.

Wollheim, Richard. *On the Emotions.* New Haven: Yale University Press, 1999.

Xenakis, Jason. "Noncommittal Philosophy." *Journal of Thought* 7 (1972): 199–205.

———. "Hippies and Cynics." *Inquiry* 16 (1973): 1–15.

Young, Edward. *Night Thoughts.* Edited by Stephen Cornford. Cambridge: Cambridge University Press, 1989.

Zagzebski, Linda Trinkaus. *Virtues of the Mind: An Inquiry into the Nature of Virtue and the Ethical Foundations of Knowledge.* Cambridge: Cambridge University Press, 1996.

———. "From Reliabilism to Virtue Epistemology." In *Knowledge, Belief, and Character,* edited by Guy Axtell, 113–22. Lanham, MD: Rowman and Littlefield, 2000.

INDEX

absurdity, 24, 30, 33, 50, 69, 71, 84, 94,
106, 113–15, 116–17, 129, 134. *See also*
nihilism; vanity
acceptance, 112–14, 116, 118, 121, 125,
132–33, 135, 139–40
aesthetic mode of life, 51, 52–64, 65–71,
73, 77, 78, 80–81, 85, 87–88, 92–93,
95–96, 119–20, 129, 131, 133
aesthetics (philosophy of art), 54, 57–58,
62–63, 66, 75–76
affirmation, 99, 100, 106, 108, 110, 113,
115–18, 121–22, 125, 130–31, 135–36
Agacinski, Sylviane, 132, 198n78
agapē, 101–3, 106–7, 139. *See also* love,
unselfish
Alexander of Aphrodisias, 156n34, 166n57,
197n71
Allers, Rudolph, 159n12
Andersen, H. C., 166n41
anger, xi, 4, 8, 12, 18, 20–22, 25, 29, 47, 49,
52, 73–74, 92, 93, 100, 105
Annas, Julia, 148n30, 151n29
annoyance, 4, 47, 112
Anthony of Egypt, 154n11
anxiety, 21, 46, 95–96, 117, 132
apathy, 3, 16, 18–20, 23, 26–27, 32–34,
36–37, 48–49, 52, 80, 101, 103–4,
113–14, 119–20, 123, 138, 193n37. *See
also* Stoicism
appraisal. *See* evaluation
appropriate emotions, 9, 29, 76–77, 117,
124. *See also* emotions, warrant for
Arendt, Hannah, 187n28, 193n37
Aristo of Chios, 32, 153n57, 154n9
Aristotle, 4, 5, 29, 42, 62, 73–74, 83, 104,
143n2, 144nn5, 8, 147n4, 148n21,
152n52, 153n7, 157n65, 163n1, 164n7,

165nn21, 27, 166nn48–49, 52,
168nn73, 75, 169n18, 174n28, 178n76,
181nn101, 106, 182n107
Arius Didymus, 144n11, 147n54
assent, 11, 14–16, 18, 67, 88, 106, 112,
129–30, 134, 138
atheism, 114, 116, 189n61
attachment. *See* care; love
attitudes, 5, 10, 13, 17, 37, 50, 53, 91, 106,
112, 114, 118, 139. *See also* belief;
dispositions toward emotion; ways of
seeing
Augustine, 9, 20, 32, 107, 151n42, 153n57,
165n23, 166n57, 178n77, 182n108,
186n27, 187n28, 190n3, 191n17
Aulus Gellius, 144n11, 145n33
authenticity, 22, 49, 54, 68, 74, 88, 95–96,
106, 112, 119, 122, 124, 129, 136, 140
axiology, 5, 10, 35, 76, 88, 91, 93, 100, 122,
124, 134. *See also* value

Barth, John, 60
Becker, Ernest, 8, 19, 82, 170n22, 188n46,
190n75
Becker, Lawrence, 152n53, 176n55
Beethoven, Ludwig van, 37, 134, 153n11,
199n87
belief, xii, 5, 14, 18, 21, 23, 45, 48–49,
54–55, 58, 63, 76–77, 79, 100, 108,
110–11, 112–14, 117–18, 119–20,
124–26, 134–35, 141
false, 5, 9, 17–19, 21, 23, 24, 27, 34, 36,
49, 55, 74, 91
Ben-Ze'ev, Aaron, 145n18, 187n34
Bergmann, Frithjof, 171n57
Bergson, Henri, 94, 109, 173n23, 191n17,
192n28

225

Berthold-Bond, Daniel, 95, 161n44
Bible, Hebrew
    Deuteronomy, 201n104
    Ecclesiastes, 7, 169n2
    Genesis, 202n1
    Job, 114–16, 188nn43–44, 56
    Proverbs, 97
    Tobit, 199n93
big and small, as metaphors for what
    appears significant or insignificant,
    xi, 4, 28, 47, 124, 140–41, 203nn14–15
Bishop, Elizabeth, 25
Blum, Lawrence, 150n24
Bollas, Christopher, 146n42
boredom, 60, 62
Bouquet, A. C., 181n96
Bowen, Gary Starr, 177n63, 189n60
Bowlby, John, 8–9
Brentano, Franz, 144n3, 161n43
Brown, Norman O., 173n16
Burns, Robert, 63
Byron, George Gordon, 27, 83, 152n46,
    160n21, 161n38

Calhoun, Cheshire, 125, 167n70
Camus, Albert, 26–27, 30, 60, 94, 117,
    150n21, 151n38, 152n45, 173n19,
    200n101
Cappelørn, N. J., 177n61, 192n30
Caputo, John D., 193n43
care, 6–11, 13–16, 18, 20–22, 25–27, 28–29,
    30, 33, 35–38, 45–47, 53, 60, 63,
    68–69, 72–73, 79, 81, 83–84, 92,
    95–96, 98–99, 101, 104–5, 108–9,
    111–12, 118, 119, 121, 130, 136, 137–39,
    177n56
    as basic mental process, 10, 92, 95–96,
        101, 108, 112, 118, 119, 137–38
    limits of, 38, 80–81, 84, 98, 95, 112, 139
    misplaced, 63, 83–84, 93, 118, 130
    See also love
Carroll, Noël, 161n33
category mistakes, 13–14
catharsis, 62, 66
Cather, Willa, 11–12
Catherine of Siena, 178n77

Cavell, Stanley, 151n33, 160n29, 202n2
character, 15, 18, 22, 51, 63, 67–68, 70,
    73–74, 87, 127. See also dispositions
    toward emotion; virtue
charitable interpretation, 100–101, 105–6,
    117, 120–21, 123–24, 128, 136, 139–40
Chaucer, Geoffrey, 144n14
Christianity, 48, 99, 101–2, 104–5, 107, 111,
    178n77, 179n81, 180n92, 183nn119,
    122, 185n22, 186n26, 190n11, 191nn13,
    20, 193n37. See also folk religion;
    religious existence
Chrysippus, 4–6, 14, 21, 27, 42, 45, 104,
    148n16, 152nn48–49, 153n6, 155nn28,
    33, 180n94, 181n100, 197n71
Cicero, 20, 42, 43, 144n11, 145nn22, 27,
    146n51, 148nn9, 18, 152n54, 171n1,
    181n95
Cioran, E. M., 36, 109
clichés, 3, 92–94, 114–15
cognition, need for broad definition of,
    12–15, 74, 146n37
Cohen, Ted, 69
coherence, 38, 65, 76–77, 83–84, 88, 92,
    97, 121–22, 129, 134, 140
Coleridge, S. T., 160n21, 161n33
color perception, 13, 54–55, 57, 73, 81,
    100, 125
Come, Arnold B., 98–99, 189n64
commitment, 59, 61, 67, 75, 85, 94–95,
    109, 112, 137–38, 182n112, 184n10
compassion, 22, 28–29, 52, 62, 108, 121
concern. See care
Connell, George, 96, 156n34, 165n38,
    173n25
consistency, as virtue of character, 23, 28,
    38, 57, 59–60, 65–66, 70, 73, 92, 95,
    120, 126, 131, 196n64
contingency, 8, 11–12, 20–23, 30, 45–46,
    48, 54, 62–63, 68, 76, 91, 96–99, 101,
    103, 110, 111, 114–16, 118, 121, 125–26,
    128, 139. See also external goods;
    vulnerability
control, 4–7, 15, 17–18, 20–22, 26, 30, 34,
    36–37, 46–47, 62, 67, 74, 86, 91, 111,
    121, 129, 132–33. See also volition

conviction, 36, 45, 46, 48, 63, 68, 82, 117, 120–21, 130, 140
correspondence, 20, 25–26, 34, 47, 92–93, 122
cosmology, 92, 114, 123, 131, 183n122
   Stoic, 22–23, 31, 35–36, 131, 152n48
crisis, spiritual, 82, 94, 111
Cynicism, 18, 22, 30, 56

Dante, 66, 121, 191n17, 199n93
Davenport, John, 168n77
Deleuze, Gilles, 195n59
depression, 13, 48, 73, 146n40
Descartes, René, 100, 155n23
desire, 52–53, 71, 83, 93–95, 102–4, 110, 120, 135
   and belief, xii
despair, 24, 50, 78, 110–11, 113, 115, 117, 134, 141, 146n40
de Sousa, Ronald, 12, 74, 119, 146n38, 147n53, 153n7, 187n29, 190n1
Deutsch, Eliot, 167n65
Dewey, John, 159n18, 196n64
Diderot, Denis, 174n42
differentiation, of subject and object, 97, 116–17, 176n55, 182n110
Diogenes Laertius, 42, 147n1, 148n8, 149nn32, 36, 39, 149n7, 150nn26–27, 152nn51–52, 153n57, 171n2, 180n94, 181nn100–101, 191n20, 193n35
Diogenes of Sinope, 18, 22, 42
Dionysius the Areopagite. See Pseudo-Dionysius
Dionysius of Heraclea, 28, 150n27
disappointment, 4–5, 21, 23, 28, 35, 68–69, 82, 105–6, 113, 117, 135, 139, 189n71
dispositions toward emotion, 5, 9–10, 15, 35, 38, 49, 67–68, 70, 73, 76, 108, 110, 112, 117, 121, 138
disproportionate emotions, 19–21, 25–26, 34, 47, 93
distinctiveness, 98, 105, 107, 112, 121–6, 128, 132, 135–36, 138, 177n60, 200n101. See also identity

distrust, 10, 20–21, 105–6, 114, 117–18, 120, 128
divine madness, 44, 45–46, 49–50, 56, 83–85, 96, 102–3, 109, 116–17, 121–22, 123, 125, 179n82, 201n103
Dostoevsky, Fyodor, 59–60, 69, 100, 141, 161n45, 163n67
doubt, 10, 49, 79, 95–96, 100, 106, 116, 124–26, 134, 139
Dreyfus, Hubert, 156n39, 170n37
duty, 75, 93, 99, 132–33, 139

elation, 9, 13
Eliot, T. S., 58, 76, 167n65, 168n74
Ellis, Ralph D., 198n78
Ellsworth, Jonathan, 150n19
embarrassment, 9–10
embodiment, 12–14, 44, 46, 48, 57, 60, 67, 73, 121, 125–26, 137
emergent properties. See supervenience
Emerson, Ralph Waldo, 23
emotions
   another name for passions, 4, 143n2
   as cognitive phenomena, 4–6, 10, 12–15, 21, 43, 45–47, 73
   escape from, 13, 18–20, 24, 30, 46–47, 125
   intentionality of, 4–7, 12–13, 15–16, 21, 38, 53–54, 57, 61, 80–81, 92, 109, 121, 144n3, 146n38
   need for clarification of, 19, 22–23, 34–35, 38, 41, 44, 48, 50–51, 55–56, 73–76, 98, 101–102, 106, 121–22, 125, 135, 137, 140, 203n15
   primary and secondary, 5, 9–11, 45–46, 96–98, 101, 106, 108, 112, 120–21, 138
   rationality of, 3–5, 10, 19, 34, 36, 48–49, 122–23, 139–41
   violent or unpleasant, xi, 5, 15, 18–20, 25, 33, 50, 52, 61, 64, 109, 112, 114–15, 118, 124, 134–35
   warrant for, xii, 7, 13, 37, 46, 49, 51, 74, 92, 101, 104
empathy, 27, 99, 109, 124, 134, 136, 138
environment, 8, 13, 36, 79, 104, 123, 125, 200n98. See also external world

envy, 16, 79, 105
Epictetus, 6, 11, 17, 19, 21, 23, 25–27,
    29–30, 32–33, 36, 39, 43–44, 47, 62,
    96, 104, 109, 122, 145n33, 147n50,
    147nn1, 2, 4, 148nn9, 19–20, 28,
    149nn39–40, 149nn5, 8, 150n18,
    151nn31, 37, 40, 152nn52, 56,
    155nn16, 18, 28, 157n54, 163n1,
    164n16, 169n11, 171n1, 175n42,
    176n45, 180n94, 181n99, 186nn23–24,
    191n20, 193nn36, 43, 197n71, 199n88,
    200n99
Epicurus, 3
episodes of emotion, 5, 9–10, 52–54, 56–57,
    59–60, 62–63, 68–70, 79, 92, 129
epistemology, 17–18, 36, 46–47, 55, 76, 81,
    87, 92, 103, 123, 125–26, 138, 141
Eriksen, Niels Nymann, 126, 130, 180n90,
    194n47, 195n52, 200n100
erōs, 101–4, 136. See also desire; love,
    romantic
estrangement, 24, 26, 30, 33, 57–59,
    80–82, 88, 93–95, 113, 125
ethical sphere, 51, 59–60, 65–77, 81–86,
    88, 91–94, 96, 102, 120, 129, 131, 133,
    138, 163n3
eupatheiai, 32, 152n53, 181n94
evaluation, 4–5, 18, 23, 26, 66, 74, 76, 83,
    87, 94, 112, 121. See also value
Evans, C. Stephen, 47, 74, 182n112
existential relevance of philosophy, 3,
    42–43, 62–63, 137
external goods, 5, 8, 18, 21, 32, 54, 57, 62,
    76, 109–10, 114, 130–31
external world, 4, 7, 10, 22, 30, 35, 50, 53,
    84, 94, 96, 98, 110, 122, 130, 152n56
    as fabric of attachments, 36, 37, 46, 74,
    104–5, 111, 118, 120, 138

faith. See belief
fallibility, 19–21, 34, 76, 135
fate, 11–12, 48, 69, 113, 114, 129
fear, 4–5, 9, 14, 20, 29, 32, 49, 58, 62–63,
    132, 161n33
Ferreira, M. Jamie, 99, 105–6, 139,
    177n56, 183n116

Fichte, J. G., 171n58, 185n14
finitude, 64, 81, 84, 96, 121, 125–26, 129,
    132, 138
folk religion, 92–93, 110–11, 114, 117–18,
    134–35, 185n16
Forster, Michael, 173n26
Foucault, Michel, 167n72
Frankfurt, Harry, 7, 35, 129, 145n27,
    177n64
Frede, Michael, 32, 150n25, 152n55,
    193n35
freedom, 22–23, 24, 56, 63, 68, 79, 81, 107,
    131, 147n51, 151n42, 171n57
Freud, Sigmund, 10, 11, 153n8, 157n57,
    159n18, 181n105, 196n65
friendship, 12, 23, 27, 29, 31, 32, 63,
    68–69, 77, 80, 85, 104, 136, 181n100,
    182n108
Fromm, Erich, 191n13
Frost, Robert, 18, 33, 128
future, 5, 14, 38, 59, 63, 87, 126, 128–30,
    140. See also hope; temporality

Gandhi, Mahātma, 22, 148n31
Gardner, Sebastian, 196n60
givenness, 97, 101, 112, 115–16, 130
God, non-metaphysical (or non-objective)
    conception of, 98, 100–101, 103–4,
    111, 113–14, 117–18, 126, 185n21,
    198n83. See also love
Goldman, Alvin I., 148n9
Gordon, Robert M., 147n52
Gouwens, David J., 112, 120, 130, 156n45,
    172n5, 187n35, 190n4, 198n82,
    200n97
Graham, George, 146n40
gratitude, 9, 46, 104, 106, 111–13, 115–17,
    125, 140, 193n38
Greek versus German philosophy, 42–45,
    154n4
Green, Ronald M., 73
Greenspan, Patricia, 166n49
Grégoire, Franz, 174nn26–27
Gregory of Nyssa, 183n122
Grice, Paul, 193n41
grief, 4, 5, 14–15, 27, 32, 46, 53, 135

Grundtvig, Nikolaj, 56
Guroian, Vigen, 174n28, 179n81,
    181n102
habit, 74, 84, 87, 93, 131
Hadot, Pierre, 22, 27, 149n2, 154n11,
    158n79, 181n98, 191n24, 193n39
Hall, Amy Laura, 194n51, 199n92
Hall, Ronald L., 46, 188n57
Hamann, J. G., 81, 169nn15–16
Hannay, Alastair, 82, 122, 157n61, 169n6,
    177nn56, 64, 178n73, 186n22,
    188n41, 196n59, 197n75, 200n98,
    201n102
happiness, 8, 18, 20–21, 26–27, 45, 56, 78,
    109–10, 112–14, 118, 119, 126, 132, 134,
    140. See also well-being
Hardy, Thomas, 113, 188n38
Hare, Richard Mervyn, 1, 33
hedonism, xii, 56, 69, 108, 138
Hegel, G. W. F., 42, 84, 96, 149n38,
    154n5, 162n60, 168n79, 170n38,
    172nn14–15, 173nn19, 26, 174nn27,
    32, 175nn37, 42, 176n53, 192n30,
    199n93, 201n102
Hegelianism, 45, 85, 93, 154n4
Heiberg, J. L., 85, 158n79, 170n47, 195n54,
    197n71
Heidegger, Martin, 8, 59, 101, 166n53,
    174n29, 193n39, 197n70
Hellenistic philosophy, 41–45, 47–49
    analogies with existentialism, 30, 44,
    149n2
    See also Cynicism; Skepticism;
    Stoicism
Helm, Bennett, 202n4
Heraclitus, 98
Heyde, Ludwig, 174n32
Hierocles, 28, 151n29
Hillman, James, 35
Holm, Isak, 194n51
hope, 4, 14, 46, 59, 110, 115, 117, 135,
    201n101
Huntington, Patricia J., 180n87
Husserl, Edmund, 162n55
Hutcheson, Francis, 29

identity, 8, 11, 26, 42, 61, 63, 68, 70–71,
    73–74, 80, 86, 98–99, 104, 106–7,
    109, 121–23, 125–26, 127, 129, 131–32,
    135–36, 182n108
Ignatius of Loyola, 37–38
imagination, 79–81, 83–85, 93–96, 101,
    120, 127–28, 130, 132, 134, 178n73,
    192n33, 196n69
impressions, 9, 11, 104, 129, 193n35
individual and society, 81–84, 86–88,
    93–96
insanity, 18–19, 49–50, 93, 134. See also
    mental illness
insight, 7, 16, 18, 30, 36, 46, 63–64, 88, 98,
    123, 141
insincerity, 32, 43–44, 54, 61, 66, 68
integrity, xii, 17, 23, 26, 31, 33, 34–36, 38,
    50–51, 56, 59, 63, 71, 73, 82, 84, 88,
    93, 95, 105, 119, 125, 128, 131, 133–35,
    137
interdependence of self and world, 120,
    122–24, 131–32, 135, 138
intersubjectivity, 74, 84, 94, 104, 111, 125,
    136
involvement. See participation
invulnerability, 20–23, 25–26, 29, 35, 51,
    110–11, 115, 119
inwardness, 74, 95–96, 101, 110–11, 121,
    129–30
Inwood, Brad, 144n13, 145n22, 152n53
irony, 42, 54, 60, 63, 68–70, 84, 123, 139
irrationality, 5, 10, 19, 34
isolated self, 26, 64, 104, 108

Jaggar, Alison, 193n42
James, William, 64, 190n7
Jankélévitch, Vladimir, 175n34
jealousy, 10, 22, 25, 79, 105. See also envy
Jefferson, Mark, 160n24
Jegstrup, Elsebet, 177n57
Joas, Hans, 185n16, 195n59
Johansen, K. F., 41–42
Johnson, Rolf, 106
joy, 5, 9–10, 13, 37, 45, 61, 68, 79, 109, 111,
    114–15, 133, 135, 139, 198n84
Joyce, James, 63, 75

judgment of value. *See* evaluation

Jung, C. G., 82, 153n16, 155n21, 170n21

Kafka, Franz, 202n9

Kant, Immanuel, 32, 151n42, 160n25, 163n1, 168n73

Keats, John, 75, 81–82, 167n67

Kenny, Anthony, 144n4

Kestenbaum, Victor, 196n64

Kierkegaard, Søren

  pseudonymous writings:

  —*The Concept of Anxiety,* 42, 56, 155n21, 157nn56, 69, 165n29,166n42, 168n76, 169n5, 195n59, 196n60, 198n80

  —*Concluding Unscientific Postscript,* 42, 45, 47, 49, 51, 54, 155n22, 156n38, 158n81, 165n25, 197n72

  —*Either/Or,* 42–43, 46–47, 48–49, 52–61, 63–64, 65–68, 70–76, 78–83, 85–87, 92–96, 120, 146n40, 153n58, 155n36, 157n56, 158nn81–82, 159nn17, 19, 161nn38, 42, 162n54, 163nn65–67, 164n11, 165n21, 166nn59–60, 168n73, 169n8, 170n37, 171n58, 172n13, 175n35, 177n60, 179nn79, 84, 181n101, 182n112, 184n12, 194n44, 195n53, 196n70, 203n14

  —*Fear and Trembling,* 46, 50, 93, 117, 172nn9, 15, 199n92

  —*Philosophical Fragments,* 48, 193n35

  —*Practice in Christianity,* 48, 133, 155n14, 157n48, 158n74, 194n50, 201n103

  —*Repetition,* 47, 80, 94, 114, 126–30, 131–32, 135, 178n73, 180n90, 187n34, 188n58, 194nn51–52, 195nn53–54, 58–59, 196n65, 197n72, 199n85, 200n101

  —*The Sickness Unto Death,* 43–44, 46, 110, 132, 165n28, 169n14, 173n24, 184n8, 185n13, 196nn66, 69, 198n80, 201nn102–3

  —*Stages on Life's Way,* 48–49, 67, 72, 83, 102–3, 117, 127, 134, 146n40,

158n81, 164nn14, 17, 184n10, 189n72, 195n53, 196nn66, 70, 199n92, 203n12

  signed (veronymous) writings:

  —*The Book on Adler,* 46, 97, 121, 158n82, 163n6, 175n41, 179n82, 191n16, 192n34, 196n64, 197n73, 203n13

  —*Christian Discourses,* 47, 100, 110, 111, 157n58, 169nn17, 19, 176n55, 177n66, 178n73, 179n78, 183n115, 185n21, 189n69, 199n92

  —*The Concept of Irony,* 42, 56–57, 69, 84, 103, 135, 155n26, 179n79, 180n89, 194nn46, 50

  —*Eighteen Upbuilding Discourses,* 95–98, 101, 103, 105–6, 110–15, 158n73, 175n41, 176nn54–55, 177n65, 184n3, 185n14, 188n58, 189n70, 202n3

  —*For Self-Examination,* 59, 76, 87, 156n38, 179n82

  —*From the Papers of One Still Living,* 82, 158n80, 162n55, 166n41

  —*The Gospel of Sufferings,* 114, 185n15, 188n50, 189n69, 190n8, 196n69, 197n76, 201n102

  —*The Instant,* 158n82, 169n3, 170n42, 186n26, 187n28

  —*Johannes Climacus,* 125, 194n49

  —*Judge for Yourself!,* 44, 101, 198n80

  —*The Point of View,* 65, 87, 158n74, 169n2, 171n65, 172n5, 201n103

  —*Purity of Heart Is to Will One Thing,* 30, 43, 49, 157nn51, 69, 175n33, 185n13, 194n48, 200n100

  —*Three Discourses on Imagined Occasions,* 45, 49, 55, 67, 96, 102, 125, 155n17, 158n73, 167n65, 175n38, 179n79, 184n4

  —*Two Ages,* 45–46, 51, 58, 80, 92, 165n22, 170nn43, 48, 190n75, 194n44

  —*Upbuilding Discourses in Various Spirits,* 60

  —*Without Authority,* 176n48, 200n98

  —*Works of Love,* 47, 82, 97–99, 101–2, 104, 106, 108, 111–12, 114, 116, 121, 128, 133, 135, 164n16, 171n54,

176nn49, 53, 177n65, 179nn78–80,
180n88, 181n106, 182nn111, 113–14,
183nn117–19, 184nn10–11, 185nn14,
21, 186n27, 193n35, 194n48, 196n69,
199nn84, 93, 200nn96, 98–99, 101,
201n103, 202n3
Kirmmse, Bruce H., 160n25
Knappe, Ulrich, 168n73
Knowledge. *See* epistemology; truth,
emotional
Kramer, Peter, 151n44
Kundera, Milan, 71, 79, 159n8, 166n46,
167n63, 170n35, 184n11, 193n38,
202n8

Lacan, Jacques, 134
Langan, Thomas, 98
language, 14–15, 44–45, 81
Larkin, Philip, 109, 139
Larmore, Charles, 160n30, 192n33
laughter, 25, 28–29, 43, 59, 79, 85, 139
Lear, Jonathan, 94, 101, 145n30, 146n45,
161n33, 190n76, 191nn19, 22, 199n90,
201n102
LeDoux, Joseph, 146n37
letting-be, 7–8, 84, 125, 129, 136, 177n57
Levin, David Michael, 153n13, 173n24
Levinas, Emmanuel, 186n24
Lingis, Alphonso, 8, 21, 178n67, 193n41
Lippitt, John, 167n69
Loewald, Hans, 182n110
logic, 10, 43, 45, 111, 125, 133
loneliness, 26, 33
Long, A. A., 21, 35, 146n47, 147n1, 149n2,
151n40, 155n16
love, 8–11, 14, 20–21, 26–27, 30, 33, 36–38,
45, 48–49, 60, 63, 66–67, 70–71,
74–75, 79–80, 85–87, 93, 96, 97–101,
102–7, 108–14, 116–18, 119–29,
130–36, 137–41
Danish words for, 45, 102, 177n56,
179nn78–80
Greek words for, 101–105, 178n77,
179n81, 180n94
measuring the lovableness of objects,
25, 38, 47, 81, 94, 101, 103–4, 112–13,

116, 118, 121, 124, 128–29, 134, 139,
140–41, 148n18
reliability of as subjective influence, 9,
20, 44, 48, 88, 96, 102–4, 107, 110–11,
114, 116, 119–20, 129, 137–38, 140
religious interpretation of, 86, 93, 96,
97–101, 102–7, 108–14, 116–18,
119–21, 124, 126, 128, 133, 136, 139
romantic, 10, 21, 47, 52–53, 60–61, 66,
71, 102, 110, 127
unselfish, 22, 99, 101–2, 104–5, 109,
120–23, 125, 128, 135, 139
Lowrie, Walter, 47, 162n54
Luther, Martin, 186n26, 192n33
Lyons, William, 146n39

MacIntyre, Alasdair, 83–84, 152n48,
166n48, 168nn75, 77, 79
Mackey, Louis, 54, 133, 154n8,
195n52
Mackie, J. L., 124, 192n31
Malantschuk, Gregor, 131, 189n74
Marcus Aurelius, 17, 21, 23, 27, 32, 37,
43, 60, 123, 145n22, 147n5, 148nn10,
31, 149n36, 150nn19, 21, 27, 151nn31,
40, 152n56, 158nn74, 79, 171n2,
181n98, 187n28, 189n63, 191nn20,
23–24, 192n30, 197n71,
200n99
Marino, Gordon, 146n40, 194n44
Marion, Jean-Luc, 123, 145n17, 176n45,
184n9, 202n3
marriage, 67, 75, 80, 83, 96, 175n34
mathematical knowledge, 125, 133
meaninglessness. *See* absurdity
memory, 12, 21, 57, 60, 62, 71–72, 130.
See also past; recollection;
temporality
mental illness, 13, 50, 151n44
Merleau-Ponty, Maurice, 147n49,
182n110, 198n80
Miyawaki, Edison, 146n43
moderation, 24–25, 32, 45
momentary emotion. *See* episodes of
emotion
moods, 13, 46, 73, 146n42

Mooney, Edward, 43, 63, 96, 104, 112,
  115–16, 133–34, 135–36, 164n19,
  166n50, 183n2, 191n18, 193nn36, 41,
  194n43
Moore, Kathleen Dean, 1, 33
moral awareness, 8–10, 14–16, 22, 26,
  28–29, 30–31, 33, 36, 42–43, 54–56,
  60, 65, 72–73, 99–100, 122–24, 131,
  135, 137–40
moral engagement. See participation
moral idealism, 36–38, 82–84, 86, 94, 117
moral perfectionism, 22–23, 74–76, 114
Murdoch, Iris, 164n8, 168n74, 178n69
musical imagery, 128, 131–34, 192n30,
  199n85
Musil, Robert, 86
Mynster, Jakob Peter, 155n34

Nagel, Thomas, 97, 191n23
Nehemas, Alexander, 195n59
Neoplatonism, 97, 102, 192n32
Neu, Jerome, 193n39
neuroscience, 4, 13, 146n43
neurosis, 82, 173n16
New Testament
  1 Corinthians, 188n50
  Ephesians, 98
  1 John, 176n54
  Luke, 60, 161n42
  1 Peter, 101
  Philippians, 111
Nicholas of Cusa, 177n62
Nietzsche, Friedrich, 34, 112, 131, 159n18,
  164n9, 171n61, 186n26, 187nn30, 34,
  189n72, 192n30, 196n59, 197n71,
  198n79, 199n93
nihilism, 1, 21, 25, 27, 30, 50, 95, 99, 110,
  112–13, 114, 116, 117–18, 125–26, 129,
  135, 139
Nishida Kitarô, 192n34
Noddings, Nel, 26
Nordentoft, Kresten, 98, 157n57, 176n55,
  179n81, 183nn119, 121, 185n16,
  188n41, 193n36, 199n90
nostalgia, 19, 55–56, 72, 127. See also
  memory; recollection

Nussbaum, Martha, 5, 9, 14–15, 44, 104,
  144n10, 146n44, 147n7, 148n14,
  151n40, 158n82, 160n30, 162n56,
  164n17, 181n98, 187n27, 193n39
Nygren, Anders, 102, 178n77

objectivity, 4, 6–8, 11, 13, 15, 30–31, 35, 50,
  56, 76, 97, 100–101, 111, 116–17, 120,
  122–23, 125, 128–29, 131, 137, 139–40.
  See also subjectivity
oceanic metaphors, 57, 97, 108, 109, 115
Ockham's razor, 116, 124
O'Hear, Anthony, 192n32
Olsen, Regine, 102, 140, 162n54, 189n63,
  202n10, 203nn11, 15
omnipotence, 30, 36, 62
Ong, Walter J., 185n22
ontological dependency, 97–98, 106–7,
  108, 111, 118, 125, 135, 137–38,
  183n119
Orange, Donna M., 202n2
Origen, 155n16, 178n77, 183n122, 192n30
Ortega y Gasset, José, 108, 189n65,
  197n75
Osborne, Catherine, 183n122
otherworldliness, 57–63, 80, 103, 111, 112,
  125–28, 130, 132, 186nn26–27, 187n28.
  See also particularity, denial of

participation, 24, 30–31, 36, 46, 53–54,
  57–59, 60–63, 65–66, 69, 79, 82,
  94–96, 101, 105, 108–9, 112, 120–21,
  123–26, 128, 131, 135–36, 138
particularity, 11–12, 14–15, 22–23, 27–28,
  42–44, 46, 62, 66, 74, 81, 103–4,
  115–16, 121–22, 124, 135–36, 138–39,
  140
  denial of, 31, 36, 42, 60–61, 63, 79–81,
  103, 111–12, 121
passions. See emotions
passivity, 6–8, 16, 67, 96–98, 106–7, 110,
  114, 120, 125, 129–30, 140, 164n17
past, 5, 12, 21, 38, 59–60, 63, 71–72, 87,
  115, 119, 125–26, 128–30, 140. See also
  memory; temporality
pathos. See suffering

Pattison, George, 61
Pelisson-Fontanier, Paul, 169n1
Peperzak, Adriaan, 144n15
perceptions
   distinguished from sensations, 4, 13,
      144n6
   of significance, emotions as, 6–10,
      13–16, 18–20, 54, 87, 91
Perkins, Robert L., 47, 172n6, 180n91
perspectivism, 105, 113, 122, 124–25, 128,
      133, 135–36, 137–41
pessimism, 108, 110–13, 116, 135
Pessin, Sarah, ix, 111
phenomenology of emotion, 4, 12–14, 25,
      38, 48, 61, 73, 96, 98, 106, 108,
      162n55
philia, 102–5. See also friendship; love
Philistinism, 81–85, 92–96, 117, 172n13,
      173n24
Philo of Alexandria, 145n33
physiology, 4, 12–14, 48
Pico della Mirandola, 83
Pinkard, Terry, 201n104
Pippin, Robert, 163n68
pity, 29, 59, 62, 121
place, emotions associated with, 11–12,
      21–22, 104, 132, 138–39
Plato, 42–43, 102–3, 125–26, 144n8, 147n7,
      149n3, 155nn16, 26, 158n70, 163n63,
      170n31, 172n10, 179nn79, 82,
      180nn88–91, 192n30, 193n43,
      194n46, 199n92
Plotinus, 42, 89, 153n15, 176n49, 178n77,
      190n9, 193n39, 199n92
Plutarch, 172n12, 180n94
Poole, Roger, 58–59, 187n35, 200n94
Porphyry, 143n1
possibility, 58, 68, 77, 81–82, 86, 95, 101,
      111, 113, 129–32, 136, 140, 196n69
praise, 108, 115–16
preferred indifferents, 28, 31–32, 150n26,
      151n40
Price, A. W., 181n94
pride, 16, 106
primary emotions. See emotions, primary
   and secondary

primitivity, 85, 95–96, 101, 103, 125, 130,
      133, 136, 140, 174n33
projection, 56, 84, 100–101, 106, 110, 120,
      140, 145n18
propatheiai, 11
Protagoras, 98
Proust, Marcel, 57, 75, 160n30, 197n74
Pseudo-Dionysius, 102, 178n77, 194n43
purpose, 68, 70, 82, 99, 109, 112, 114, 116–17

qualia. See raw feeling
Quinney, Laura, 190n5

raw feeling, 12, 48, 53–55, 57, 61–62,
      69–70
realism, 7, 46, 77, 106–7, 111, 122, 124, 128
reasons for loving, 10–11, 30, 48, 101,
      103–4, 112, 118, 120–21, 139
receptivity, 8, 30, 36, 56, 67, 86–88, 97,
      100, 104–7, 109–10, 120, 123–29, 130,
      133, 135, 138–39, 164n19, 190n9
recollection, 57, 60, 125–26. See also
   memory
religious existence, 51, 91–101, 102–7,
      108–18, 119–21, 124–29, 133–34, 136
remorse, 48, 59
repetition, 126–30, 131–34, 195n54,
      196n65, 197n71
Rescher, Nicholas, 77, 144n15, 167n69
resentment, 112, 134
resolution, 67–75, 87, 113, 121, 129–30,
      132–33, 140
responsibility, 29, 58–59, 63, 67, 74–75,
      111, 130, 138
reverence, 93, 102, 104, 108, 110, 114, 118,
      121, 135
revolt, 80, 85. See also estrangement
Rhees, Rush, 125, 193n38
Ricoeur, Paul, 166n62, 167n68
Rilke, Rainer Maria, 26, 39, 75, 89, 159n17
Roberts, Robert C., 45–46, 54, 143n2,
      145n28, 146n47, 155n29, 156n38, 172n7
Roberts, Tyler T., 197n71, 198n83
Romanticism, 49, 55, 63, 80, 83–84,
      87–88, 101, 120, 134, 160n21, 178n73,
      190n5, 192n33, 200n99

Rorty, Richard, 93, 106–7, 165n30, 169n4
Rosenzweig, Franz, 201n104
Rosset, Clément, 198n84
Rudd, Anthony, 47, 83, 85, 190n5, 193n36

sacred, the, 97–98, 104, 108, 110, 116, 118
sadness, 9, 13, 61, 63, 73
Salinger, J. D., 164n13
Sandbach, F. H., 144n13, 149n8
Santner, Eric, 201n104
Sartre, Jean-Paul, 161n36
Scheler, Max, 10, 150n13, 163n6, 166n62, 178n77, 180n92, 190n75, 193n37
Schelling, F. W. J., 94–95, 173n25, 175n43, 189n62
Schiller, Johann, 159n6
Schlabach, Gerald, 123
Schlegel, Friedrich, 178n73
Schofield, Malcolm, 180n94, 181n100
Schopenhauer, Arthur, 25, 111, 117, 133, 139, 148n16, 152n49, 160n30, 184nn4, 6, 186nn25–26, 188nn38, 57, 189nn62, 71–72, 193n39, 200n99
scientific detachment, 29, 43, 55, 60, 101, 113, 116, 122–24, 140, 151n40, 191n24
Scopetea, Sophia, 155n16, 180n87
Scruton, Roger, 144n3, 161nn33, 40, 164n13
secondary emotions. See emotions, primary and secondary
seeing. See ways of seeing
self, as network of relations, 8, 26, 36, 37, 67–68, 73, 81, 107, 108, 111, 118, 120, 126, 130, 138, 140. See also identity
self-deception, 21, 33, 34, 48, 55–56, 71, 99, 106, 110–11, 114, 121, 124, 129, 132–33, 160n26
selfishness, 22, 26–28, 33, 36, 101, 105, 110, 112, 121, 125, 135, 200n101
self-sufficiency, 20–23, 25–27, 30, 36, 86, 96, 104, 106–7, 123, 125–26, 130
Seneca, 18–19, 21–23, 24–26, 27–29, 42–43, 47, 145n33, 147n4, 148nn11, 16, 149n36, 149n5, 150n9, 151n43, 155nn17, 28, 157n49, 169n4, 171n1, 172n10, 181n98, 190n2, 198n76

sensations, 4, 12–14, 48, 54–55, 62, 69, 146n41
sentimentality, 32, 34, 47, 48, 49, 53–56, 58–59, 61, 70–72, 117–18, 121, 127, 130, 135, 159nn6, 8, 18
Sextus Empiricus, 42, 152n52, 153n57, 173n16, 192n30, 193n35
Shakespeare, William, 58
Shelley, Percy Bysshe, 63
Sherman, Nancy, 147n1, 150n24, 152n53
Shestov, Lev, 192n33
Sibbern, F. C., 42, 48, 154n2, 155n34, 173n24
significance, 6–9, 11, 13, 17–20, 23–24, 26, 30–32, 35, 46, 48–51, 53, 54–56, 62–64, 65–67, 70, 72, 74–75, 77, 79–80, 82–83, 85–88, 91–94, 95–97, 100–101, 104–6, 108, 109–10, 111, 113, 115, 117–18, 120, 122–26, 128–29, 131–36, 137–38, 140
as illusory, 17–18, 20, 24–25, 50, 79, 133, 137
as non-metaphysical, 6, 13, 70, 100–101, 144n15
Singer, Irving, 92
Skepticism, 20–21, 45, 48, 105, 124–25, 128
Sløk, Johannes, 77, 120, 173n24, 197n72
Slote, Michael, 160n26
Smilansky, Saul, 176n45
Smith, Adam, 152n46
Smith, Stevie, 43
Smyth, John Vignaux, 63, 170n42
social-consensus theory of truth, 85, 93–96, 103–4, 173n26, 175n37, 201nn102, 104
social practices, 75–77, 83–85, 92–96, 136, 173n24
Socrates, 28, 42–43, 44, 47, 83–84, 102–3, 122–23, 147n7, 153n4, 155nn16, 26, 180n89, 192nn29–30
Solomon, Robert, 4, 144n5, 150n14, 174n26, 190n11
Søltoft, Pia, 181n99
Sorabji, Richard, 22, 144n9, 148n27, 151nn37, 40, 152n53
sorrow, 23, 25, 29, 48, 57, 109, 115